Ohio

Brad Crawford
Photography by William Manning

COMPASS AMERICAN GUIDES
An imprint of Fodor's Travel Publications

Compass American Guides: Ohio

Editor: Paula Consolo   Designer: Siobhan O'Hare

Compass Editorial Director: Paul Eisenberg   Compass Creative Director: Fabrizio La Rocca

Compass Senior Editor: Kristin Moehlmann   Editorial Production: Linda K. Schmidt

Photo Editor and Archival Researcher: Melanie Marin

Map Design: Mark Stroud, Moon Street Cartography

First Edition
ISBN 1–4000–1394–1

Compass American Guides, 1745 Broadway, New York NY 10019
PRINTED IN CHINA
10 9 8 7 6 5 4 3 2 1

For Michelle

C O N T E N T S

Topical Essays and Sidebars

Literary Extracts

Maps

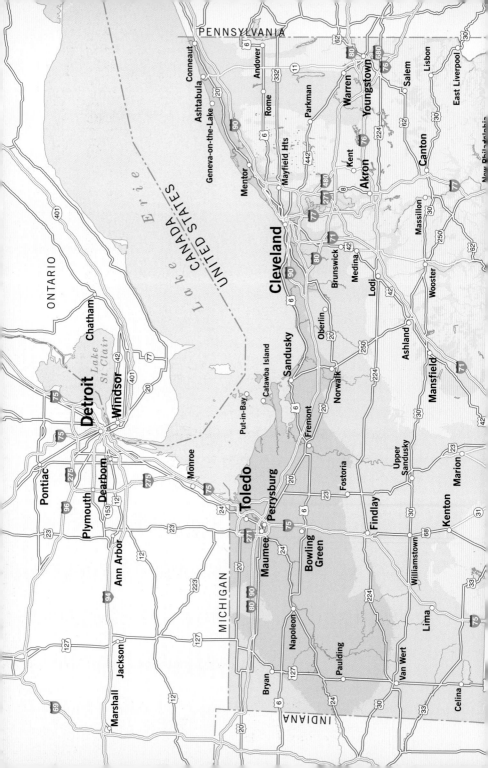

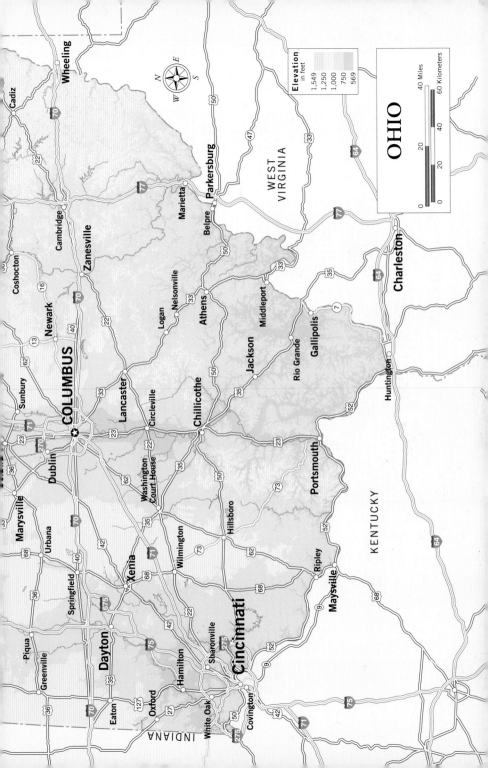

OHIO FACTS

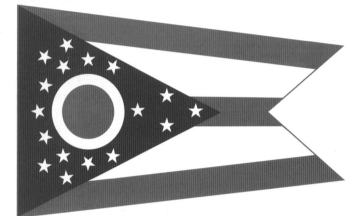

NICKNAME:
The Buckeye State

CAPITAL:
Columbus

STATE MOTTO:
With God, all things are possible.

STATE FLOWER:
Scarlet carnation

STATE BEVERAGE:
Tomato juice

STATE ANIMAL:
White-tailed deer

STATE BIRD:
Cardinal

STATE SONG:
"Beautiful Ohio"

ENTERED THE UNION:
March 1, 1803, 17th state

POPULATION:
11,353,140 (2000 U.S. Census)

Three Largest Cities by Population
Columbus   711,470
Cleveland   478,403
Cincinnati   331,285

TOP EMPLOYERS:
General Motors, Kroger Company, Delphi Automotive, Wright-Patterson Air Force Base, Cleveland Clinic Health System

Geography and Climate

The state comprises 44,828 square miles and eighty-eight counties. The largest county is Ashtabula, at 711 square miles, and the smallest is Lake County, at only 232 square miles. They are adjacent to each other on the Lake Erie shore.

Highest point: Campbell Hill (Bellefontaine), 1,550 feet
Lowest point: Ohio River (near Cincinnati), 455 feet
Water: 3,499 square miles of Lake Erie; 44,000 miles of rivers and streams
Highest recorded temperature: 113 degrees Fahrenheit, recorded on July 21, 1934, near Gallipolis
Lowest recorded temperature: -39 degrees Fahrenheit, recorded on February 10, 1899, at Milligan

Interesting Facts

▸ Ohio has the only state flag that isn't square. It's a pennant with two points, known as a burgee.

▸ Ohio boasts the world's largest Amish population, which is largely concentrated in Holmes, Wayne, and Tuscarawas counties.

▸ Twin Days in Twinsburg, Ohio, is an annual celebration of multiple births that draws thousands of twin sets every year—not to mention triplets and quadruplets.

▸ The famous Heimlich maneuver, designed to save choking victims, was created by a native Cincinnatian, Henry Heimlich.

▸ Ohio can claim some of the greatest figures in history, among them Tecumseh, Ulysses S. Grant, and John Glenn, as well as some of the most notorious—Jeffrey Dahmer, George Armstrong Custer, John Brown, Charles Manson, and the exonerated Dr. Sam Sheppard, whose story inspired *The Fugitive*.

▸ 83 percent of Ohioans 25 and older are high school graduates, versus 80.4 percent nationwide; 21.1 percent hold at least a bachelor's degree, versus 24.4 percent nationwide.

▸ Colo, the world's first captive-bred gorilla, was born at the Columbus Zoo in 1956.

▸ The world's tallest and fastest roller coaster is Top Thrill Dragster at Cedar Point amusement park in Sandusky, Ohio. Riders experience a 420-foot drop and speeds of 120 mph.

INTRODUCTION

> "Where exactly is Ohio? I have always replied, 'It is the farthest west of the east, and the farthest east of the west, the farthest north of the south, and the farthest south of the north, and it is probably the richest area of its size in the world.' "—Louis Bromfield

Pity Ohio. Lacking the easy labels reserved for states in New England, the South, or about any other American region you care to name, Ohio's identity becomes muddled beyond its own statehood. "Midwest" seems a misnomer. (Does anyone from Iowa or Kansas feel a regional kinship with Ohioans?) "Near West" is more like it. For those on the Atlantic Coast, there's no difference between Ohio and Oklahoma. The only people who consider Ohio to be East are Californians, Hawaiians, and the folks who drew up the time zones. "Great Lakes" as a regional label brings to mind Michigan or Wisconsin, not Ohio, despite its 262-mile Lake Erie shoreline.

Yet Ohioans know where they belong. They possess a quiet confidence, a clarity of purpose, a security in place. Humorist and famous *New Yorker* contributor James Thurber, a Columbus native, wrote, "Half of my books could not have been written if it had not been for the city of my birth." Ohio's steady, nurturing feel comes in part from an economy that, from its inception, has been almost perpetually healthy and made it a place of possibility for a dozen generations. In 1909 Wilbur Wright told an audience, "If I were giving a young man advice in how he might succeed in life, I would say to him, pick out a good mother and father and begin life in Ohio."

Many did. Ohio's population quintupled between 1800 and 1810. But as Ohio filled in, some Ohioans moved farther west in search of cheaper land and more opportunity. The Ohio River, and then later the National Road, provided what passed for convenient access to western lands, while Lake Erie, the Ohio, and the Appalachian Mountains made the state the small end of a funnel through which many would pass to populate the rest of the continent.

Roads and crops form geometric patterns in Wayne County's Amish Country, part of the largest Amish community in the world, about forty thousand strong.

The Ohio Gate, the old entrance to the Ohio State Fairgrounds, was torn down in 2002.

The National Road, the first major road-building effort to link the East Coast and the newly acquired lands west of the Appalachian Mountains, was authorized by Congress in 1806; construction began in 1811. When completed, it ran more than 600 miles from Cumberland, Maryland, to Vandalia, Illinois, and was a major cultural influence and factor in Ohio's settlement. Now known as U.S. 40, it runs through Zanesville, Columbus, and Springfield.

Because so many settlers passed through Ohio and because the state has such well-preserved and meticulously kept records, genealogists from around the country come here to document their ancestors. (The Ohio Genealogical Society is the largest such state society in the country.) So, many Americans' forebears were Ohioans at one time, even if briefly, and to some extent all indulged in the abundance and opportunity that it afforded. "It will be our own fault if we are not the happiest people in the union," the author and politician Caleb Atwater said in 1838.

Recent times have been harder. Fierce global trade and migration of companies to southern and western states have hit many cities and counties hard, especially those that rely on manufacturing. In 2003 Ohio lost more jobs than any other state except Michigan. On the upside, Ohioans have become more competitive, reinvested in communities and culture, and transformed Ohio into an eminently livable space and a wide-ranging travel experience. Cleveland is Exhibit A: the onetime punch line has given us a bustling waterfront playground, popular entertainment districts, and a network of first-class parks. Overall, it's one very attractive city. Around the state the story is similar: new museums, parks, and entertainment; improved planning; revitalized streetscapes; restored historic districts; and renewed energy.

The best part is that much of this cultural resurgence has embraced the past instead of erasing it. The old hat has been patched and embroidered to yield funky new headgear. Thus there are new, recreational uses for the old canal system; renovated loft-style housing in historic urban districts; and reclaimed mining land, like that of the Wilds, an exotic-animal park near Cumberland.

Recognizing the importance of outdoor recreation, Ohio has cleaned up its act environmentally. Both Lake Erie and the Ohio River are cleaner than they've been in years and are popular attractions for fishing and boating. Top float streams for canoeing—the Mohican, Little Muskingum, and Little Miami—draw many groups in spring and summer. The state park system has been recognized as the best in the country. And Appalachian Ohio—a crescent-shaped slice of southeast Ohio that runs from south of Canton to just east of Cincinnati and has historically been the state's poorest and most underdeveloped region and is considered part of Appalachia—has emerged as the state's outdoor playground, in part because of the topography and a move toward recreation over industry.

As a cradle of Americana, Ohio has its share of celebrities and highly regarded figures, many of whom are so ingrained in the popular imagination that they transcend its borders. In a state claiming eight presidents, Orville and Wilbur Wright get top billing (as much a statement about Ohio's presidents as the Wrights). Among the host of other notable Ohioans are John Glenn, Neil Armstrong, Annie Oakley, Tecumseh, Bob Hope, and Toni Morrison. The names keep coming, figures from all walks of life who confirm a synchronicity between what Ohio has produced and what people see as essentially American. Jesse Owens, John D. Rockefeller, Gloria Steinem, Paul Newman.

Morning fog creeps over Holmes County farm fields in Amish Country.

Ohio became a state not long after Vermont and drew its share of New England settlers just as Vermont did. That might be where the similarities end. Since the early 1990s a small but sincere group of Vermonters has campaigned to make the state an independent republic. The plan isn't as crazy as it might seem; Vermont was a sovereign nation from 1777 until 1791, when it became the fourteenth state. Similar movements have arisen in other states. But can anyone imagine Ohio entertaining such an idea? Were citizens here to feel overburdened and underheard by the federal government, they would instead mount a campaign to put candidates into every elected office in Washington. They'd have Ohioans running for *Virginia's* Senate seats. Winston Churchill's quote about the United States applies equally to Ohio: "The United States is like a gigantic boiler. Once the fire is lit, there is no limit to the power it can generate."

Procter & Gamble's headquarters pays homage to Cincinnati's art deco tradition.

Before the Civil War some of the town of Oberlin's more aggressive abolitionists fueled the conflicts leading to war by freeing a runaway slave from jail in nearby Wellington. Many in the group, known as the Rescuers, were tried, but they eventually were released on the condition that they leave northern Ohio. The incident galvanized opposition to slavery in Ohio. During World War II the state's enormous manufacturing base—composed of General Electric, General Motors, Goodyear, Firestone, Crosley, and many others—was a major part of the production machine that secured an American victory. And when necessary, Ohioans have also spoken out vociferously against war, as the tragedy at Kent State continually reminds us.

This sense of determination, of high stakes and resourcefulness, has played out again and again in Ohio's culture. You can see it in innumerable innovations—all-American developments such as the electric traffic light, the pop-top can, and the coed swimming pool. You can see it on the state's high school football fields, where the game is less a sport and more a way of life, and at Ohio State, where the Horseshoe can draw more than one hundred thousand fans. And you can see it in the people who live here generation after generation and are intent on making it a great place to play and explore.

The pages that follow are my interpretation of Ohio. It doesn't come close to exhausting everything there is to see and do, and you won't find admission prices and restaurant reviews. Rather, this is a guide to be read. I have searched for what's best and notable, whether facts or destinations, and tied them together in a way that will allow you to make informed travel choices and better understand the places you're visiting, or just leisurely explore the state from an armchair.

There is one other possibility for a regional label for Ohio, one I'm drawn to despite its license-plate overtones and somewhat ambiguous meaning: the Heartland. For two hundred years, Ohio has been building an empire at home and sending ambassadors into the world at large to explore, conquer, govern, invent, entertain, and create—and then return home to recharge. If it's true that the United States couldn't survive as we know it without Ohioans, then I know of no better name. Welcome to the Heartland.

HISTORY AND CULTURE

To settle in Ohio is to be satisfied. More than anything, the place means comfort, a stable haven where people flourish in realms of their own making. From the beginning, people have come to carve out their own piece of America, seen as due to them in a new land of opportunity. It's a place where the most miraculous events have taken place—epic battles, groundbreaking inventions, and fiery speeches—though modesty and practicality usually reign. An outsider, or even an insider, likely couldn't put a finger on what makes Ohio Ohio, because it's at once everything and nothing, an amalgam and an enigma.

Among Americans at large, a man-on-the-street survey about Ohio would probably yield two vague impressions: that it's short on diversity and that it is in some way connected to buckeyes. The first notion is not exactly true. Place-names, architectural styles, and a range of ethnic cuisines speak of the incredible diversity the state has seen, although most of those do come from groups that long ago integrated and tapped the accompanying economic advantages. Germans and Irish are the largest ethnic groups associated with Ohio; African-Americans also have a significant presence. Recent immigration has been more modest, with a small but growing Hispanic population, particularly in the northwest, and a similar trend with Asians in major cities and university communities. But it is true that Ohio will never see the overwhelming diversity of a New York or California by virtue of its sandwiched location.

The buckeye connection is more accurate, although too many people are hazy on what a buckeye is. The name comes from the buckeye tree, the state tree, which produces five-leaf clusters and dark-brown, polished-looking nuts with a tan circle that resembles a deer's eye. Ohio lore has it that Indians applied the name to Col. Ebenezer Sproat, one of the state's earliest settlers, for his imposing stature and presence. The gritty Sproat enjoyed his nickname, and over time "Buckeye" came to represent white settlers in general. (Later, it also became a tasty confection consisting of peanut butter balls dipped in chocolate.) The nut serves little purpose beyond aesthetics and folklore—it's bitter and poisonous—but the tree is tenacious and intent on growing everywhere. Pioneers had a hard time killing it; even after being cut and used to build cabins, buckeye logs would put out new leaves. The perfect symbol for Ohio.

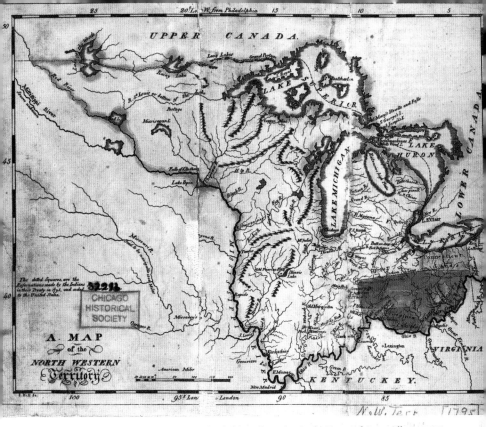

The shaded area on this map shows land ceded by Ohio tribes in the Treaty of Greenville in 1795.

If there's a common thread among Buckeyes, it's a strong work ethic. In Ohio, they say, the barns are bigger than the houses. But it doesn't matter whether Ohioans live on the farm or in the city. The typical answer for people here is hard work and dedication, regardless of the question. And from the beginning, they've had a lot to work with.

■ ORIGINAL OHIO

For centuries before the first Europeans arrived in Ohio, the land offered indigenous tribes a richness almost beyond compare. The entire state was part of a forest stretching from the Atlantic seaboard to Missouri and as diverse as it was broad. Oak and hickory forests in the southeastern portion of the state gave way to mixed beech forests and then elm and ash in the swamplands of the northwest. Game was abundant, and crops could be planted to supplement the food supply. Relatively even terrain made travel more manageable than in the Appalachians to the east and south, and while winters could be harsh around the lake, there was also shelter in the hills and many rivers for food and transportation.

One way to measure the bounty of the land is to look at the cultural sophistication of prehistoric tribes. Early cultures like the Adena and Hopewell built earthworks based on various solar and astronomical alignments and crafted elaborate pipes, jewelry, headdresses, talismans, and other objects out of materials unavailable in Ohio. Based on those relics, archaeologists have mapped out an extensive trade network that included inhabitants from the East Coast to the Rockies and from Canada to the Gulf of Mexico. All of this required spare time, organization, and socialization that people in a less forgiving land would have found an impossible luxury.

Ohio was the nexus of a mound-building culture centered on the rich river bottoms of the eastern United States. Upon arriving, frontier settlers encountered thousands of these mounds, small and large, conical and flat-topped, round, oblong, and rectangular. The names of both the Adena and Hopewell come from 19th-century landowners on whose property mounds from those cultures were discovered. The mounds could have served several purposes, depending on their location and the peoples who built them. Some are burial mounds, the product of religious rituals that necessitated an intricate process of digging, lodge construction, and layering of soils. Others seem to correspond to astronomical alignments and may have been used for telling time. No one knows for sure how many mounds might have been destroyed as new arrivals cleared the land and pressed it into agricultural service, but it's a safe bet that many more existed than we know about today.

The same natural wealth that supported ancient cultures also nurtured strong latter-day tribes in Ohio, including the Shawnee, Miami, and Delaware. The military units and early settlers who pushed into the Ohio Country met fierce resistance that surely frustrated white leaders who assumed settlement was a given. By that time the Delaware already had been moved west from their traditional lands. Ohio tribes had not just the physical prowess and technical capability to defend the territory, thanks in part to European allies, but they also had the necessary political organization. They formed alliances with the French, who set up forts in the Great Lakes region and eastern Canada, to keep the British colonists at bay. French outposts such as Fort Niagara, Fort Detroit, Fort Duquesne at Pittsburgh, and Fort Miami at Toledo threatened Britain's interests in the Ohio Valley. The tribes aligned themselves with the French in the 1754–1760 French and Indian War, which the British won when Montreal fell in 1760.

Ironically, after the war the British became the Indians' tenuous allies as colonists' loyalty to the crown wavered in the face of increased taxes and a proclamation prohibiting settlement west of the Appalachians. Britain's alliance was expedient rather than principled. After the expense of the French and Indian War, it couldn't afford to quell more insurrections in the North American colonies. When the Revolution began in 1775, natives hoped that the British could put down the American rebellion, uphold colonial law, and prevent native lands from being overrun. The Ohio Country was a land worth defending.

■ BATTLE FOR OHIO

Once the Americans gained clear ownership of the Ohio Valley with victory over Great Britain in 1783, squatters began venturing over the Appalachians and settling along the Ohio River. The Confederation Congress ordered Josiah Harmar and a small contingent of other soldiers to flush illegal settlers out of Ohio and protect early surveyors until Congress could set forth a governmental structure for the entire Northwest Territory, including Ohio. He built Fort Harmar at the confluence of the Muskingum and Ohio rivers. (Ironically, squatters looked to Fort Harmar for protection from hostile Indians in the area.) The necessary organization came in the Northwest Ordinance of 1787, a seminal document establishing freedom of religion, civil rights, and freedom from slavery in the Northwest Territory, and laid the groundwork for most later state constitutions in the west. At the time, even the original thirteen states did not outlaw slavery. Marietta, the first permanent settlement in the Northwest Territory, became a paragon of democratic governance. "No colony in America was ever settled under such favorable auspices as that which has just commenced at the Muskingum," George Washington said. But unlike the rest of southern Ohio, which would be settled by Virginians and other southerners, Marietta was settled by migrants from the Northeast, a group more commonly associated with northeast Ohio.

The territory's first settlements were all along the Ohio River because of hostile Indians north of the river. The United States pushed for greater access and sent first Harmar and then Gen. Arthur St. Clair (also the territorial governor) to do battle and clear the land for settlement. Both suffered crushing defeats, with St. Clair's

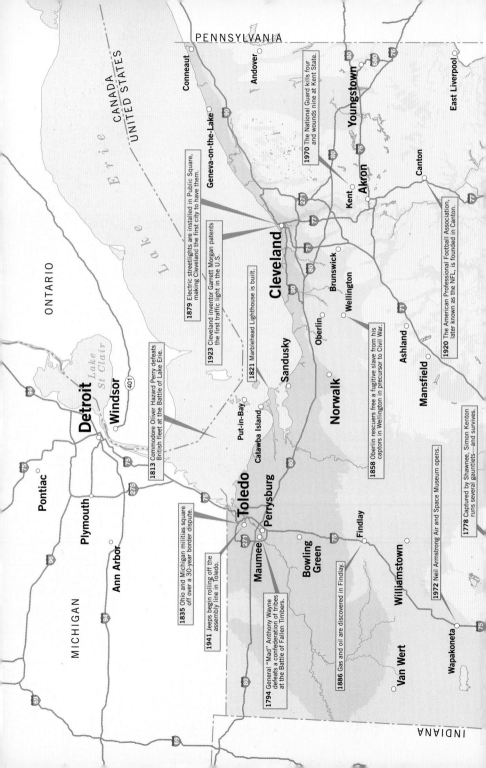

PENNSYLVANIA

CANADA
UNITED STATES

ONTARIO

MICHIGAN

INDIANA

Lake Erie

Lake St. Clair

Conneaut

Andover

Geneva-on-the-Lake

Youngstown

East Liverpool

Akron

Kent

Canton

Cleveland

Brunswick

Wellington

Oberlin

Ashland

Sandusky

Mansfield

Norwalk

Put-in-Bay

Catawba Island

Detroit

Windsor

Pontiac

Plymouth

Ann Arbor

Toledo

Maumee

Perrysburg

Bowling Green

Findlay

Williamstown

Van Wert

Wapakoneta

1879 Electric streetlights are installed in Public Square, making Cleveland the first city to have them.

1923 Cleveland inventor Garrett Morgan patents the first traffic light in the U.S.

1821 Marblehead Lighthouse is built.

1970 The National Guard kills four and wounds nine at Kent State.

1920 The American Professional Football Association, later known as the NFL, is founded in Canton.

1858 Oberlin rescuers free a fugitive slave from his captors in Wellington in precursor to Civil War.

1813 Commodore Oliver Hazard Perry defeats British fleet at the Battle of Lake Erie.

1835 Ohio and Michigan militias square off over a 30-year border dispute.

1941 Jeeps begin rolling off the assembly line in Toledo.

1794 General "Mad" Anthony Wayne defeats a confederation of tribes at the Battle of Fallen Timbers.

1972 Neil Armstrong Air and Space Museum opens.

1778 Captured by Shawnee, Simon Kenton runs several gauntlets—and survives.

1886 Gas and oil are discovered in Findlay.

HISTORIC OHIO

Elevation in feet
1,549
1,250
1,000
750
569

0   20   40 Miles
0   20   40   60 Kilometers

Modern freeways shown in gray

WEST VIRGINIA

KENTUCKY

Charleston

1782 A Pennsylvania militia kills 96 Christian Indians in the Gnadenhutten Massacre.

1785 Martin's Ferry, then called Mercer, becomes the first white settlement in Ohio.

1804 Ohio University becomes the first university in the Northwest Territory.

1899 Milligan hits a low temperature of -39°F., the lowest on record in Ohio.

1863 Union troops defeat Brig. Gen. John Hunt Morgan at the Battle of Buffington Island, after a string of Confederate cavalry raids in Indiana and Ohio.

1825 Work begins on Ohio's canal system at Licking Summit.

2003 Series of I-270 shootings alarms central Ohio residents.

1802 Mount Logan inspires the design of the Ohio State Seal.

1884 Disgruntled miners in New Straitsville set fire to the coal mines, which still burn underground today.

1934 Gallipolis hits a high temperature of 113°F., the highest on record in Ohio.

1974 Severe tornado in Xenia kills 36 and destroys much of the city.

1866 John A. Roebling Suspension Bridge, prototype for the Brooklyn Bridge, is completed.

1904 After Kitty Hawk, the Wright brothers make experimental flights at Dayton's Huffman Prairie.

1933 First official Soap Box Derby is held.

goes 4-3-2 in his first year at Ohio State.

Martin's Ferry
Wheeling
Zanesville
Parkersburg
Belpre
Athens
Logan
Lancaster
Marysville
Piqua
Greenville
Dublin
COLUMBUS
Chillicothe
▲ Mt Logan
Gallipolis
Xenia
Wilmington
Portsmouth
Dayton
Hamilton
Cincinnati
Covington
Ripley
Maysville

Territorial Governor Arthur St. Clair kept a log while in the Northwest Territory.

the largest loss of men the United States would ever see in Indian wars—more than twice as many as at the Battle of the Little Bighorn. Gen. "Mad" Anthony Wayne led the Americans' third campaign with a force trained in the frontier tactics that St. Clair had failed to use. Wayne and two thousand other men marched north from Fort Washington, present-day Cincinnati, and established Fort Recovery at the site of St. Clair's defeat. Although stricken with a bad case of gout, Wayne routed the Indians and their white leader, Blue Jacket, near Britain's Fort Miami (Toledo) at the Battle of Fallen Timbers in 1794.

The British offered no help to prevent the decisive victory; the Indians had no choice but to agree to withdraw from Ohio. The Treaty of Greenville, which General Wayne negotiated in 1795, finalized that fate. Only the northwest corner of the state remained viable for the Miami, Shawnee, Wyandot, Delaware, and other tribes that agreed to the treaty, and Ohio's expansion wrested even that from them in the decades to come. The Miami chief Little Turtle, who had led the two successful campaigns against Harmar and St. Clair, indirectly summarized the weighty implications of tribal displacement on a later trip to Philadelphia: "When

I walk through your streets, I see people busy at their work, making shoes, hats, selling cloth. I say to myself—which of these can you do? And I answer: not one. I can make a bow, an arrow, catch fish, kill game. But none of these is of use in your city. Old age comes and I must be in my own country."

■ ROAD TO STATEHOOD

With the Treaty of Greenville making most of the state safe for average citizens and families to settle, southern Ohio boomed. Owning land was a primary goal for most everyone at the time—for farming, status, and resources. In 1800 two developments made moving to Ohio even more appealing. The Harrison Land Act cut down the acreage a settler was required to buy and extended credit to the purchaser, who could make payment over several years. A buyer could secure 320 acres for as little as $2 per acre. Also in 1800, Connecticut relinquished its claim to the Western Reserve, a slice of land in northeast Ohio extending along Lake Erie and including Cleveland and Akron. The Western Reserve had been given to Connecticut to compensate the state for lands it had given up to New York State. Although most of the Western Reserve was later sold to a land company, it brought many Connecticut settlers and other New Englanders to Ohio. Connecticut offered land in the western part of the reserve, known as the Firelands, to certain Connecticut residents as compensation for property lost or destroyed during the Revolution. Moses Cleaveland and the Connecticut Land Company surveyed the reserve east of the Cuyahoga River—conducted separately and using a different style from that used for federal land surveys—which would see rapid settlement by New Englanders. (The town of Cleaveland on the Cuyahoga was among the places platted, in 1796. Later the name would be shortened to Cleveland.)

The Northwest Ordinance of 1787 dictated that a territory must have sixty thousand inhabitants before it could petition for statehood. By 1800, the territory was well on its way, with a population of forty-five thousand. Chillicothe, in south-central Ohio, was the center of activism for statehood. Thomas Worthington and his brother-in-law Edward Tiffin, two well-to-do Virginia transplants, had bought land in Chillicothe and were soon immersed in territorial politics. Worthington served in the territorial legislature, as did Tiffin, who later became Speaker of the Ohio Statehouse. Both pushed for statehood and, as Democratic-Republicans, opposed the policies of the territorial governor, Arthur St. Clair. St. Clair, known for losing the worst Indian battle in American history, was a Federalist and in the minority on the frontier. He hoped to delay statehood until the Federalists could gain a stronger hold in Ohio and recommended that the Scioto River be the Ohio Territory's western boundary (which would split the population needed for statehood and exclude Chillicothe). With help from Democratic-Republican Thomas Jefferson, Tiffin, Worthington, and the other constitutional delegates overrode this measure and passed a state constitution calling for limited government that received approval from the U.S. House and Senate in 1803. Tiffin became the first governor of Ohio, the seventeenth state.

■ TECUMSEH AND THE WAR OF 1812

The population quintupled between 1800 and 1810 as word spread of the opportunities and fertile land available in the new state. The borders of Indian territory defined in the Treaty of Greenville (with the Cuyahoga River, now in the middle of Cleveland, marking the Indians' eastern perimeter) soon appeared ill-conceived to residents in the Western Reserve who had been promised some of the land now being given to the Indians. Ohio negotiated round after round of treaties with the natives, who, under duress, ceded more land to the settlers' government. Weakened and outnumbered, the Indians had little choice but to sign.

There was some small hope for the Indians. The British had never fully complied with the 1783 Treaty of Paris, which was negotiated with the United States to end the Revolutionary War. This treaty required them to withdraw from the territory between the Appalachians and the Mississippi, but the British continued to exact revenge for their defeat by raiding American merchant ships, forcing U.S.

Colonel Richard Johnson defeats Tecumseh's forces at the Battle of the Thames, October 5, 1813.

seamen into service on naval ships, and, critically, equipping native tribes with weapons and supplies to continue attacks on Ohio settlements. The older chiefs who had seen the bloody fighting of previous campaigns were inclined to move west and forsake whatever territory would appease the settlers, but the young warriors wanted to take a stand.

The charismatic Shawnee warrior Tecumseh led these efforts with his brother, Tenskwatawa, a purported mystic known as the Prophet. Tecumseh visited many tribes in the Old Northwest—Indiana, Wisconsin, Illinois, and Michigan—to build support for a unified resistance. They began gathering at Prophetstown, a camp on the Tippecanoe River in Indiana. The Indiana territorial governor William Henry Harrison knew about Tecumseh's plans, however, and was determined to crush any insurrections. In 1811, while Tecumseh was away persuading more warriors to join the cause, Harrison led a force of a thousand men encamped near Prophetstown. Against Tecumseh's wishes, the Prophet rallied the warriors for a preemptive strike on the camp. Harrison's army repelled the attack and burned the lodges and supplies the tribes had amassed at Prophetstown. The last best chance for the confederation of Indians to regain control of their lost range was gone. When Tecumseh returned a month later, he recognized what had happened and led what remained of his followers to Canada to seek aid from the British.

American settlers' feelings of vulnerability to Indian attack and Britain's support of the natives contributed to the War of 1812. In Ohio the war centered on the defense of the Lake Erie shoreline, Fort Meigs on the Maumee River, and Fort Stephenson at present-day Fremont, near Sandusky Bay. The settlers' plan was to take the British's Fort Detroit and Fort Malden, on the Canadian side, in order to cut off port access to the British fleet on Lake Erie. The Americans tenaciously, and successfully, defended their key forts—despite the superior artillery, supplies, and troops of the British—and demoralized the alliance of English and Indians by causing heavy casualties. But it was young Commodore Oliver Hazard Perry who forced the British to retreat from Ohio. Perry's shipbuilders had hastily constructed a small fleet in Pennsylvania in hopes of wresting control of Lake Erie from the

THE BATTLE OF LAKE ERIE, COMMODORE O.H.PERRY'S VICTORY.

Commodore Perry declared: "We have met the enemy and they are ours . . ."

British captain Robert Barclay. With a core crew of sailors augmented by inexperienced soldiers and volunteers, Perry headed to western Lake Erie and, some weeks later, encountered Barclay and his fleet near South Bass Island. Perry's *Lawrence* and *Niagara* led a fleet of nine against Barclay's six vessels and in an intense three-hour battle forced their surrender, culminating in Perry's famous message to Harrison: "We have met the enemy and they are ours: two ships, two brigs, one schooner, and one sloop." The Battle of Lake Erie marked the turning point in the war; at the time, it was the worst defeat ever of a British fleet.

■ TWIN MISTRESSES: AGRICULTURE AND TRANSPORTATION

With few exceptions, the early white settlers in Ohio were farmers. In 1830, 96 percent of the population still lived in rural areas. Outside of the Appalachian hill country, soils were generally fertile, but new residents had to clear the land first, an exhausting task. Corn was the staple crop because of its ability to thrive in a variety of soils. The farm work was done by hand, and large jobs such as cabin raisings and corn husking were social occasions that called for help from the entire family as well as neighbors.

The prairie states traditionally thought of as America's breadbasket—Illinois, Iowa, Kansas, Nebraska—were not yet a force in agricultural production. Ohio at times led the country in some farm production, including corn, wheat, and sheep, and even as western states emerged, Ohio's production of corn and hogs continued to grow. This was in part thanks to technological advances and to gains in arable land. Around 1850 the introduction of machine-made clay drainage tiles literally paved the way for the conversion of northwest Ohio's marshes to ultrarich farmland.

Agriculture in the state developed alongside the country's interior infrastructure. Even before the War of 1812, the first steamboat had made the trip from Pittsburgh down the Ohio and Mississippi rivers to New Orleans; a decade later, commercial steamboat traffic on the Ohio was brisk and popular. Cincinnati, the country's primary western city besides New Orleans, flourished as a major port and builder of steamboats. Around that time, Congress was making plans for a primary thoroughfare that would link Washington, D.C., with key states to the west. The National Road, which had reached Wheeling, West Virginia, by 1818, further improved the market for Ohio farm goods and eased the way for westward migrants, who had previously traveled by river or circuitous wagon trails.

Still, the biggest boon for the state was the completion of the canals that connected the Ohio River with Lake Erie and united the most populous regions of the state. The idea came from New York, where the canals connecting the Hudson River and Lake Erie had worked so well. In Ohio there were two main canals—the Miami & Erie Canal between Cincinnati and Toledo, and the Ohio & Erie Canal between Portsmouth and Cleveland—and two spurs, to Athens and Marietta. Trade in towns along the canals improved, and transient villages were transformed into viable cities. Ohio now had an infrastructure as good as or better than its promising young economy. The placement and corresponding sizes of Ohio's cities still testify to the canals' economic effects.

■ SLAVERY AND THE CIVIL WAR

Before the Civil War, Ohio, like many Northern states, was in the curious position of opposing slavery and inhumane treatment for African-Americans while denying them basic rights and deterring their migration here. In keeping with Ohio's constitution, African-Americans could not vote, that being the province of free white men. They could not serve on juries, send their children to public schools, or join the militia. "Black laws," although frequently skirted, required that they post a $500 bond and furnish evidence of their free status upon entering Ohio. Nevertheless, there were more opportunities for African-Americans to live the good life here than in the South. The New Englanders of the Western Reserve were particularly accommodating.

From the 1830s on, abolition was a significant force in Ohio politics, and as a border state, Ohio was bound to become a battleground. Merchants and businessmen in southern Ohio who dealt with Southern companies found it expedient to adopt a sympathetic view of slavery, genuine or not. On the other side, Southern progressives who received little tolerance from the slave-owning populace for their abolitionist stances migrated to Ohio. The antislavery movement in Ohio found its most ardent supporters in religious circles, notably the Quakers, Presbyterians, Methodists, and Congregationalists. The preacher Lyman Beecher, father of Harriet Beecher Stowe, founded Cincinnati's Lane Theological Seminary, a school that became a rallying point for abolition. Congregationalist Oberlin, southwest of Cleveland, was a strong center for the anti-slavery movement and Underground Railroad activity revolving around Oberlin College, the first in the country to admit black students. Oberlin professors Charles Grandison Finney and Theodore

Weld instilled in students an enthusiasm for abolition that caught on far beyond the town's borders. And John Brown, infamous for his quixotic siege of the Harpers Ferry armory in a precursor to the Civil War, helped conduct fugitive slaves as a young boy near Akron.

These righteous campaigns masked the mixed and complicated views of many Ohioans, including those of abolitionist radicals, and when Confederates attacked Fort Sumter, South Carolina, in April 1861, it wasn't a given that Ohio would support a war against the South. Ironically, the state's southern counties met their recruitment quotas for soldiers during the war better than the Western Reserve counties, where the draft had to be instituted. In the congressional elections of 1862, Democrats won fourteen of Ohio's

Lyman Beecher, preacher, abolitionist, and father of Harriet Beecher Stowe.

nineteen seats. The next year Clement Vallandigham ran for governor against John Brough, a newspaper publisher and longtime democratic politician who broke with the Democratic Party that year. Vallandigham ran as a "Peace Democrat" who opposed slavery but also opposed civil war and had called for Lincoln's impeachment. He was imprisoned as a traitor before the election yet enjoyed wide support and still carried eighteen counties. Lincoln expressed his gratitude to Brough, who supported the Union, in a telegram afterward: "Glory to God in the Highest. Ohio has saved the Union."

Those contentious aspects of Ohio's Civil War–era history are mostly forgotten now, because the men who did fight spawned a celebrated legacy. Ohio produced more soldiers for the Union, some three hundred and fifty thousand, than any other state save the more populous New York and Pennsylvania. In two generations Ohio had matured from frontier backwater to political heavyweight. Some of the

ALL OF OHIO'S MEN

For fifty-four heady years from 1869 to 1923—not counting the monthlong presidency of Virginia-born William Henry Harrison—Ohioans dominated the country's highest office. Of the fourteen elections between 1868 and 1920, Ohioans won nine. Many of these presidents were dark horses or compromise candidates who somehow rose to the top of the ticket. These were party men, best known for not rocking the boat, rather than for displaying the brash, controversial leadership that shines in history books. The state's status as a bridge between East and West, its wealth of Civil War heroes, and its reputation for steady, centrist leadership made people from Ohio a safe choice. Unfortunately, these things also made the names of these people difficult to recall. A refresher follows. (Non-Ohioan presidents are listed in italics to help set the stage.)

1841 *William Henry Harrison* (1773–1841). "Old Tippecanoe" spent his adult life in North Bend, Ohio, although he was born in Virginia. Despite his aristocratic origins, Harrison capitalized on perceptions of him as a backwoods roughneck with a "log cabin" campaign, which subsequent presidents, including Lincoln, would use to great effect. His campaign slogan, "Tippecanoe and Tyler Too," invoked Harrison's victorious battle against an Indian insurgency at Tippecanoe led by the Prophet, Tecumseh's brother, in 1811. (John Tyler was Harrison's vice presidential candidate.) The rugged war hero met his match in bitter temperatures at his inauguration, where, underdressed, he gave a long-winded speech and died of pneumonia a month later, the shortest tenure of any president.

1869–1877 **Ulysses S. Grant** (1822–1885). Grant, frankly, was a brilliant military strategist and a marginal politician. Nevertheless, being a war hero was enough to offset his inadequacies as a politician in the court of public opinion. His biggest problem was mis-

(left) William H. Harrison. (right, clockwise from top left) Grant, Hayes, Benjamin Harrison, Garfield.

placed trust in appointees, who were intent only on profiting from it. His last great act was writing his memoirs, which stabilized his family's financial situation before his death and are still a compelling read.

1877–1881   Rutherford B. Hayes (1822–1893). Hayes never intended to serve more than one term and was more than happy to be rid of the presidency and return to Fremont, making his struggle to the White House all the more ironic. Hayes won the most bitterly contested election up to that time, over the Democrat Samuel Tilden. Backdoor party deals brought Hayes South Carolina, Florida, and Louisiana after recounts that gave him one hundred eighty-five electoral votes to Tilden's one hundred eighty-four. Critics called him "Rutherfraud."

1881   James A. Garfield (1831–1881). Garfield's magical oratorical ability won him the presidency and sealed his fate—assassination at the hands of a spurned would-be appointee. He dazzled delegates at the 1880 Republican Convention with a speech nominating John Sherman for president, who, it turns out, never stood a chance. Garfield didn't want to be president; he accepted out of duty. His intellect and classical education didn't translate into strong leadership, and he succumbed to the demands of party bosses.

1881–1885   Chester Arthur

1885–1889   Grover Cleveland

(above) McKinley speaks at his 1897 inauguration with Cleveland looking on.
(right, at top) Taft never matched Roosevelt's legacy. (right, at bottom) Harding addresses a crowd at the Capitol.

1889–1893   Benjamin Harrison (1833–1901). Harrison grew up in North Bend, Ohio, home of his grandfather William Henry Harrison, and studied at both Miami University and the University of Cincinnati. Another powerful orator but a cold individual, Harrison wrestled with the same patronage system that had undone James Garfield: "When I came into power, I found that the party managers had taken it all to themselves. . . . They had sold out every place to pay for the election."

1893–1897   Grover Cleveland

1897–1901   William McKinley (1843–1901). A kind and respectable man, McKinley was known for his staid demeanor and conservative economic policies, which made him the safe choice over the Populist William Jennings Bryan in 1896. In 1901 he won the same race again on the strength of emerging imperialism. McKinley doted on his invalid wife, Ida, and took care to protect her even after he was shot, warning an aide to be careful in breaking the news to her. He was probably the best of the Ohioan presidents.

1901–1909   Theodore Roosevelt

1909–1913   William Howard Taft (1857–1930). With his girth and handlebar mustache, Taft might have made a good strongman. Having been the vice president for people's favorite Teddy Roosevelt, he was a strong politician whose legacy has been hampered by comparison to Roosevelt's and by his own beliefs in strict interpretation of presidential powers. Taft was more progressive than he gets credit for and might be better remembered under different circumstances: in the 1912 election, when T.R. ran again, Taft got hammered as both the pro-Roosevelt and anti-Roosevelt president. (He was considered too close to T.R. for those who disliked Roosevelt's progressive politics.)

1913–1921   Woodrow Wilson

1921–1923   William G. Harding (1865–1923). Harding fell into politics as the publisher of the *Marion Star,* a small-town newspaper. Indisputably the worst of the Ohioan presidents, he lacked the political savvy to lead effectively and the good character judgment to choose people who could. Harding's famous quote about his scandal-plagued administration sums it up: "I can take care of my enemies all right. But my damn friends, my God . . . they're the ones that keep me walking the floor at night." Harding died in office while in San Francisco, shortly before his scandals broke.

war's most illustrious Union figures were Ohioans or had been raised there: Gen. Ulysses Grant, who first led volunteer forces from Illinois but grew up in Point Pleasant, near Cincinnati; Lancaster native Gen. William Tecumseh Sherman, one of the most colorful individuals of the era, a gritty hero unafraid to speak his mind and dismissed by his detractors as crazy; and Gen. Philip Sheridan, a valiant fighter and able cavalry leader best remembered for a 20-mile journey to rejoin and rally his troops near Winchester, Virginia, known as Sheridan's Ride. In addition, the Civil War credentials of Ohioan presidents to come—including Grant, Rutherford Hayes, James Garfield, Benjamin Harrison, and William McKinley—would reinforce the state's contribution to the war in later years.

■ INDUSTRY COMES OF AGE

Even more so than during its early farm period, Ohio's location made it the place to be as industry steadily supplanted agriculture after the Civil War. In the first part of the 19th century, the Appalachians had shielded the state's farm economy from the bigger markets to the east and given it a chance to thrive in isolation. But as the population moved west and transportation became cheap, Ohio found itself in the middle of it all—better positioned to serve the western markets than East Coast states and vice versa.

With the new age, power began shifting from Cincinnati and the southwest to the northeast. Louisville and St. Louis now rivaled Cincinnati for river-city dominance. Cleveland, meanwhile, was ideally situated to process crude oil discovered in western Pennsylvania and manufacture iron and steel from the iron ore common around Lake Superior. Industry prospered throughout the state and endowed cities with reputations that endure today. Local clays in East Liverpool, Steubenville, Zanesville, Perry County, and Cincinnati spawned pottery businesses. Marietta thrived on brick making. There was steel in Youngstown and Canton, glass in Toledo, rubber in Akron, and gas and oil in Findlay, where Marathon Oil still has a presence. Cincinnati was known for pork processing and soap making, which used pork fat in its manufacture and aided the rise of consumer giant Procter & Gamble.

The incredible success and integration that ensued created the first modern corporations, operating on unprecedented scale and leveraging volume and capital to grow ever larger. John D. Rockefeller's Standard Oil Company is the classic example, built on credit and through Rockefeller's aggressive strategy of buyouts and vertical integration, in which he consolidated the entire process of oil production, from drilling to retail sales, to control costs and service and to crush competitors. Depending on whom you talk to, the man was either a robber baron (the Sherman Antitrust Act eventually brought about Standard's dissolution) or one of the greatest philanthropists and businessmen who ever lived (he donated $600 million to nonprofits). Mark Hanna, the famous industrialist who funded William McKinley's presidential bids, called Rockefeller "mad about money, though sane in everything else." One thing is certain: Rockefeller took full advantage of the government's lack of preparedness for capitalism on this scale and of the pro-business, status quo attitude of late-1800s presidents.

■ Ohio's Golden Age: 1896–1929

Somewhere between the news of the Wright brothers' accomplishments in flight and the election of William Howard Taft, the seventh Ohioan president, Ohio hit its stride. It continued as a crossroads of cultures and grew by 40 percent between 1900 and 1920 as workers streamed into the state to supply expanding businesses. New arrivals, including Germans, Irish, Czechs, Hungarians, Italians, Poles, Greeks, and Jews, infused much of the state with new languages and cultures and a relentless energy. Cleveland was by far the most ethnic city, meaning it was home to the largest number of first- and second-generation Americans of various ancestry.

Social reforms began to address corporate monopolies and the working conditions of the lower classes. In the state legislature, the African-American congressman Harry C. Smith helped pass the Smith Act in 1896, to prevent lynchings, and the Ohio Civil Rights Law, which made public discrimination based on race illegal. Around the same time, the reformist Toledo mayor Samuel "Golden Rule" Jones instituted an eight-hour workday for police and private contractors, built playgrounds and parks, brought kindergartens to the schools, and introduced a merit system to the police department. Similarly, during four terms in office, Cleveland mayor Tom Johnson began municipal garbage collection and secured cleaner water for the city; he worked to have streets paved, lighted, and cleaned; and he supported the revitalization of a decaying downtown through the influential Cleveland Group Plan, which involved construction of a series of municipal buildings in the downtown core that incorporated green space and attractive public areas.

The Ohio State University began teaching a cooking class in Hayes Hall in 1896.

Not everything was copacetic. As the industrial economy took hold in the late 1800s, the gap between rich and poor grew to record levels, and although the widening of this gap was mitigated, the gap itself continued into the 20th century. Economic prosperity and the influx of laborers to the cities precipitated out-of-control growth, overcrowding, and the corresponding problems of substandard housing, poor air quality, insufficient sewage management, and crime—some of the same issues that had led to reform in the first place. Intense competition for jobs prompted bitter labor disputes, particularly in the Appalachian region, among miners, who faced some of the worst working conditions imaginable. But the state was at the height of its powers, the country's population was still centered in the Midwest and Northeast, and growth and innovation continued to fuel a sense of limitless opportunity while progressive voices tempered the harshest consequences.

Prior to Ohio's golden age, it had a strong economic base but deplorable pollution and working conditions. During its golden age, Ohio had a strong economic base and an infusion of progressive politics that curbed some of the consequences of industrialization. After its golden age (i.e., during the Depression), the state lost much of its economic strength but retained a progressive bent. Thus, the second period, when the state had both economic prosperity and a sense of social justice, could be considered Ohio's historical peak.

One reason for Ohio's golden age was the rise of the automobile. In a real sense, the state created its own jobs. Before Henry Ford revolutionized the industry, Cleveland was its major center, and there's evidence that an Ohio City man built the first U.S. automobile, in 1891. Even after Detroit became the undisputed car capital, cities such as Cleveland, Akron, Toledo, Youngstown, Canton, and Dayton thrived as primary suppliers. Local inventors ensured that work. Charles Kettering, probably the state's most prominent inventor after the Wright brothers, developed the electric starter, quick-drying auto paint, and safety glass, and other inventors made significant progress with automobile-related projects. Much of the car culture we know today originated or was refined in Cleveland: the traffic light, the eight-cylinder car, automatic windshield wipers, hydraulic shock absorbers, and a process for making gasoline from fuel oil. Later, Ohioans and Ohio companies would invent the radar detector, the road striper, and the tubeless tire.

The breakthroughs weren't limited to cars. Inventions and new discoveries arrived at a breakneck pace and changed not just the way people in Ohio worked but also the way the entire country lived. In 1907 janitor James Murray Spangler of Canton invented the vacuum cleaner and shortly thereafter sold the rights to W. H. Hoover. Thomas Midgley, part of Charles Kettering's research team, invented Freon, a "miracle compound" still indispensable for refrigerators and air conditioners today. The myriad golden age inventions included polyvinyl chloride (PVC), Procter & Gamble's Crisco, Formica, and the KitchenAid mixer.

After World War I the social reforms continued. The state and country were changing dramatically, just as they would after World War II. Women gained the right to vote with the Nineteenth Amendment and in general enjoyed freedoms that wouldn't have been acceptable for respectable women of the Victorian era: more provocative dress, short hair, and smoking. Prohibition divided Ohioans and essentially killed off a once-vibrant brewing industry. The movement to go dry had deep roots in Ohio dating to the Reconstruction era, when it became a perennial political issue; Cleveland church women founded the influential Women's Christian Temperance Union in the 1870s. The other major force, the Anti-Saloon League, had national headquarters in Westerville, north of Columbus, for many years. The dry/wet debate illustrated the cultural disconnect between urban and rural. Rural counties were heavily religious and inclined to see drinking as a social evil. Urban counties, by contrast, had much higher immigrant populations, more relaxed values, and saloon keepers and commercial interests that depended on liquor sales. Under the sway of a shrinking rural electorate, Ohio voted for statewide prohibition by a slim margin, some twenty-five thousand votes.

On the national level, the debate was just as contentious. Prohibition was unenforceable, and many in power seemed to feel the rules were intended for others. "These miserable hypocrites in the House and Senate," President Woodrow Wilson fumed. "Voting to override my veto of the bill—many with their cellars stocked with liquors and not believing in Prohibition at all—jumping at the whip of lobbyists!" Presidential candidate Warren Harding, of Marion, Ohio, was one object of Wilson's anger. Senator Harding had helped pass the Volstead Act, which codified enforcement of Prohibition, but once elected president, he was known to serve liquor at White House poker games. Harding's attorney general even accepted bribes from bootleggers, as did police officers across the country.

■ MID-CENTURY

Labeling 1929 as the end of Ohio's golden age implies that the state's fortunes since then have been in a downward spiral, and that isn't true. Through the Great Depression, World War II, and the subsequent boom years, Ohio had its ups and downs like every other state. World War II demanded just the sort of large-scale production that Ohio's heavy industry was built for, and innovation again helped the state pull through. Cincinnati's Crosley Corporation, for example, created a "proximity fuse," which used a radio transmitter to detonate an explosive as it neared its target; this was one of the keys to winning the war. After the war, companies returned to consumer production, and both job growth and demand for goods soared. Veterans seeking an education on the GI bill streamed into Ohio's many universities. For a while, there was a new level of comfort and promise.

For a variety of reasons, the year 1929 did, however, mark the beginning of the state's waning importance on a national scale. Stricter immigration policies in the 1920s curtailed the ready supply of laborers and the mosaic of cultures they brought. Ohio's percentage of the national population has generally headed downward in each census since. The interstate highway system made the automobile not just a tool of weekend forays or inter-neighborhood commutes but also a practical way to separate work and home lives and to flee the poorer classes taking over the cities. In the course of twenty years, everything seemed to reverse. Cities, long associated with the generation of wealth, became poor, and rural areas became

The National Guard clashed with students at Kent State on May 4, 1970.

upwardly mobile. As the Democratic Party took up the cause of civil rights, some Democrats became Republicans and vice versa. Ohio's well-developed industrial infrastructure became a liability as manufacturers found it more expedient to build new facilities in the South and West rather than upgrade existing ones at home. Air-conditioning and, in the West, massive new water projects made it appealing to follow those jobs.

A growing discontent, a sense of the social machine drifting out of control, became concrete in the late days of April and early May 1970. The Vietnam War appeared to be unwinnable, and opposition to it had become the majority view. When President Nixon announced plans to invade Cambodia to pursue Vietcong (who would attack and then take refuge across the border), the public reacted immediately. Protests erupted at campuses around the state. The National Guard descended on Ohio State to quell vandalism and unrest. In Kent, northeast of Akron, protestors turned violent and burned the ROTC building on the Kent State campus. The governor, James Rhodes, called in the National Guard to restore order and denounced the protestors, but that only escalated confrontations. On Monday, May 4, at a rally of some three thousand students that university officials banned, the Guard fired suddenly into a crowd, killing four and wounding nine. Two of the students who were killed were walking to class; one was shot in the back.

Because of the circumstances leading up to the deaths, the sex and race of those who died—two of the dead were women and all four were white—and the public outcry afterward, Kent State has become synonymous with Vietnam dissent as well as with the entire counterculture movement. The shootings there set the political and cultural tone for the decade. Ten days after Kent State, highway patrolmen killed two students at Jackson State University in Mississippi; more than nine hundred colleges and universities had closed by the end of May. President Nixon began taking measures to ensure his reelection that eventually lead to the Watergate scandal. Neil Young wrote the song "Ohio," which used Kent State to dramatize the anger and alienation felt by anti-war Americans. And Kent State became an object lesson for police and military on how not to handle crowds of protestors.

Although politics and social issues were tumultuous through the 1960s, Ohio appeared as robust as ever in the traditionally strong areas of manufacturing, science, and technology. The space program of the 1960s had Ohio written all over it, affected as it was by the roles of Wright-Patterson Air Force Base in Dayton and the Lewis Research Center in Cleveland (renamed the Glenn Research Center in 1999) and contributions of such Ohio legends as John Glenn and Neil Armstrong. Glenn piloted the *Friendship 7* solo to become the first American to orbit the earth and the courageous guinea pig in a grand experiment. Before Glenn's flight, scientists didn't know for sure how a person would react to actual weightlessness during a rigorous flight at more than 17,000 mph. "People always tend to say, 'Well, what are you going to learn?' " Glenn says of space exploration. "If you already knew what you're gonna learn, you wouldn't be doing this in the first place."

The high-water mark of modern Ohio history was Armstrong's 1969 moon landing. As the commander aboard *Apollo 11,* with the lunar module pilot "Buzz" Aldrin and the command module pilot Michael Collins, Armstrong became the first person to walk on the moon—and thus began the perpetual complaints about comparatively inferior technologies ("If they can put a man on the moon . . . "). In addition to an American flag, Aldrin and Armstrong left a plaque on the moon that reads HERE MEN FROM THE PLANET EARTH FIRST SET FOOT UPON THE MOON, JULY 1969, A.D. WE CAME IN PEACE FOR ALL MANKIND. Ohio, the birthplace of aviation, has continued to be an integral part of the aerospace industry: twenty-four Ohio natives have been astronauts, more than from any other state.

■ THE THIRD FRONTIER

The past thirty-five years also have thrown Ohioans for a bit of a loop. We're accustomed to being at the center of things, a large, stable cog in the national machine. The population has ticked steadily upward, but this growth is nothing like it was a hundred years ago or like some Southern states are seeing now. And Ohio is growing more slowly than the nation as a whole. In the 1960s Texas passed Ohio in population, and in the 1980s Florida did too. In the post–Civil War era, Ohio transitioned from agricultural dominance to manufacturing dominance, albeit not without growing pains. Today the expectation is that we'll weather this change too—and come out stronger. Still, manufacturing jobs continue to migrate toward cheaper labor, and Ohio's agriculture, while highly efficient, no longer provides a solid economic base.

Ohio's leaders are on a mission for jobs. So-called Third Frontier companies, those based in the Knowledge Economy, are now the holy grail. Success on this front has been disappointing, but it is not a lost cause. The Knowledge Economy is more than economics: it's a way of living. It's why people move to Vegas, North Carolina, and Florida. It includes good schools and health care; attractive shopping destinations; clean, well-planned communities; and first-class entertainment. What politicians are really talking about is a Lifestyle Economy, an economy with high-end "service" jobs that companies can't outsource to Mexico or Asia—including medical professionals, landscapers, fitness instructors, masseuses, and package-delivery people.

"Knowledge" workers and free agents are increasingly geographically independent, and these people will seek out places that best fit their lifestyles. In this contest Ohio stacks up pretty well. Environmental reform, growing rails-to-trails networks, and an excellent state park system provide inviting outdoor opportunities. Big cities and small towns around the state are fighting to keep their downtown commercial districts thriving. Many of them have joined the National Trust for Historic Preservation's Main Street Program, which aims to reintroduce downtowns as the lifeblood of American communities. In 1996 Wooster was one of five towns nationwide honored with the Great American Main Street Award, and in 2001 Mansfield earned the same distinction. A huge range of colleges and universities add to the state's economic stability; they help keep young adults in Ohio and provide an array of cultural diversions. The state's three biggest cities, Cleveland, Cincinnati, and especially Columbus, have diversified economies in such sectors as health care, banking, insurance, government, and education, making downturns easier to bear.

Neil Armstrong, commander of Apollo 11, *was born in Wapakoneta, Ohio.*

In a larger sense, the secret to Ohio's successes has remained the same throughout its history: diversity and balance. Whether it is a political bellwether, cultural mosaic, or scientific proving ground, Ohio accepts all types, all identities, and uses everything it has to craft its traditions, principles, and lore. As long as the state's people pursue new ideas and apply them with a dash of zeitgeist and a healthy measure of hard work to the challenges at hand, the spirit of Ohio will live on.

Historical and Cultural Time Line

1787   The Northwest Ordinance passes, formalizing settlement and a governmental structure for present-day Ohio, Indiana, Illinois, Michigan, and Wisconsin.

1788   Revolutionary War veterans settle Marietta, the first permanent settlement in the Northwest Territory, at the mouth of the Muskingum River.
Cincinnati is founded by Mathias Denman, Robert Patterson, and Israel Ludlow.

1794   Gen. "Mad" Anthony Wayne defeats a confederation of tribes at the Battle of Fallen Timbers. The victory leads to the Treaty of Greenville, in which Indians concede most of their Ohio lands.

1796   Moses Cleaveland plats his eponymous city on Lake Erie. A printer shortens the name to Cleveland to fit a newspaper masthead in 1831.

1803   Ohio enters the Union as the seventeenth state. Chillicothe is the state's first capital.

1810   The state capital moves to Zanesville.

1812   The dance continues; the state capital returns to Chillicothe.

1813   Commodore Oliver Hazard Perry defeats the British navy on Lake Erie: "We have met the enemy, and they are ours."

1816   Columbus is laid out on the Scioto River as a formal capital city. Its central location is a key factor.

1826   William Holmes McGuffey, creator of the McGuffey Readers, becomes a professor at Miami University.

1832   The Ohio & Erie Canal, which runs from Cleveland to Portsmouth, is completed.

1836   President Andrew Jackson settles a border dispute between Ohio and Michigan. Ohio gets Toledo, and Michigan gets statehood along with the Upper Peninsula.

1841   As the first Ohioan president, North Bend's William Henry Harrison sets the stage for a string of "log cabin" presidents.

1845   The Miami & Erie Canal, running from Toledo to Cincinnati, is completed.

1849   The first Ohio State Fair is held.

1850   U.S. Congress passes the Fugitive Slave Act.

1851   Harriett Beecher Stowe's *Uncle Tom's Cabin,* based partly on her experiences while living in Cincinnati, first appears in serial form in the *National Era,* an abolitionist newspaper.

1858   A group of abolitionists from Oberlin gets fugitive slave John Price released from jail in nearby Wellington. The incident raises rancor on both sides, a factor in the North-South division leading to the Civil War.

1861   The Greek Revival–style Ohio Statehouse, twenty-two years in the making, is finished.

1864   Ulysses S. Grant attains the rank of lieutenant general and assumes command of all the Union armies.

Gen. William Tecumseh Sherman burns Atlanta before his March to the Sea.

1868   Ulysses S. Grant wins the presidency in a landslide over Democrat Horatio Seymour.

1869   The Cincinnati Red Stockings become the first professional baseball team.

1870   John D. Rockefeller organizes the Standard Oil Company.

Cedar Point opens as a modest resort getaway.

1876   Perhaps the least known of the unknown presidents, Rutherford B. Hayes begins his only term. Hayes is the first president to win office while losing the popular vote.

1879   Charles F. Brush installs electric streetlights on Cleveland's Public Square, making the city the first to have them.

1881   President James Garfield is shot by a disgruntled lawyer passed over for a consular post. Garfield dies two and half months later.

1888   Benjamin Harrison, the son of a president and grandson of a signatory on the Declaration of Independence, becomes the twenty-third president and the last one to have a beard.

1896   Canton's William McKinley wins the presidency over the young upstart William Jennings Bryan.

1901   In his second term President McKinley is shot by anarchist Leon Czolgosz at the Buffalo Pan-American Exposition. He dies eight days later.

1903   Dayton brothers Orville and Wilbur Wright make their first successful flight with a powered, heavier-than-air "flying machine." The twelve-second flight, covering 120 feet, is shorter than a 747's wingspan.

1907   Bob Hope and his family immigrate to Cleveland from England.

1912   William Howard Taft of Cincinnati suffers the worst defeat ever for an incumbent president. He goes on to become the chief justice of the Supreme Court, the only president ever to do so.

1912   Zane Grey's *Riders of the Purple Sage* is published. The book goes on to sell 2 million copies.

1920   Football teams convene in Canton and create the American Professional Football Association, the future NFL. The members select Jim Thorpe as president.

1923   The last Ohioan president, Warren Harding, dies in San Francisco amid a flurry of corruption by political appointees.

1926   *Canton Daily News* editor Don Mellett is murdered for exposing organized crime and corruption.

1927   Columbus native James Thurber gets a job as a writer and editor at the *New Yorker*. His first cartoons appear three years later.

1930   Dayton schoolteacher Irna Phillips creates *Painted Dreams*, recognized as the first soap opera, for radio. She later becomes known for such popular TV soaps as *Days of Our Lives* and *As the World Turns*.

1933   A *Dayton Daily News* photographer organizes the first Soap Box Derby. In 1935 the race moves to Akron.

1935   The Reds play the Major Leagues' first night game, at Crosley Field in Cincinnati.

1938   Superman, the creation of Cleveland writer Jerry Siegel and artist Joe Shuster, appears on the cover of *Action Comics* #1.

1939   Cadiz native Clark Gable stars in *Gone with the Wind*.

1952   At the Cleveland Arena, twenty thousand fans crash the gates to get into DJ Alan Freed's "Moondog Coronation Ball," considered the first rock concert. Freed coins the term "rock and roll."

1959   The state legislature establishes the Ohio Civil Rights Commission.

1962   John Glenn becomes the first American to orbit the earth. One of Ohio's most revered and respected public figures, Glenn is elected to the U.S. Senate in 1974.

1967   Dayton's WLWD-TV begins airing the *Phil Donahue Show*.

1969   Neil Armstrong, from Wapakoneta, Ohio, becomes the first person to walk on the moon.

       An oil slick on the Cuyahoga River near Cleveland catches fire, bringing national attention to the polluted river and hastening environmental reform.

1970   The National Guard kills four Kent State students and wounds nine during Vietnam War demonstrations.

1974   Cincinnati city councilman Jerry Springer resigns after a police raid reveals he patronized a prostitute—and paid with a personal check.

1975–1976	The Big Red Machine, boasting such players as Johnny Bench, Pete Rose, Joe Morgan, Ken Griffey, and Tony Perez, wins back-to-back World Series.
1977	Jerry Springer wins forgiveness from voters and serves as mayor of Cincinnati until 1981.
1982	*WKRP in Cincinnati* goes off the air after a four-year run.
1986	Cleveland is selected to be home to the Rock and Roll Hall of Fame and Museum.
1993	Lorain, Ohio, native Toni Morrison wins the Nobel Prize in literature.

The Apollo 11 *astronauts were heroes when they returned home.*

1994	The Cleveland Indians' Jacobs Field opens for business as one of the finest parks in the majors.
1995	The Dayton Peace Accords, signed in Dayton, Ohio, officially end the war in Bosnia.
1998	John Glenn, at seventy-seven, becomes the oldest astronaut to go into space. Cincinnati native Sarah Jessica Parker debuts on *Sex and the City*.
2000	Cuyahoga Valley National Recreation Area, between Cleveland and Akron, becomes Ohio's first national park.
2001	Cincinnati makes national headlines for its race riots in Over-the-Rhine.
2003	Ohio celebrates its bicentennial, and the centennial of flight, with ceremonies and festivals around the state. A former mayor of Cleveland and a U.S. Representative from Ohio, Dennis Kucinich runs for president.
2004	The Ohio Legislature passes a Defense of Marriage Act, which asserts that gay marriage is against the "strong public policy" of the state and denies domestic partner benefits to state employees.

YANKEE OHIO

Ohio's northeast quadrant, with its New England influence, is the best known of the state's regions, but it wasn't the first region to be settled, and in most ways it is hardly representative of the rest of the state. This is the precise point where the Northeast meets the Midwest, the happy overlap in a Venn diagram, where blazing fall foliage, wooden churches, and town commons mesh with fertile rolling hills, a temperate Ohio climate, and friendly faces.

This section of Ohio lay directly west of Connecticut, which before the American Revolution extended its western border far into the unexplored hinterlands of what are now part of New York, Pennsylvania, and Ohio. Although Connecticut ceded much of this territory to Congress in 1786, the state retained some lands as compensation for those it had given up. The Connecticut Western Reserve, or just the Western Reserve, extends 120 miles west from what is now the Pennsylvania border, between Lake Erie and the forty-first parallel (a bit south of U.S. 224 and Youngstown). The old western border of the reserve reaches into today's Huron and Erie counties.

A more favorable climate and better soils led Connecticut farmers to take their chances in the Western Reserve, and the Amish came from Pennsylvania to settle what would become the largest Amish community in the country. In Yankee Ohio you'll find the same picture-perfect Federal and Greek Revival homes and well-preserved covered bridges as in New England but without the wandering, impractical layouts of many of those towns. It's as if the settlers of New England called out "Do over!" and built their revised, perfected communities in Ohio.

A large percentage of the Western Reserve's inhabitants come from Connecticut stock, and that ancestry still plays out in the predominance of Democratic voters and left-leaning politics in many of these counties, while most of Ohio, save the urban centers, leans right. This is where passengers on the Underground Railroad made the final push to Canada, where Oberlin College became the first in the country to admit women, and where the maverick abolitionist John Brown spent his boyhood.

Yankee Ohio is an industrial stalwart as well as an agrarian haven. It continues a close association with unions, from steel to auto manufacturing, and has been hardest hit by the hundreds of thousands of mostly manufacturing job losses in the past few years. Still, the region, which here includes Cleveland, Akron, Canton, Youngstown, Warren, and Massillon, as well as the surrounding towns and coun-

(above) The restored Lanterman's Mill in Youngstown grinds grains as it did more than one hundred fifty years ago. (following spread) An Amish farmer uses horses to cut down his corn in Holmes County.

tryside, remains the most important in the state: it has the largest population, the largest economic base, a crucial strategic location, and a sizable cultural influence on the rest of the state.

■ ASHTABULA COUNTY *map page 56, C-1*

The name Ashtabula (ash-tuh-*byoo*-luh) comes from a similar-sounding Indian word describing the wealth of fish in the Ashtabula River. It refers to the city of twenty-one thousand on Lake Erie, the surrounding township, and the county itself, geographically the largest in the state, at 705 square miles.

Smack-dab between Cleveland and Erie, Pennsylvania, Ashtabula County embodies the multiple personalities of the Western Reserve. Its origins lie to the east with the intrepid New Englanders who first settled here, but its focus has long been the lakeshore, site of a major shipping and fishing port. In the 1800s

Ashtabula grew comfortably as a key railroad hub, and in the middle of the last century it drew Appalachians and Southerners for jobs in manufacturing and newly constructed chemical plants. Today its namesake city is also a far eastern outpost for Cleveland workers, a few thousand of whom commute from here.

In the county at large, Ashtabula is synonymous with covered bridges: there are sixteen of them here, more than anywhere else in the country. Every year the town of Jefferson, 10 miles south of the city of Ashtabula, hosts the **Ashtabula County Covered Bridge Festival** the second full weekend in October. The celebration has become a community institution, as much about pride of place as the actual bridges. It includes a draft horse pull, a calendar photo contest, and bridge tours.

The city of Ashtabula exhibits a more industrial flavor, as illustrated by the **Ashtabula Harbor Lift Bridge,** which at one time accommodated ore freighters rather than recreational watercraft. From May to September, the bascule-design

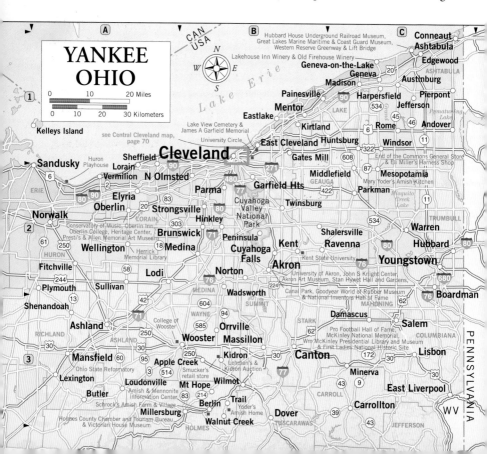

bridge, a type of drawbridge, is raised on the hour and half hour. The city celebrated its bicentennial along with Ohio's in 2003. It has developed an extensive long-term revitalization plan for the downtown, centered on the Harbor District and the unusual Lift Bridge, now lighted in blue thanks to community fund-raising efforts. The revitalized area will complement two established must-sees, the **Great Lakes Marine Maritime & Coast Guard Museum** (1071 Walnut Boulevard; 440-964-6847) and the **Hubbard House Underground Railroad Museum** (1603 Walnut Boulevard; 440-964-8168). As a former residence for lighthouse keepers, the marine museum affords sweeping views of Ashtabula Harbor and includes paintings, scale models, and a pilot's house from an ore freighter. Hubbard House was a northern terminus for the Underground Railroad and is loaded with period photographs and furniture, maps, and artifacts. The museum consists of two exhibits: an Underground Railroad exhibit and a Civil War–Americana exhibit.

Another recent development is the **Western Reserve Greenway,** a rails-to-trails initiative that includes 27 miles in Ashtabula County. When complete, this hiking and biking trail will run south through Trumbull, Mahoning, and Columbiana counties to the Ohio River. Also known simply as the Greenway, the trail starts at West Avenue on the southwest side of town. It is closed to motorized vehicles except for snowmobiles—and the area gets enough snowfall each winter that permission to use them isn't hollow.

Ashtabula's working-class tradition takes center stage at **Geneva-on-the-Lake,** the state's first summer resort and one that has more in common with the old New Jersey boardwalks than with contemporary big-box theme parks. Over the years the town has hosted such nouveau riche vacationers as Henry Ford, John D. Rockefeller, and Harvey Firestone, but working-class families from all over northeast Ohio and western Pennsylvania made it a vacation hot spot from the 1930s into the 1960s. In the late 1960s excessive rowdiness, Lake Erie pollution, beach erosion, and a love affair with newer, faraway theme parks led to a decline in the area's tourism business. But by the 1980s, as people began taking a renewed interest in simple pleasures, they returned to Geneva-on-the-Lake for summertime basics: swimming, boating, camping, fishing, and eating deliciously greasy food. The Strip includes state-fair–style Erieview Amusement Park, miniature golf, an arcade, summer concerts, fireworks, and a range of bars and restaurants. Plenty of rental cottages and B&Bs dot the area, and a new, hundred-and-nine-room resort lodge opened at Geneva State Park in 2004.

UNDER COVER: ASHTABULA'S BRIDGES

Beyond preserving its twelve historic covered bridges, Ashtabula County has taken the welcome step of building *new* ones. The county's latest covered bridge, slated for completion in 2006, will span the Ashtabula River and is expected to be the longest in the United States. That project will bump the county's bridge total to seventeen, five of them built after 1983. Here is the rundown on bridges, listed in a convenient order for touring and with the date of their completion in parentheses:

Netcher Road Bridge (1999): About 3 miles east of Jefferson, this bridge is of a neo-Victorian design.

South Denmark Road Bridge (1890): This Town Lattice bridge spans Mill Creek. It is no longer on the main route but stands near South Denmark Road.

Caine Road Bridge (1986): A Pratt truss design in Pierpont Township on the west branch of the Ashtabula River, this bridge was built for Ashtabula County's hundred-and-seventy-fifth anniversary.

Graham Road Bridge (date unknown): Rebuilt after a 1913 flood, this bridge is in a park just south of Graham Road and directly north of the Caine Road Bridge. It is closed to vehicles.

Root Road Bridge (1868): Rehabilitated in 1983, this Town Lattice bridge spans the Ashtabula River about 7 miles north of Pierpont.

Middle Road Bridge (1868): This Howe truss design bridge is in Conneaut Township, south of Conneaut. It was reconstructed in 1984.

State Road Bridge (1983): This Town Lattice bridge is in the northwest corner of Monroe Township.

Creek Road Bridge (date unknown): This Town Lattice bridge over Conneaut Creek, southwest of Conneaut, was renovated in 1994.

Benetka Road Bridge (ca. 1900): This Town Lattice with Arch bridge spans the Ashtabula River in northwestern Sheffield Township, just south of I-90. It was renovated in 1985.

Olin Bridge (1873): On Dewey Road in northwestern Plymouth Township, Olin Bridge is named after a longtime local family. Renovated in 1985, it crosses the Ashtabula River.

Giddings Road Bridge (1995): This newer Pratt truss bridge crosses Mill Creek northwest of Jefferson.

Doyle Road Bridge (1868): Spanning Mill Creek northwest of Jefferson, off Route 307, this bridge was renovated in 1987.

Harpersfield Bridge (1868): This is presently the longest covered bridge in the state and probably the most unusual. It stretches 228 feet over the Grand River to join a steel span, added after a flood altered the river channel. Located in Harpersfield Township, the bridge was renovated with a walkway in 1992.

Mechanicsville Road Bridge (1867): Thought to be the oldest covered bridge in the county, Mechanicsville crosses the Grand River northwest of Armington Lake, in western Austinburg. It was renovated in 2003.

Riverdale Road Bridge (1874): This bridge straddles the Grand River west of Route 45. It was reinforced and updated in 1945, 1981, and 1987.

Windsor Mills Bridge (1867): The outlier among Ashtabula's covered bridges, Windsor Mills is in the extreme southwest corner of the county, 15 miles from Riverdale Road Bridge in Windsor Township. The bridge spans Phelps Creek just south of U.S. 322, on Wiswell Road. It was renovated in 2003.

Netcher Road Bridge is one of the newest covered bridges in Ashtabula County.

Geneva-on-the-Lake has two wineries that provide another kind of simple pleasure: the **Lakehouse Inn Winery** (5653 Lake Road East; 440-466-8668), a cozy bed-and-breakfast with cottage rentals, and the **Old Firehouse Winery** (5499 Lake Road; 440-466-9300 or 800-862-6751), located in the original Geneva-on-the-Lake firehouse, still home to the department's first fire truck. Both have full lunch and dinner menus, the latter only during the summer.

There is in fact an extensive collection of wineries in Ashtabula and neighboring Lake County. The lake's warming effect extends the growing season and has made northern Ohio, known as the Lake Erie Grape Belt, the best place in the state for viticulture. The lake plains east of Cleveland hold more than half the state's wine-grape crop. Wineries here produce outstanding native wines such as Catawba as well as more familiar varieties such as Riesling and chardonnay. The largest cluster of wineries—ten in all—is in western Ashtabula County south of Geneva and in eastern Lake County and northeastern Geauga County south of Madison.

■ **MESOPOTAMIA** *map page 56, C-1/2*

You would probably never wind up in Mesopotamia if you weren't aiming for it. On Route 534 about 23 miles south of Geneva, this little postcard of a town is the sort of place you visit not so much to do something but to observe, contemplate a lifestyle vastly different from your own, and question why more towns haven't assembled or preserved something special like this. Mesopotamia—"Mespo" if you want to sound in the know—is a classic New England village in the heart of Trumbull County's Amish Country. The entire township has about twenty-six hundred people, more than half of whom are Amish.

Although admirable, Mespo's preservation came about through a government scare rather than a grand plan. For thirty years, an on-again, off-again Ohio Statehouse proposal to put the town at the bottom of a transportation reservoir chilled interest in development and investment. The death of that damning idea was fitting. Mesopotamia, after all, takes its name from the Middle East's fertile crescent, the land *between* two rivers (the Tigris and Euphrates), not under them. Town fathers proposed the name Mesopotamia for the town's similar position between the Cuyahoga and Grand rivers.

The village has a startling array of 19th-century wooden homes, churches, and buildings; the oldest dates to 1816. The structures, often modest but durable, are all the more picturesque when seen against the maple-lined town commons, which

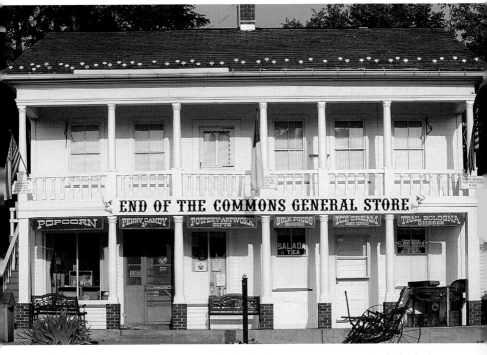

The hitching rail at this general store in Mespo is often in use.

recalls New England so clearly. One highlight on the quarter-mile-long commons is **End of the Commons General Store** (8719 Route 534; 440-693-4295), a former post office and bulk-food store that's no less charming for being a popular travel destination. The owners aren't Amish, but many of its patrons are, and the hitching rail out front is often in use.

Inns, crafts and gift shops, bed-and-breakfasts, and furniture stores round out the town's offerings. Don't leave without exploring **Eli Miller's Harness Shop** (4390 Route 87; no phone), a leather shop and country store with a working saddle maker. For a taste of authentic Amish cooking, consider traveling to the nearby Amish community of Middlefield, where you'll find **Mary Yoder's Amish Kitchen** (14743 Route 608; 440-632-1939). The Fourth of July brings the **Mesopotamia Ox Roast & Flea Market,** a multiday summer favorite.

■ **OBERLIN** *map page 56, A-2*

From the beginning, Oberlin and Oberlin College have brought controversy, unwavering principles, and a renowned intellectual environment to Ohio's cultural landscape. Thirty-five miles southwest of Cleveland in Lorain County, the scenic town of eighty-two hundred carries a social weight far out of proportion to its size, not unlike Yellow Springs, home to Antioch College east of Dayton. The two communities, both closely connected to the universities and their progressive values, share commitments to tolerance, human rights, and personal responsibility. Both boast idyllic locations close to major cities but retain their local color and sense of independence. The National Trust for Historic Preservation named Oberlin in 2004 one of its Dozen Distinctive Destinations and cited its reputation as "the most cosmopolitan small town in America."

Many who know little else about Oberlin are aware of the college's world-class music program, the **Oberlin Conservatory of Music.** The conservatory is elite, with an enrollment of only six hundred, and bears mentioning in the same breath as Juilliard and Eastman. For residents and visitors that means nearly unlimited concerts from some of the best musicians in the world: faculty, students, and internationally known performers. The Oberlin campus averages four hundred concerts per year; among those is the popular Artist Recital Series, an annual tradition since 1878 that has brought to town such respected musicians as Yo-Yo Ma, Vladimir Horowitz, and Isaac Stern. Performers in the series also stay to conduct student workshops. *77 West College Street; 440-775-6933.*

Oberlin's other claim to fame is just as impressive—a hundred-and-seventy-year record of progressive social activism that includes being the first college in the country to admit women (in 1833) and first in the country to admit African-American students (in 1835) as a matter of policy. Oberlin and Oberlin College essentially came into being at the same time. The evangelist founders intended to build a model society in untamed country where students and residents would be free to live the values they espoused: evangelism, peace, temperance, women's rights, and abolition. Heady ideals to be sure, but Oberlin proved up to the task.

The famous preacher Charles Grandison Finney became pastor of First Church here in 1835 and president of Oberlin College in 1851. Although Finney didn't advocate controversy to bring an end to slavery, the fiery preachers that subscribed to his brand of reformed evangelism, some of whom set eastern Ohio aflame with antislavery speeches, were known as Finney's Band. The movement came to a head

(above) The Underground Railroad Sculpture *recalls Oberlin's turbulent past. (following spread) Coach John Heisman (second row, far left) poses with his first team at Oberlin College.*

in 1858 when slave catchers captured runaway John Price near Oberlin and hauled him south to Wellington with the intention of returning him to Kentucky. Once the news spread, an angry and daring group from Oberlin stormed the American House Hotel in Wellington and returned Price to freedom, in violation of the Fugitive Slave Act of 1850. Thirty-seven rescuers were indicted for their part in "the Rescue," and the outcome left hard feelings among both pro-slavery and anti-slavery forces. The event so entrenched opposing views that Oberlin has become known as "the town that started the Civil War," the title of historian Nat Brandt's 1990 book on the controversy.

To say that Oberlin was a big part of the Underground Railroad, then, is an understatement. Take note of the ***Underground Railroad Sculpture,*** installed in 1977 as a gift from the graduating class, across from the conservatory on South Professor Street. In a literal interpretation of the movement's name, students angled railroad ties and tracks to disappear underground. No runaway slaves in Oberlin were ever returned to slavery.

OBERLIN VARS

Activism in Oberlin wasn't limited to abolitionists. The Ohio Anti-Saloon League formed in Oberlin in 1893, the same year a national organization of the same name came together in Washington, D.C. The organizations merged two years later to become the Anti-Saloon League of America. Along with the Women's Christian Temperance Union, which had been founded in Cleveland twenty years earlier, the organization was instrumental in pushing politicians of the era to a "dry" platform and eventually securing nationwide prohibition.

The **Oberlin Heritage Center** (78 South Professor Street; 440-774-1700) is a good place to get more information about the town's history, but start your trip at **Tappan Square,** the spiritual heart of town and campus. The square is bordered by College, Professor, Lorain, and Main streets and is the site of summer concerts and the Juneteenth Festival, a celebration of June 19, 1865, the day Texas slaves learned about the 1863 Emancipation Proclamation. (They were the last American slaves to be emancipated.) During Oberlin commencements, graduating seniors pass under the square's **Memorial Arch,** a monument recognizing Oberlin missionaries who were killed in China's Boxer Rebellion in 1900. Sunday of graduation weekend brings Illumination Night, when the entire square is lighted with Japanese lanterns, a party revered by students, faculty, alumni, and townspeople alike. In 2002 Oberlin students and residents started a new tradition: the **Big Parade,** a celebration held in early May and aimed at maintaining strong town-gown relations. The parade ends on Tappan Square, and colorful costumes, dancing, floats, food, and, of course, live music are all part of the mix.

From the square it's a short walk to any number of downtown shops and restaurants. The **Oberlin Inn** (7 North Main Street; 800-376-4173), a good choice for diners and travelers, has beautifully landscaped grounds in a prime location across from the square. **Presti's of Oberlin** (580 West Lorain Street; 440-775-2511) serves classic Italian about a mile away. The conservatory is just east of Main Street. Admirers of the visual arts should not forego visiting the **Allen Memorial Art Museum** (87 North Main Street, on campus; 440-775-8665), among the best college art collections in the country.

If you find yourself with additional time, consider venturing the 8 miles south to **Wellington,** a bastion of well-preserved architecture, former cheese capital, and hometown of Archibald Willard, the artist who painted *Spirit of '76*. Both it and several of Willard's other paintings are on display in Wellington's **Herrick Memorial Library** (100 Willard Memorial Square; 440-647-2120).

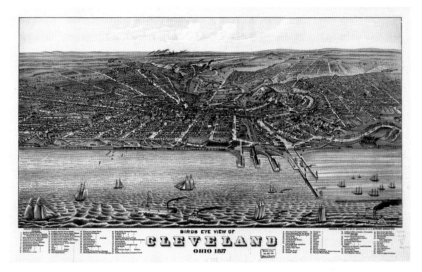

Cleveland was a burgeoning American power in 1877.

■ CLEVELAND *map page 70*

Great cities start with great locations, and Moses Cleaveland snatched up the best one in Ohio in 1796. Some attributes, such as its frontage on expansive Lake Erie and the winding Cuyahoga River, must have been obvious to Cleaveland when he platted the city; others he couldn't possibly have foreseen. After all, he stayed only three months. Aside from its prime lakeside location, Ohio's alpha city ended up being just the right distance from a bunch of places: it is halfway between New York City and Chicago; a stone's throw from the iron ore of southwestern Pennsylvania that made it a player in the steel revolution; and, although it lost the race to be Motown, close enough to Detroit—less than three hours away—to be an important supplier to the auto industry.

Cleveland has had its ups and downs, but fortunately, the city has never seemed overly concerned with what other people think. It was still a mosquito-infested backwater when Cincinnati was earning notoriety as the Queen City of the West. Only when the Ohio & Erie Canal became a reality in the 1820s did Cleveland spring to life as a distributor of goods to the rest of the state. A few decades ago, when people mocked it as past its prime, an oxidizing relic of the industrial age, Cleveland turned its rusty belt into a cool new fashion accessory.

The key to Cleveland's appeal is authenticity. Planners have spruced up what already existed, leaving the character of the city intact. In the past ten years or so, the self-styled Comeback City has been dubbed "most culturally fascinating city in the U.S." by *TravelSmart* and second-best spot in the country for recreation by *Places Rated Almanac,* but it hasn't become antiseptic.

Sometimes called the Forest City, Cleveland has a commendable system of fourteen MetroParks that people say encircle it like an emerald necklace. It's one of Cleveland's greatest strengths, but visitors too often overlook it because they have an image of the city as a place of outmoded industry fixed in their minds. Truth is, when you're in Cleveland, you're never far from a beautiful park.

The city is large but its many neighborhoods make it approachable. For a good introduction to the town's sightseeing highlights, consider taking a Lolly the Trolley tour, which will cover as much ground as you might in a week of exploring on your own. Guides are knowledgeable and have a memorable story for most any building you are interested in. If you don't mind hitting the pavement, Walking Tours of Cleaveland has guided, two-hour foot tours of downtown Cleveland and Ohio City. These provide a narrower, more in-depth view of Cleveland. And if you still don't get to do everything you had planned during your visit, don't sweat it. There's more than one reason they call it the Comeback City.

Although Cleveland was founded by New England settlers, you have to look closely to find what's left of those roots. The waves of European immigrants who joined the city in the late 19th and early 20th centuries proved to be the most influential. In 1900, 75 percent of Cleveland citizens were first- or second-generation American citizens, making it Ohio's most ethnic city. Immigration from Eastern Europe was especially heavy; it included Hungarians, Czechs, Jews, Poles, Austrians, Russians, and Slovenes. Italians and Greeks also came in large numbers.

The respect most Americans now have for our multicultural heritage was hard to come by at the turn of the 20th century in Cleveland, and it was not easy being a non-English-speaking immigrant. The city was more a mosaic than a melting pot. Immigrants formed their own neighborhoods, worshipped in their own churches, and generally followed their old traditions, at least in the first generation. Assimilation, economic vagaries, and the march of time have blurred the boundaries, but it isn't hard to pick out some of these neighborhoods: Slovenes in Euclid

The Fountain of Eternal Life *dominates Memorial Plaza in Cleveland.*

(home to the National Cleveland-Style Polka Hall of Fame), Italians in Little Italy, Greeks and Poles in Tremont, and Czechs and Poles in Slavic Village. Many of these neighborhoods still serve great ethnic foods, one of the strongest remaining connections to the Old World cultures.

Although manufacturing is still important in northeast Ohio, Cleveland has succeeded in diversifying its economy and concentrating its expertise on growth industries, two of which are banking and insurance. Another is health care: Cleveland enjoys a strong reputation as home of the Cleveland Clinic, University Hospitals of Cleveland, MetroHealth Medical Center, and Mt. Sinai Medical Center.

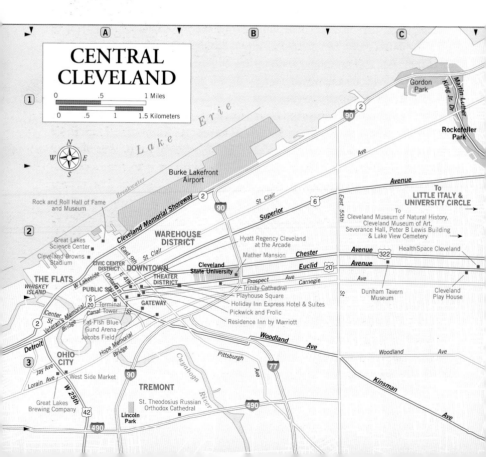

■ NORTH COAST HARBOR AND THE LAKEFRONT

map page 70, A/B-1/2

A critical part of the city's downtown revitalization plan, North Coast Harbor, created in 1988, is postcard Cleveland and the district that introduces the rest of downtown. Route 2 and the Cuyahoga River cut it off from the urban core, so it sits alone, a shoreline playground. Cleveland is lucky to have it. In the mid-nineteenth century the city turned over the lakeshore to the railroads, making for an unsightly and—for the public—unusable shoreline. By the 1930s officials realized their mistake and recovered by creating new shoreline with landfill, the site for today's

Alan Freed coined the term "rock and roll."

North Coast Harbor. During the summer all types pack the sidewalks for great views of both the city skyline and the lake and for the Cleveland National Air Show and the Grand Prix auto race at Burke Airport each August. The area is a rather traditional development of stadiums and museums, the kind modern cities tend to build on their prime real estate, whether fronting ocean, bay, river, or lake. And it might be entirely forgettable if those traditional attractions weren't so good.

If you're from out of town, your first stop is the **Rock and Roll Hall of Fame and Museum.** Arguably the city's biggest tourist attraction and most iconic building, it's *the* must-do in a city filled with must-dos. If you mention visiting Cleveland, friends will quiz you about whether you made the pilgrimage. Why Cleveland rather than Memphis, Detroit, or another notable rock city? Alan Freed. Freed coined the term "rock and roll" on his WJW radio show out of Cleveland. Calling himself Moondog, Freed brought rhythm and blues to a broader audience that, by 1954, would explode when he moved to WINS in New York. Ten years later he was convicted on charges of payola and faced a ruined career, but in 1986 the Hall of Fame inducted him as a nonperformer.

Famed architect I. M. Pei was instrumental in creating the Rock and Roll Hall of Fame, which anchors downtown Cleveland's cultural hot spots.

From the outside, the pyramid-shaped building is almost templelike, seemingly too formal to reflect the great unwinding—old-timers might say great unraveling—of American culture. Inside, it feels spare and industrial, and the exhibits convey reverence and knowledge in equal parts. Costumes and ephemera from most any band you ever knew make up the bulk of displays. Kitsch and spectacle are the main reasons to go, but an attempt is made to put rock and roll in a social context and explain the progression of the music from early pre-rock influences to the present day. *1 Key Plaza; 800-493-7655.*

Next door to the Hall of Fame, the **Great Lakes Science Center** is a pleasant departure from what you might expect to find among waterfront attractions. More than four hundred hands-on exhibits dot the facility, including a simulated indoor tornado and a blimp that visitors can pilot. An entire floor is dedicated to the Great Lakes region, one of the most important and magnificent natural resources in the country. *601 Erieside Avenue; 216-694-2000.*

Cleveland is once again home to the Browns, the football team residents rabidly supported until Baltimore stole it in 1996. **Cleveland Browns Stadium,** right on the lakefront next to the Great Lakes Science Center, is the new football palace the city built on the site of Municipal Stadium, the ancient venue that led embittered owner Art Modell to move the team in the first place. A new Browns franchise replaced Modell's team in 1999, and all is right again in the world of Cleveland football. *1085 West Third Street; 888-891-1999.*

■ THE FLATS *map page 70, A-2*

The meandering Cuyahoga (which comes from a Mohawk word meaning "crooked river"), a rather shallow waterway, separates east from west in Cleveland. Historically, its shores have been the domain of barges, mills, refineries, and other industry, but in the 1980s, in its push to move beyond its industrial past, Cleveland redeveloped the flat terrain where the Cuyahoga River meets Lake Erie, transforming it into the Flats entertainment district, with more than fifty restaurants and nightclubs. The location is prime, perfect for a mild evening when you can sit, margarita in hand, on one of the patios or decks overlooking the river and watch boats come and go.

The district actually consists of two parts: the east bank and the west bank. The west bank is the larger of the two, a sprawling destination that still shares space

The Warehouse District burnishes Cleveland's already-stellar bar and restaurant scene.

The New England influence was evident in Cleveland's Public Square in 1912.

with salt trucks from the mines on Whiskey Island and with some very modest housing just to the west. The **Powerhouse,** a hundred-year-old building holding several clubs and pubs, anchors the west bank. Beyond the Powerhouse, the boater's favorite **Shooters on the Water** (1148 Main Avenue; 216-861-6900), a tropical-themed restaurant, and the raucous beer-and-rock bar **Pat's in the Flats** (2233 West Third Street; 216-621-8044), are longstanding traditions. The *Nautica Queen* (1153 Main Avenue; 800-837-0604) cruise ship operates off the west bank and affords views of the downtown skyline you can't get anywhere else. Go for the sightseeing and not the food. To get to the west side from downtown, get on the Veteran's Memorial Bridge and take the first right; if you are on the east side, drop down to Canal Road/Center Street and follow it across the river.

The east bank, just down the hill from the Warehouse District on the downtown side of the river, is smaller and has fewer establishments than the west. The east bank caters more to clubgoers and draws a younger crowd.

■ **WAREHOUSE DISTRICT** *map page 70, A/B-2*
Although the Flats remains a draw, the Warehouse District, closer to downtown and more upscale, has become the new "in" spot in town. Bounded by West Third Street, West 10th Street, and Superior Avenue, the Warehouse District has the advantage of being just a block or two from Public Square. The prestigious address, home to the **Rockefeller Building** and the **Bradley Building,** which led the housing trend in the district, makes a dream commute for people who work downtown.

Higher prices, both for housing and entertainment, tend to attract an older crowd than in the Flats, although there's enough diversity to go around. Trendy coffeehouses and restaurants pop up around the district. The critically lauded New Orleans–style restaurant and blues club **Fat Fish Blue** (21 Prospect Avenue; 216-875-6000) gives a sense of the neighborhood's tone. The regular Wednesday-night talent is the band of Robert Lockwood Jr., believed to be the only surviving bluesman to have learned guitar from blues god Robert Johnson.

■ **DOWNTOWN** *map page 70, A/B-2/3*
Downtown Cleveland includes the Civic Center District, north of Public Square and south of Memorial Shoreway; the Theater District (including Playhouse Square); and the Gateway District, with Jacobs Field.

The indisputable center of downtown is **Public Square,** the four blocks surrounding the junction of Superior Avenue and Ontario Street. Euclid Avenue cuts in from the east. The Cleveland inventor Charles Brush installed his patented arc lights here in 1879, making Public Square's streets the first in the world to be lighted with electricity. **Terminal Tower** (50 Public Square) embraces the square from the south corner. The neoclassical masterpiece has been a Cleveland icon since 1928 and holds great meaning for residents. It is a hub for downtown bus routes and was once the city's railroad terminal. With traditional railroads no longer important in the downtown core, the rear of the building was converted to a sweeping, successful shopping mall, Tower City Center. Until 948-foot Key Tower, just to the north, was finished in 1992, Terminal Tower was the tallest

Jacobs Field set the standard by which new retro ballparks are measured.

building in the city. If you venture inside, take note of the seven murals in the tower's portico painted by the well-known muralist Jules Guerin.

Catercorner to Terminal Tower is the **Civic Center District,** home to many of the major government buildings: the Federal Courthouse, Federal Reserve Bank, Cleveland Public Library, and a half dozen others. This district runs from West Third Street to East 18th Street and from Lakeside Avenue to Superior Avenue. With a solid government base and stable corporate tenants, it has been a dependable downtown anchor, while other sections of downtown have been more tenuous.

Ten years ago, when revitalization was taking hold in many sections of Cleveland, the downtown area lagged behind. Like other urban centers across the country, downtown Cleveland struggled to find a way to supplement its nine-to-five population with a 24/7 thriving community. The city started by luring sporadic pleasure seekers. The revival of **Playhouse Square** (216-771-4444) was an early component. The five theaters on Euclid—the State, Ohio, Palace, Allen, and Hanna—all opened between 1921 and 1922 as grand destinations on a grand street. After struggling through the middle of the 20th century, the theaters were saved by the Playhouse Square Association. The Ohio reopened in 1982, followed by the Palace and State in the late eighties and the Allen in 1998. In 2000 the association reopened the Hanna, which had closed in the eighties, for cabaret.

A fan's-eye view of "the Jake."

Playhouse Square has the largest concentration of theaters in the United States outside of New York City.

The Gateway District is home to **Jacobs Field,** which, despite the controversy over its substantial public funding and cost overruns, has succeeded in making the Indians a relevant baseball franchise again. The retro styling of "the Jake" was borrowed from the Baltimore Orioles' seminal Camden Yards, and teams around the country have followed suit. While the design opens the outfield to an appealing urban streetscape, the park is actually isolated on the southern end of downtown, not far from I-90. It is part of the Gateway Complex, along with Gund Arena, home of the Cleveland Cavaliers. Together Jacobs Field and Gund Arena have contributed to Cleveland's turnaround, and developers have created new, upscale apartments and housing in historic buildings around the Gateway District. If you can't get a ticket to the game or the Indians are on the road, you can still tour the park Monday through Saturday during the season. *2401 Ontario Street; 866-488-7423 for tickets; 216-420-4385 for tour information.*

Renovated historic housing and commercial space, the master stroke for city planners and preservationists alike, has taken hold around downtown, particularly in the Gateway District. Loft and apartment developments have sprung up all over Euclid Avenue. A medley of city, county, and private financing returned the glamorous Arcade at Fourth and Euclid to its former glory in 2001 as the **Hyatt Regency Cleveland at the Arcade** (420 Superior Avenue East; 216-776-4572). The Arcade was among America's first indoor shopping malls and is one of the jewels of Cleveland, a four-story monument to ostentation with 100-foot ceilings and intricate cast-iron balcony railings. Hyatt wasn't alone in its move to become a downtown presence. **Residence Inn by Marriott** (527 Prospect Avenue; 800-331-3131) opened in the **Colonial Marketplace** arcade across the street in 2000, and **Holiday Inn Express Hotel & Suites** (629 Euclid Avenue; 800-465-4329) remains open in the old **National City Bank** building as it revamps. The restaurant-cabaret **Pickwick and Frolic** (2035 East Fourth Street; 216-241-7425) serves up American rustic cuisine, excellent martinis, original comedy, and magic shows around the corner. And **House of Blues,** a growing national chain of clubs that books acts across the musical spectrum, has plans for a music hall and restaurant in Cleveland at Fourth and Euclid, which opened in November 2004.

■ **OHIO CITY** *map page 70, A-3*
The west side of the Cuyahoga, more residential than the east and filled with wood-sided homes, seems like it could be a different city. Indeed, it once was. Ohio City didn't become part of Cleveland until 1854, and that was much debated. Ohio City and the ridges on the west bank overlook downtown and the river valley. Early on, when poorer settlers lived on the swampy land along the Cuyahoga, Ohio City was the domain of the rich. Some of their houses have survived, easy to pick out for being both noticeably older and larger than the usual stock. When upwardly mobile river dwellers began moving onto property farther up the hill, entire wealthy families packed and moved to the east side of the river, around Euclid Avenue. They even exhumed their late family members and took them too.

Urban pioneers in the 1970s looking for diversity and character did the reverse, moving from downtown across the river—albeit without their ancestors' bodies. Three decades later the neighborhood has become a promising area full of activity and diversity. The Irish Catholic and German Protestant immigrants who once dominated the area have been replaced by mainly working-class Hispanic immigrants and young professionals.

Lorain, which runs east–west, formed the dividing line between the Irish to the north and the Germans to the south. Today it is an important artery through Cleveland's west side and provides access to specialty shops, markets, and numerous bars and restaurants.

Wood siding tends to wear quickly, so homes in Ohio City, which are generally small, look either rundown or good enough to eat. A trip down **Jay Avenue,** off of 25th Street, will give you a feel for how the better renovations have turned out.

West Side Market (West 25th and Lorain) is a social hot spot and popular shopping destination in the neighborhood for people all over the city. The nearly hundred-year-old market is open four days a week year-round. Vendors carry everyday foods as well as specialty foods, including Irish and Hungarian sausages. A more recent addition is **Great Lakes Brewing Company** (2516 Market Street; 216-771-4404), a friendly brewpub started by two local brothers. Bullet holes here are said to have been caused by Eliot Ness, author of *The Untouchables* and former safety director of Cleveland.

■ TREMONT   *map page 70, A/B-3*
Tremont, south of Ohio City, has become a trendy urban neighborhood and focus for developers. New town houses and condos are squeezed between well-restored and unrestored older homes. Tremont has stronger ethnic ties than Ohio City; people of thirty different nationalities have lived here at one time or another. One church, St. John Cantius, offers services in English, Polish, and Spanish.

You'll know you're officially in Tremont when you reach **Lincoln Park,** at Kenilworth Avenue and West 14th Street, long the heart of the neighborhood. Tremont is best known for its ethnic churches, especially **St. Theodosius Russian Orthodox Cathedral** (733 Starkweather Avenue). St. Theodosius is said to be modeled after Church of Our Savior in Moscow, and its oxidized onion domes make it one of the most distinctive churches in the city.

■ UNIVERSITY CIRCLE   *map page 70, C-2*
Since Euclid Avenue's erstwhile Millionaire's Row is no longer up to the task, University Circle stands alone in its testament to the tremendous money, power, and vision of Cleveland's great industrialists and philanthropists during the city's mightiest years. The district covers a square mile where Euclid Avenue bends to the northeast at 105th Street and is named for the trolley turnaround at what is now the Children's Museum of Cleveland. Based around the campus of Case Western Reserve University, University Circle has the largest concentration in the world of cultural institutions in a single square mile. There are museums, theaters, and galleries, schools and universities, public gardens, beautiful churches, and great restaurants. Pick one or two sites that interest you and survey the rest as you have time.

EUCLID AVENUE: MILLIONAIRE'S ROW

A century after its heyday, Euclid Avenue is still the most important street in the city. Euclid begins at Public Square, runs east past many of downtown's most important buildings to University Circle, and then turns northeast and skirts the Lake Erie coast as U.S. 20. A hundred and sixty years ago, when Cleveland was beginning to grow in earnest, the stretch of Euclid between downtown and University Circle was the outskirts of town, an elite enclave for people with means to escape the city. For seventy or eighty years, superrich industrial titans, inventors, and businessmen lived here.

Through the Industrial Revolution others joined their ranks, and homes got bigger. Rockefeller lived here. So did inventor Charles F. Brush and, at times, New York architect Stanford White. At Euclid's peak in the 1880s and 1890s, some considered it the most beautiful street in the world, trumping New York's famed Fifth Avenue. Much has been made since of its decline—to poor zoning, overcommercialization, and antagonistic city government. Many mansions were demolished for the freeway. Some residents ordered their mansions destroyed rather than allow them to suffer subdivision and/or decay at the hands of market forces.

The fact remains, however, that Cleveland's fate hangs on Euclid. Downtown and University Circle are the city's cultural anchors, and the sixty or so blocks in between are an urban-planning high wire. Present-day Euclid is not without redeeming features, but its location alone confers importance. Just east of Playhouse Square, **Cleveland State University** adds to the street's appeal; it uses one of the few old homes left on Euclid, the 1910 **Mather Mansion** (2605 Euclid Avenue), for its Division of University Relations. (Samuel Mather made a fortune in iron ore and was the founder of Case Western Reserve University's medical school.) The **Trinity Cathedral** (2230 Euclid Avenue), down the block, offers the chance to see how millionaires worshipped—and no, not to altars piled with money. Mather contributed to construction of the cathedral, built just a few years before his mansion.

The Euclid Avenue corridor also contains the 1824 **Dunham Tavern Museum** (6709 Euclid Avenue; 216-431-1060), Cleveland's oldest building still on its original site; the **Cleveland Play House** (8500 Euclid Avenue; 216-795-7000); and **HealthSpace Cleveland** (8911 Euclid Avenue; 216-231-5010), formerly the Health Museum of Cleveland. HealthSpace Cleveland is right at home across from the **Cleveland Clinic,** the cutting-edge hospital facility that dominates the blocks

At the end of the nineteenth century, Euclid Avenue was home to the superrich.

west of University Circle and is Cleveland's largest employer. City planners know exactly how important this corridor is. Plans are in the works for a Bus Rapid Transit line between downtown and University Circle by late 2006. The transit line will combine the flexibility of buses with the convenience of light rail, using dedicated lanes, center-median transit stations, priority right-of-way at intersections, and proposed diesel-electric buses. An East Side Transit Center at Prospect Avenue and 21st Street would serve riders and provide layover space for buses.

The beauty of the circle is not just that there are so many attractions but also that so many are so good. The **Cleveland Orchestra** has a sterling reputation as one of the best orchestras in the world. Conducted by Franz Welser-Möst, the orchestra plays in **Severance Hall** (11001 Euclid Avenue; 800-686-1141), where there's truly not a bad seat in the house. Severance Hall underwent a $36 million renovation and expansion between 1998 and 2000. Blossom Music Center in Cuyahoga Falls is the orchestra's summer venue.

In the same league is the **Cleveland Museum of Art,** which may well be the best University Circle has to offer. The *New York Times* calls the museum "one of the nation's premier collections"; it is recognized in particular for its pre-Columbian and Asian art. *11150 East Boulevard; 216-421-7340.*

The natural sciences take on a life of their own at **Cleveland Museum of Natural History,** with just a little imagination required. Exhibits range from a reproduction of Lucy, the world's oldest human fossil, to full-on dinosaur skeletons. The Shafran Planetarium and Astronomy Exhibit, open only since 2002, is a high point of a visit to the museum. *1 Wade Oval Drive; 800-317-9155.*

Even the Weatherhead School of Management at Case Western has gotten into the superlative act with its Frank Gehry–designed **Peter B. Lewis Building** (Ford Drive and Bellflower Road), the new centerpiece of Weatherhead, housing classrooms, faculty offices, and meeting areas. Lewis, chairman of Cleveland-based insurance giant Progressive, was lead donor for the building, a swirling concoction that suggests an unfortunate run-in with stainless-steel space junk. Contact the school to inquire about tours (216-368-4771).

The flawless landscaping and peaceful parks of University Circle also make it a special place. In honor of the city's hundredth birthday, in 1896, John D. Rockefeller donated 270 acres to create **Rockefeller Park,** a lush strip of land that jogs north from University Circle to meet Gordon Park at Lake Erie. This narrow green corridor feels secluded and boundless when you're driving through it on Martin Luther King Jr. Drive. International gardens along the drive pay homage to the various cultures—from Irish to Hebrew—that have helped create Cleveland.

■ **LAKE VIEW CEMETERY** *map page 70, C-2*
Lake View Cemetery (12316 Euclid Avenue) isn't really that different from University Circle: it's elegant, lushly landscaped, and full of influential people. The

Ohioan President James Garfield stands tall inside a monument at Lake View Cemetery.

cemetery was created in the mid-1800s, when people saw burial grounds as places for solitude and reflection, dedicated to the living as well as the dead. Lake View is the perfect place to go if you've spent too much of your day indoors at museums and galleries.

In truth, Lake View is a museum itself, albeit with more refreshing surroundings. You can learn as much about the history of Cleveland and its people here as you might in any number of other places. It is the final resting place of John D. Rockefeller; Marcus Hanna, the senator and financial backer of President William McKinley; Leonard Case, founder of the Case School of Applied Science (later merged with Western Reserve University); iron baron Samuel Mather; Henry A. Sherwin, founder of the paint company Sherwin-Williams; and the Van Sweringen brothers, who built Shaker Heights and Terminal Tower.

The biggest memorial is the **James A. Garfield Monument,** a tribute to President James Garfield, who is mostly forgotten outside of Ohio and almost famous for being unknown. The monument is on the highest point in the cemetery, and visitors can see downtown and Lake Erie from the second floor. Garfield served a brief few months as president before being assassinated by a disgruntled, passed-over cabinet candidate. He was, however, a master orator and accomplished scholar known to be able to write Greek with one hand and Latin with the other—simultaneously.

■ CUYAHOGA VALLEY NATIONAL PARK *map page 56, B-2*

Not far from downtown Cleveland, a thin green band cuts through what has traditionally been one of the most industrial areas in the country, wending its way past railroad lines, freeways, bridges, various industry, and the Southerly Wastewater Treatment Plant. South of I-480, the unlikely green space bulges and swells into a genuine sanctuary, one of the hottest destinations for recreation in the Cleveland, Akron, and Canton metro areas and clearly the fat jewel in Cleveland's oft-touted "emerald necklace" of parks. Much of it is now 33,000-acre **Cuyahoga Valley National Park** (15610 Vaughn Road, Brecksville; 216-524-1497 or 440-546-5991), promoted from Cuyahoga Valley National Recreation Area in 2000. It is Ohio's first and only national park.

The park preserves beech-maple forests, open fields, and rare wetlands along a 22-mile stretch of the Cuyahoga River that feels surprisingly remote considering its proximity to both Cleveland and Akron. Unlike traditional national parks, Cuyahoga Valley is a patchwork of spaces comanaged by Cleveland Metroparks and Summit County's Metro Parks. (The southern two-thirds of the park is in Akron's Summit County.)

A quorum of individuals and state and local governments helped save the green space when development loomed in the 1960s. In light of the area's pattern of settlement and previous uses, it can't duplicate the pristine wilderness experience an outdoorsman might enjoy in one of the capstone parks. There actually are no public campgrounds here; bed-and-breakfasts fill the need for overnight visits. Cuyahoga Valley is more a series of historic sites that are set in unusually pleasant surroundings and that present the area as it was—an important transportation corridor that enriched the industrial cities strung out along it.

The **Ohio & Erie Canal Towpath Trail,** or just the Towpath Trail, is the backbone of the park and splits it into east and west. The even surface of the crushed-gravel path, the relatively modest changes in incline, and the meandering route along the canal and the Cuyahoga help resolve the National Park Service's traditional problem of appeasing a diverse public with competing interests. Visitors come to walk, run, bike, cross-country and downhill ski, and horseback ride. As construction crews were building the trail in the early 1990s, hikers and cyclists followed in their wake. From the trail it's possible to see deer, beaver, herons, turkeys, and the occasional coyote.

Because it's part of the towpath, the trail offers great views of the canal and a chance to better understand how the canal worked and what effect it had on nearby towns. **Peninsula,** a village near the center of the park, is a classic example of the communities that sprang up to serve traffic on the Ohio & Erie Canal. Its prominence on the canal later snared it a stop on the railroad, and it has since served travelers escaping the city with galleries, restaurants, bike rentals, and train tours.

The **Cuyahoga Valley Scenic Railroad** (800-468-4070) runs a number of routes through the valley with classic coach cars from the thirties and forties; some itineraries include ventures to Akron and Canton. The tracks within the park generally run on the opposite side of the river from the towpath, so passengers get a different perspective from hikers and bikers. In fact, many choose to take the train (bikes are allowed on board) for the first leg of a hiking or biking trip. The railroad offers ranger-led trips and theme-based trips, including the Murder Mystery Express and the children's favorite Polar Express in November and December.

Like the Towpath Trail, the entire park, which first became a national recreation area in 1974, caters to a wide range of interests and reflects the diverse uses of the valley before federal protection. In the summer, park goers can choose from *four* public golf courses and in the winter from two downhill ski resorts, Boston Mills and Brandywine. Kids flock to Kendall Hills for prime sledding. And the view from Tinkers Creek Gorge could inspire a stanza or two.

Only 20 or so miles of the Towpath Trail is in the national park, but the trail runs for nearly 100 miles through the **Ohio & Erie Canal National Heritage Corridor,** which Congress designated in 1996. Compared with the national park, the heritage corridor comprises an even looser network of parks and easements that stretches from downtown Cleveland to New Philadelphia. Volunteer groups, non-profit organizations, parks departments, and others are working to connect parks, historic sites, and communities along the corridor with sections of trail.

The urban green-space movement in the Cuyahoga Valley is a welcome development that should go far in enhancing recreational opportunities for city dwellers while preserving a rural landscape that likely would not have survived another twenty years. Land managers and coalitions want to preserve not just the natural landscape and resources but also the human landscape. The National Park Service leases land in the park to private individuals willing to run environmentally and commercially sustainable farms. Called the Countryside Initiative, the program is part of a wider effort to represent the park's agricultural past.

■ **AKRON** *map page 56, B-2*

Akron's name comes from the Greek *akros,* meaning "high place." The Akron area is actually part of a continental divide, less vaunted than its rocky counterpart to the west, that sends the Cuyahoga River north to Lake Erie and the Tuscarawas River south to the Ohio and ultimately the Gulf of Mexico. Akron sits at the apex, 479 feet above Lake Erie. Before European settlement, the area was so prized that no one tribe claimed the land; it was shared as an important portage route between the Cuyahoga and Tuscarawas rivers. Not long before the Ohio & Erie Canal opened in 1827, there was a scattering of farm villages here, but the location proved strategic, and a city bustling with canal trade and mills emerged.

These days the city is on its way back up after sustaining a massive job exodus from the rubber industry in the 1970s and 1980s. What was once the end of the earth in frontier days is now a conduit for commerce of all kinds. Roughly halfway between New York City and Chicago, Akron is using its proximity to large populations to recast itself as a center for business and travel. It has invested more than

Old and new come together in the General Store in Akron's Old Quaker Oats Building.

$600 million in its downtown core in the past ten years and is at work on another $700 million. Akron's high-tech convention center, the **John S. Knight Center** (77 East Mill Street; 330-245-4254), and the AA Akron Aeros' ballpark, **Canal Park** (300 South Main Street; 800-972-3767), anchor a resurgent downtown, which has new restaurants and nightclubs. The **Akron Art Museum** (70 East Market Street; 330-376-9185) is slated for a new building designed by the Austrian firm Coop Himmelb(l)au, to be completed in 2006. And there are renovated apartments downtown and the draw of Cuyahoga Valley National Park.

Polymers are a path for the future at four hundred Akron companies that employ more than thirty-five thousand people. The **University of Akron**'s highly rated College of Polymer Science & Polymer Engineering is an invaluable research facility as well as an important training ground for the next generation in the field. The trucking industry also provides a big boost. More than a hundred and fifty trucking companies serve the city, and the Roadway division of Yellow Roadway has headquarters here.

Whatever Akron's progress in new industry and technology in the past ten years, it will be some time before the city outgrows its identity as the Rubber Capital of

the World. The manufacturing jobs are gone, but Goodyear headquarters and Firestone offices are still here. Through current and former employees, cultural events, museums, the skies, streets, and neighborhoods, rubber is ingrained in the collective psyche. B. F. Goodrich was the first to manufacture here, in 1876, followed by Firestone and Goodyear. Understandably, the industry hit a fever pitch with the arrival of the automobile and Ford's mass-produced Model T. Between 1910 and 1920 Akron tripled its population, making it the fastest-growing city in the country during that time span.

Already an industry town, Akron saw the rise of company neighborhoods, namely Goodyear Heights and Firestone Park. With today's rush to the suburbs northwest and south of the city, Firestone Park looks like a quaint remnant of old Akron, filled with durable Sears kit

(clockwise from top left) There are lots of winners at the All-American Soap Box Derby World Championships; the finish line at Derby Downs; tucking in for a fast time; making some final adjustments.

homes and interested buyers. Harvey Firestone took his cue from Goodyear's company neighborhood and laid out homes around a shield-shaped park representing the Firestone logo.

As Firestone Park was getting started, Goodyear founder Frank Seiberling was finishing construction of Stan Hywet Hall (stan *hee*-wit), an imposing 64,500-square-foot Tudor Revival manor on the northwest side of town that looks much older than it is. The family mansion was finished in 1915. (*Stan Hywet,* Old English for "stone quarry," acknowledges the old quarry on the property.) Like Cleveland and other cities where superrich industrialists made their fortunes, Akron reaped some rewards—through philanthropy and the power that the city's elite commanded. After Frank Seiberling's death, his family established **Stan Hywet Hall & Gardens** (714 North Portage Path; 330-836-5533) as a public museum and cultural center, opened to the public in 1957. Spring or summer is the best time to visit; the gardens on the 70-acre estate are almost as impressive as the mansion itself.

Seiberling had to turn Goodyear over to a Wall Street group after post–World War I financial struggles, but the company remains an Akron institution. If you care to uncover the mysteries of rubber, or just want to take in a quirky museum that's pure Akron, visit the **Goodyear World of Rubber Museum** (1144 East Market Street; 330-796-7117). Located in Goodyear's headquarters, the museum includes a reproduction of the workshop of Charles Goodyear, who invented vulcanized rubber; it also houses Indy cars, tires from a vehicle used on the moon, and the requisite exhibits on rubber making and tire building.

The city's biggest event of the year comes every July and might be the only reason kids around the world have ever heard of Akron—the **All-American Soap Box Derby.** (Despite its name, kids from several other countries compete.) It's difficult to imagine an event that better exemplifies Akron. Champions from a hundred and fifty regional races come to compete before crowds of fifteen thousand at Derby Downs. The entrants, anywhere from eight to seventeen years old, build their own cars and come away with an unforgettable experience. During Derby Week they're the center of attention. In 1949 Jimmy Stewart even postponed his honeymoon and brought his wife to Akron to watch the derby. Celebrity appearances are the norm, and that tradition should continue with NASCAR as a partner.

The enshrinees at the **National Inventors Hall of Fame,** on the other hand, aren't what most people would regard as celebrities. The celebrated historical figures you'd expect to see here—Thomas Edison, George Washington Carver,

Samuel Morse, etc.—have their places, but lesser-known inventors that neverthe-less contributed mightily to breakthroughs in engineering and science also get their due. Adults will recognize some names, although most are more likely known through their creations, such as George de Mestral's Velcro or Dr. Hans J. P. von Ohain's jet engine. As fascinating as many of the inventors' biographies are, the real action is on the museum's bottom floor, which holds the mother lode of hands-on and interactive stations. Kids will enjoy tinkering with lasers and strobe lights; in the Take-Apart area, they can break down old machines to learn how they work. *221 South Broadway; 330-762-4463.*

■ CANTON *map page 56, B-3*

Although Canton is home to the Pro Football Hall of Fame, the city didn't create football, and it didn't produce the first professional players. In fact, universities in the Northeast, mostly those in the Ivy League, adapted football from rugby and soccer, and many of those same schools—Yale, Princeton, Harvard, University of Pennsylvania—were surely paying key players to compete by the 1880s. Canton's legacy lies in the creation of the National Football League at a meeting in the city in 1920, with Canton Bulldogs superstar Jim Thorpe named as league president.

Ohio, and especially Canton and nearby Massillon, had constituted the zenith of football for years in the Ohio League, where the very best of the amateur and pro teams were playing by the early 1900s. Canton and Massillon competed every year, and frequently Akron, Columbus, and Toledo fielded teams as well. The Canton Bulldogs were the Ohio League champions in 1916, 1917, and 1919, los-ing only in 1918 during World War I, when most teams didn't play a full schedule and lacked their usual talent. But the Ohio League had a loose structure that hin-dered fair play and broad fan appeal.

By 1920 the formation of an official league was long overdue. The practices of fixing games, poaching (stealing other teams' players), and paying amateur players under the table were damaging the game's integrity and creating a fair amount of chaos at a time when momentum was key. By the time Jim Thorpe stepped up as president of the new league, he had already played five seasons with the Bulldogs, in addition to winning gold medals in the decathlon and pentathlon at the 1912 Stockholm Olympics. He was the icon of the league and gave its image the luster necessary for early success.

Even without Thorpe, Canton and northeast Ohio would have been a force in football, if not as well known as they are today. Canton-Massillon was a classic rivalry in the early 1900s, and it remains so on the high school level. Both schools use the mascots of their respective former pro teams, and both are among the top ten winningest high school football teams in history, the edge going to Massillon.

The legendary Paul Brown lends a mystique to Massillon, where he served for nine years as head coach (1932–1940). His team won more than 90 percent of games played, including six state championships and four national championships. (Brown later coached the Ohio State Buckeyes, and he coached and owned the Cincinnati Bengals.) With a similar pedigree, Canton McKinley High has ten state titles, including back-to-back titles in 1997 and 1998; it plays in Fawcett Stadium, the site of the NFL's Hall of Fame Game and adjacent to the Pro Football Hall of Fame. The *Sporting News* has rated the stadium, which has capacity for more than twenty-three thousand, the number-one high school football venue in the country.

So, the **Pro Football Hall of Fame** draws as much on the lore of football in northeast Ohio as the local teams here benefit from having it in their backyard. Everything you'd expect is here: the solemn Enshrinement Gallery; the Super Bowl Room; displays dedicated to specific games; famous uniforms, game balls, helmets, and related memorabilia; franchise histories; interactive exhibits and trivia; and the Gameday Stadium, which shows highlights of many games. A favorite is the 1st Century of Pro Football, the Hall's first exhibit, which spotlights a number of the game's greatest players from the 20th century and mixes in audio stations with display cases, mannequins, video footage, and memorabilia—a great overview that sets the tone for the visit. Enshrinement ceremonies and the Hall of Fame Game take place each year in early August. *2121 George Halas Drive NW; 330-456-8207.*

Canton's other claim to fame doesn't quite fit with the character of the rough-and-tumble factory town, where steely amateurs lined up on the gridiron and gangsters once operated as they pleased. The city is where President William McKinley served as Stark County prosecutor, where he ran his front-porch campaign before the 1896 election, and where his wife, Ida, returned to live after McKinley was assassinated in September 1901, just six months after beginning his second term.

McKinley had been a popular president, bolstered by a U.S. victory in the Spanish-American War. Planning for a memorial began almost immediately, and President Theodore Roosevelt came for the dedication of the **McKinley National**

More than two hundred busts circle the Enshrinement Gallery at the Pro Football Hall of Fame.

Memorial in 1907. McKinley, Ida, and their two daughters, Katie and Ida, both of whom died in childhood, are entombed at the memorial, a domed Neoclassical Revival structure accessed by a long flight of stairs.

Every year on the Saturday closest to McKinley's birthday, January 29, the adjacent **Wm. McKinley Presidential Library & Museum** celebrates McKinley Day with a wreath-laying ceremony and a full day of Civil War reenactments and living-history displays. Don't brush off the museum over a lack of interest in McKinley. It is a major cultural center for Canton and includes several attractions, including Hoover-Price Planetarium and Discover World, which are both hits with kids. Discover World has hands-on exhibits covering space, natural history, and ecology—think towering dinosaurs, fish ponds, and fossil remains. Upstairs, the Street of Shops makes the historical accessible. Re-created late-1800s storefronts literally provide windows into the past, some with interpretive staff, and include a large model-train collection and an expansive working railroad layout. For students, historians researching local history, and genealogists, the presidential library has the largest collection of McKinley papers and photographs in the world and is also home to the comprehensive records of the Stark County Historical Society. The park surrounding the building is an attractive place for a picnic and a pleasant foreground for the view from atop the steps of the McKinley National Memorial. *800 McKinley Monument Drive NW; 330-455-7043.*

In a town of seventy-eight thousand where people tend to stick around, it seems many families have a McKinley story passed down through generations. The museum is all the more important because the McKinleys' Canton home is long gone. The old house on the southwest corner of Eighth Street and Market Avenue North where McKinley ran his campaign was moved to Meyer Park to make way for a hospital expansion and was razed during the Depression for lack of maintenance funds. Ida grew up in Canton, the daughter of James Saxton, the well-to-do founder and president of Stark County Bank. Ida's childhood home, known as the Saxton McKinley House, is now the **First Ladies National Historic Site** (331 Market Avenue South; 330-452-0876), across the street from the McKinley Marriott Grand.

McKinley will never have the notoriety of a Roosevelt, but he did reemerge as an icon in political circles a few years ago when George W. Bush adviser Karl Rove publicly revealed his admiration for McKinley and compared the two presidencies.

The childhood home of First Lady Ida McKinley is a museum in downtown Canton.

McKinley, Rove says, saw that he was entering a new era in politics, when the United States would transition from an isolationist republic to an international power, and effectively repackaged the Republican message to appeal to an increasingly diverse country, to laborer and businessman alike. Whether the comparisons hold water or not, McKinley has been introduced to a new generation that might give him a closer look beyond his mountain in Alaska and membership in the club of "presidents elected in a year ending in zero who were shot or died in office."

■ **WOOSTER** *map page 56, A/B-3*

About 55 miles southwest of Cleveland in Wayne County, Wooster is beautiful and staid and has a rich mix of agriculture and business. As small towns across the country struggle to maintain their economic and population bases and steadily lose the charm that once made them attractive, Wooster (*wus*-ter) improbably prospers on all fronts. Wayne County is a major producer of dairy products, and Wooster is home to the corporate headquarters of Rubbermaid Home Products, part of Newell Rubbermaid.

Like Oberlin, Wooster packs a lot of culture into a small town. Victorian facades and streetlamps add to the urbane, well-manicured feel in a thriving downtown. The **College of Wooster** (1189 Beall Avenue; 330-263-2000), a high-tech, widely respected liberal arts college, radiates academic importance. The grounds are dominated by gray Gothic buildings beneath stately old trees. The **Ohio Light Opera,** which performs at Freedlander Theatre (330-263-2345) on the Wooster campus, has achieved international recognition for its productions; it is the only professional company in the United States devoted entirely to operetta. Rubbermaid runs a huge retail store in the city with more than twenty-five hundred products, including Little Tikes play equipment and outlet specials.

Wooster itself isn't part of Amish Country, but it is a jumping-off point for it. Certainly Amish frequent the town, but they aren't part of the dominant culture here the way they are in the outlying hamlets. Just outside Wooster there are old country stores, antiques shops, and furniture retailers in towns such as Apple Creek and Kidron, which is home to **Lehman's** (1 Lehman Circle; 330-857-5757), an Amish version of Sears. Lehman's carries hardware and appliances—gas lamps, woodstoves, wrought iron, weather vanes, and about anything else you might need to set up a homestead. The store also has a smaller, less bustling location in Mt. Hope.

To get a bit closer to the action and take in more of the culture directly, you might consider attending a livestock auction. The **Kidron Auction** (Kidron Auction Barn, Kidron and Emerson roads; 330-857-2641) is Ohio's oldest weekly livestock auction and is held every Thursday starting at 11 A.M. (10:15 for hay and straw). The auction brings a good cross-section of locals and the animals they make their living on, from hogs to sheep to cows.

Amid all the rusticity, **Smucker's retail store** (333 Wadsworth Road; 330-684-1500) scarcely seems out of place. Just a few miles north of Kidron, in a classic barn befitting the Smucker's image, the store carries a plethora of jams, jellies, gift baskets, and related products not far from Smucker's headquarters in Orrville.

■ AMISH COUNTRY *map page 56, B-3*

The term Amish Country ought to be confusing in Ohio, because there are so many settlements scattered throughout the state, often wherever there is good farmland, wide-open spaces, and a reasonable cost of living. Somehow, though, when someone speaks of Ohio's Amish Country, it's clear enough what is meant— Holmes, Wayne, Tuscarawas, and Stark counties, which together compose the largest Amish settlement in the world, approximately forty thousand people. Holmes accounts for the largest proportion: close to half of its thirty-nine thousand residents are Amish.

The landscape here is beautiful and familiar. It's the one you imagine come winter when everyone joins in on a round of "Over the River and Through the Woods." White frame farmhouses give an observer perspective on tree-flecked ridges and valleys full of patchwork crops. Although the descriptions have been overused and rendered nearly trite, Amish Country really does sit in the anatomical "heart" of Ohio, and history does "come alive" inside its borders. Most Ohioan ancestors were not Amish, and Ohio did not develop around the Amish culture, but the lives lived today in Holmes and its neighboring counties tell us volumes about where we are and where we've been. Only in the last generation has Amish society moved from social curiosity to full-blown tourist industry—and it isn't the Amish who have changed.

The customs of the Amish have remained much the same since Jacob (or Jakob) Ammann led a faction of Mennonites to split from the main church in Switzerland in 1693 over the issue of whether excommunicated church members should be partly shunned or completely shunned. (Ammann's group believed in total shunning.) Ammann's strict offshoot group became known as the Amish. Religious persecution in Europe in the early 1700s led Amish and Mennonites to put down roots in Pennsylvania, where fertile valleys and religious freedom drew many from the Old World. A century later, as these settlements became more crowded, some Amish moved westward and eventually settled in communities in Ohio, Indiana, Illinois, and Iowa.

The farmland we know today as Amish Country became predominately Amish relatively recently, thanks to the fact that the Amish tend to have large families. Non-Amish settled the region first, and in the 19th century only a small percentage of the population in Holmes County was Amish. In 1940 it stood at about 15 percent, and today it has grown to nearly 50 percent. The inversion that has taken place since then, from the minority to the dominant culture in this area, has to be a sea change—though perhaps a welcome one—for the Amish, the ultimate outsiders.

(above) Folks use buggies to run errands near Berlin. (following spread) Amish farms abound in Holmes County.

The Old Order Amish avoid political involvement; they disdain materialism, machines, and unnecessary talk with non-Amish. They interpret the Bible literally and practice adult baptism, believing that the participant must be mature enough to understand the importance of this rite. They also are pacifists; settle disagreements, should they arise, by discussion or arbitration rather than in court; shun public relief programs; and refuse to buy on credit. Many non-Amish in the area are Mennonites. Mennonites stem from the same Anabaptist order as the Amish and hold essentially the same beliefs but accept modern conveniences and dress.

A visit to Amish Country is an embrace of simple pleasures. The area has become commercialized in response to overwhelming consumer demand, but it remains a place of inquiry and exploration more than entertainment. There will be no Amish line dances, no tractor pulls, no bachelorette parties at the bed-and-breakfasts. Instead, you might sample hearty made-from-scratch cooking, watch a farmers' auction, troll for antiques, or hole up in an inn for the weekend. Whatever activity you decide on, the most important thing you can do is *slow down.* Horses and buggies rule these roads, although cars can create congestion in the towns, particularly on weekends. Slowing down is the best way to soak in the subtleties of the culture and is a sign of respect and goodwill toward the stewards of this dazzling country.

■ BERLIN AND MILLERSBURG *map page 56, A/B-3*

Holmes County, the heart of Amish Country, has only two towns of any size: Berlin and Millersburg. **Berlin** (pronounced *ber*-lin, unlike the capital of Germany) is the smaller of the two, an Amish town of about one thousand people in the eastern half of the county. There's no wrong way to see Amish Country. The place *is* the spectacle, and wandering the back roads, shopping in crafts and furniture stores, visiting demonstration farms, and exchanging news with the locals at roadside produce stands are all equally worthy ways to pass the time. A good start, however, is the **Amish & Mennonite Information Center** (5798 Route 77; 330-893-3192) in Berlin. The center includes a 265-foot mural depicting the history of the Amish, Mennonites, and Hutterites, a third Anabaptist group organized under Jacob Hutter around the same time as the Mennonites. You can pick up maps and leaflets to plan your time and learn more about Amish beliefs, traditions, and taboos. Taking pictures of the Amish, for instance, is frowned upon.

An easy way to experience the Amish way of life without feeling like a brazen voyeur is to visit one of the demonstration farms in the area. **Schrock's Amish Farm & Village** (4363 Route 39, east of Berlin; 330-893-3232) provides tours of a 19th-century farmhouse and insight into daily work, along with buggy rides, a petting zoo, and, on Saturday afternoon, an hour-long lecture on life in Amish Country. **Yoder's Amish Home** (6050 Route 515; 330-893-2541), between Trail and Walnut Creek, is a 116-acre working farm with two farmhouses, an 1860s farmhouse and a contemporary dwelling. Like Schrock's, Yoder's offers buggy rides and has an animal petting area. Both are closed on Sunday, as are many of the sites in this area. Sunday makes a good day for travel or independent exploration.

The maze of roads winding through hill and dale in farm country doesn't always make sense. But it's good to get a little lost. Mennonites and the "English" are the ones who take advantage of high-traffic locations to serve the robust tourism industry. The Old Order Amish tend to stick to the back roads, where traffic is much lighter and slower, or to use busier roads at off-peak hours. They tend to avoid all the hubbub we create by going there, so meandering with consideration and curiosity through the countryside will net you the most authentic experience. Countless bed-and-breakfasts, especially around Berlin and Charm, to the south, will expose you to the peace and simplicity that await off the beaten path.

To the west lies **Millersburg,** in the middle of Holmes County. Millersburg is the county seat and so is not strictly an Amish community, although that element is definitely present. Millersburg and its revamped Victorian downtown can make a good base of operations or a good resupply point when the simple life becomes too simple. If you start your trip here, the **Holmes County Chamber of Commerce & Tourism Bureau** (35 North Monroe Street; 330-674-3975) is another good source for information on the area but is closed on weekends. The prize in Millersburg is the **Victorian House Museum** (484 Wooster Road; 330-674-0022), operated by the Holmes County Historical Society. The onetime home of Cleveland industrialist L. H. Brightman, the restored Queen Anne structure dates to 1902 and is even more intricate, exquisitely furnished, and well tended than you'd expect. Among the house's twenty-eight rooms are a fourth-floor ballroom and a basement sauna and steam room.

■ Travel Basics

Getting Around: Northeast Ohio is dominated by a spiderweb of major highways. The Ohio Turnpike (I-76 from Pennsylvania to Youngstown, I-80 from Youngstown to Cleveland, and I-80/90 from Cleveland to the Indiana border) snakes into the region from Pennsylvania and continues westward north of Akron. I-71 and I-77 come in from the south, while I-90 and I-76 run east–west. Interstates 271 and 480 form a loop of sorts around Cleveland. While most of the region requires a car, you'll find ample public transportation in Cleveland, with both bus and train service. The city is also adding a much-needed Bus Rapid Transit line from the central business district to University Circle, slated for completion in late 2006. Public bus service is available to a lesser extent in Akron and Canton. For a quiet afternoon in the country, try one of these scenic drives: Route 534 between Damascus and Harpersfield, U.S. 322 between Gates Mills and Huntsburg, or Route 303 between Hinkley and Shalersville.

Climate: Sitting on the Appalachian plateau—and the Lake Erie plains near the shoreline—northeast Ohio enjoys all four seasons across its gentle hills and valleys. Temperatures range from below freezing in January to the 80s in July. Summer and fall offer moderate weather perfect for sightseeing. In the winter prepare for icy lake winds and the occasional pummeling snowstorm. Annual precipitation is roughly 38 inches, with annual snowfall nearing 50 inches. Both numbers tend to be higher than in southern parts of the state due to lake-effect moisture. The lake coast doglegs northeast at Cleveland and often blankets the hills on the east side of town with snow even as towns farther west get nothing. Chardon, 35 miles east of Cleveland, in particular gets hit with snow out of proportion to surrounding areas. A belt around Wooster and Canton, too far south to benefit from the lake's warming effects, gets some of the coldest winter temperatures in the state.

In Ohio, the barns tend to be bigger than the houses.

APPALACHIAN
HILL COUNTRY

Although the Appalachian Mountains don't run through Ohio, the southeast portion of the state is nevertheless culturally part of Appalachia and known as Appalachian Ohio. It is the most culturally cohesive and distinct of Ohio's regions, and it looks the part, all weathered hills of sandstone and shale, thick second-growth forest, coal mines both open and reclaimed, and roads that would shame the Big Three automakers' proving grounds. People who gripe about Ohio being flat have never been south of Cleveland or else just like to complain. The southeast corner of the state was the only section left unscathed during the last Ice Age, and this has shaped its very essence: not just its topography but also its culture, biological diversity, settlement patterns, and economy.

Appalachian Ohio has no cities. Zanesville comes closest, with a population of twenty-six thousand. Like most of Appalachia, the hill country was something to endure on the way to places with better soils and economies, but it did see a boomlet during the early years of settlement. Towns like Marietta and Portsmouth served as waypoints for riverboat traffic and settlers headed west. The National Road, today's U.S. 40, ran from Baltimore to Columbus (and ultimately Vandalia, Illinois) to link crops with their consumers, settle the interior, and allow travel to and from the coast. The Ohio & Erie Canal sustained towns like Coshocton with its watery lifeline between Cleveland and Portsmouth.

Germans, Scots-Irish, and English settled Appalachia in the early 19th century, with Germans tending to form their own communities in the valley bottoms and Scots-Irish settling the mountainsides. (Along the Ohio River, Germans tended to settle on the Ohio side because they disapproved of slavery.) The genuine isolation of rural mountain life at the time preserved many European customs and culture and buffered inhabitants from outside influences so well that today the federal government actually identifies Appalachians as a distinct ethnic group, despite the fact that they represent a range of ancestry. Linguists can trace some elements of the Appalachian dialect to Anglo and Gaelic roots. For example, using "on" as part of a verb phrase to convey affection for someone (as in "He was hugging on her all night") is a Gaelic construction, as is using "what" in place of "that" ("I don't know what I wouldn't do it myself").

APPALACHIAN HILL COUNTRY

Youngstown

Shelby   Ashland   WAYNE   Orrville   Ohio & Erie Canal   62   STARK   9   11
Bucyrus   39   250   Wooster   21
30   Massillon   Canton   MAHONING
314   Mansfield   3   250   Wilmot   77   43   East Liverpool   1
71   ASHLAND   Loudonville   241   800   43
42   RICHLAND   39   83   Dover   Carrollton   43   JEFFERSON   7
Mount Gilead   514   HOLMES   Millersburg   New Philadelphia   43
13   62   New Philadelphia   Steubenville   22
42   Mt Vernon   KNOX   Millwood   83   Uhrichsville   36   800   250   Cadiz
Delaware   657   13   Utica   541   36   93   TUSCARAWAS   HARRISON
71   62   Coshocton   77   Wheeling
Westerville   60   Longaberger Homestead   GUERNSEY   22   St Clairsville   250
Newark   Frazeysburg   Dresden   70   Moundsville   250
Gahanna   LICKING   Longaberger Basket Company   Cambridge   800   BELMONT
COLUMBUS   National Road-Zane Grey Museum   513
270   Pickerington   70   Zanesville   Zanesville Art Center & Alan Cottrill Sculpture Studio & Gallery   New Martinsville
FAIRFIELD   Somerset   22   National Ceramic Museum and Heritage Center   Cumberland   MONROE   Woodsville
664   Crooksville   Roseville   Wilds   Caldwell   78
23   Lancaster   37   60   Malta   NOBLE   800
22   93   PERRY   13   60   77
Circleville   HOCKING   MORGAN   Logan   Burr Oak State Park   377   339   Marietta
159   Conkles Hollow State Nature Preserve   180   93   Nelsonville   WASHINGTON   550   Lafayette Hotel, Harmar Village, Campus Martius Museum, Mound Cemetery & Washington County Public Library
Hopewell Culture National Historical Park   374   664   Hocking Hills State Park   Chauncey   Parkersburg
Chillicothe   Adena State Memorial, Ross County Courthouse, Tanglewood, Willis/Cook/Briggs House, Ross County Historical Society Museum & Mountain House   Armitage   Strouds Run State Park   50
23   50   Athens   33   50
ROSS   35   VINTON   ATHENS   River
PIKE   32   681   Darwin   MEIGS   47   Ohio University, Kennedy Museum of Art, Dairy Barn Southeastern Ohio Cultural Arts Center & Hockhocking Adena Bikeway
Jackson   Wellston   7
124   JACKSON   124   Middleport   124
Buckeye Furnace   554
35   Bob Evans Farm   Point Pleasant
Rio Grande   Ohio   33
Portsmouth's Floodwall Murals & Southern Ohio Museum   Gallipolis   77   WEST VIRGINIA
23   335   140   GALLIA   141   218
Scioto   93
Portsmouth   LAWRENCE   79
52   141   35
Shawnee State Park   Ironton   775   243   79
Ashland   Huntington
Grayson   Charleston
KENTUCKY   52   10

Ohio & Erie Canal

N

W   E

S

Elevation
in feet

| 1,549 |
| 1,250 |
| 1,000 |
| 750 |
| 569 |

0   15   30 Miles
0   15   30   45 Kilometers

The bonds of rugged independence and economic hardship make Appalachian Ohio feel secretive and more exclusive than other parts of the state. Travelers from outside the area often cite an "otherness" that feels no less tangible for being difficult to describe.

In more recent years, many from Appalachia have sought opportunity in cities and blended in amid the urban lifestyle, but the fact remains that Appalachians are probably the last minority group in the United States that may be ridiculed and parodied with widespread public approval. The jokes are everywhere in popular culture—in novelty toys and games, movies, and prime-time comedies such as *The Simpsons*—and they date back to *The Beverly Hillbillies, The Andy Griffith Show,* and before. When late-night bar talk grows slow in Cincinnati, Columbus, or Cleveland, Appalachian Ohio still fills in as the occasional butt of jokes. Ohioans in the region, naturally, make fun of West Virginia, and West Virginians in turn make fun of Ohio.

People accept the jokes, it seems, because they see elements of Appalachian culture as a chosen lifestyle that's fair game and because Appalachians are not perceived as an ethnic group (and perhaps because if you don't laugh, you have to cry: a public-service billboard on Highway 23 in the Scioto Valley warns, "Don't let your date become your due date").

There's no denying that parts of southeast Ohio are economically troubled. The Appalachian Regional Commission (ARC), set up by the Kennedy administration to combat poverty in the area, mostly has succeeded in furnishing richer counties with infrastructure to aid business development instead of bringing social services to poorer counties, as was originally intended. As of 2004 the ARC classified *six* of Ohio's twenty-nine Appalachian counties as "distressed" (meaning they had unemployment and poverty rates 50 percent higher than national averages and a per capita income 33 percent below average). In 1960 seven Ohio counties qualified.

Ironically, for many years southeastern counties fueled the Ohio economy with the raw materials necessary for heavy manufacturing in Cleveland, Toledo, Youngstown, and elsewhere. The arrival of the steam engine created a large market for coal, used in everything from lake vessels to factories and railroads. By 1900, 90 percent of factories in Ohio depended on coal-powered steam engines. Coal was and still is the most important mineral mined here; the mines are concentrated in the eastern part of the state, and the coal from them primarily ends up generating electricity at coal-burning power plants. Counties such as Belmont and Noble in

Men sort coal at the Sunday Creek Coal Company in Hocking County in the 1940s.

the east but also Meigs and Vinton counties farther south contribute mightily to the state's coal production. Ohio's total output has decreased even as the value of coal has risen, however, and the time isn't far off when miners won't be able to rely on this work.

Many operations have closed for good, and the transition hasn't been easy for workers *or* for the land. The roads, heavy equipment, deforestation, and dramatic new contours resulting from strip mining leave both miners and land changed, so that the memory of mine work lingers long after the last chunk of coal has headed down the Ohio and the land has returned to form. In her poem "The Mountains Have Numbers," Laura Treacy Bentley writes, "They tell me even now, though most of the mines are boarded up, directions are given in numbers, not mountains. 'You go past Holden 22. If you pass Hewitt Creek, you've gone too far.' "

Many have sought better economic prospects in the cities—Cleveland, Pittsburgh, and Columbus—and at least as many urbanites have sought refuge in

THE ROOTS OF FORT HENRY

Zane Grey's ancestors were pioneers on a much earlier frontier. Before the popular Western novelist tackled sagebrush and Mormons, he told the story of his great-grandfather Col. Ebenezer Zane and his great-great-aunt Betty Zane, who lived on the edge of the Ohio Country. Colonel Zane is best known for his blazing of Zane's Trace, the early Ohio trail he cleared for settlers that ran from Wheeling, West Virginia, through Zanesville, Ohio, and southwest to Maysville, Kentucky. Fort Henry was near the mouth of Wheeling Creek, site of present-day Wheeling.

One bright morning in June, 1769, the figure of a stalwart, broad shouldered man could have been seen standing on the wild and rugged promontory which rears its rocky bluff high above the Ohio river, at a point near the mouth of Wheeling Creek. He was alone save for the companionship of a deerhound that crouched at his feet. As he leaned on a long rifle, contemplating the glorious scene that stretched before him, a smile flashed across his bronzed cheek, and his heart bounded as he forecast the future of that spot. In the river below him lay an island so round and green that it resembled a huge lily pad floating placidly on the water. The fresh green foliage of the trees sparkled with glittering dew-drops. Back of him rose the high ridges, and, in front, as far as eye could reach, extended an unbroken forest.

Beneath him to the left and across a deep ravine he saw a wide level clearing. The few scattered and blackened tree stumps showed the ravages made by a forest fire in the years gone by. The field was now overgrown with hazel and laurel bushes, and intermingling with them were the trailing arbutus, the honeysuckle, and the wild rose. A fragrant perfume was wafted upward to him. A rushing creek bordered one edge of the clearing. After a long quiet reach of water, which could be seen winding back in the hills, the stream tumbled madly over a rocky ledge, and white with foam, it hurried onward as if impatient of long restraint, and lost its individuality in the broad Ohio.

This solitary hunter was Colonel Ebenezer Zane.

—Zane Grey, *Betty Zane* (from the Ohio River Trilogy), 1903

these misty, ancient hills. Between 1970 and 1998 Appalachian Ohio grew three times as fast as the state overall. It's evident now, with city dwellers looking for a more connected, relaxed, and meaningful lifestyle, that southeast Ohio has become a top draw for tourism and weekend getaways. Travelers come for the best hiking and camping in the state—all of Ohio's national and state forests lie in this region, part of the most biologically diverse forest of its kind in the world—and an arts culture that's intentionally not slick but well done and enjoyable. Athens's Dairy Barn, Chillicothe's summer production of *Tecumseh!*, the Zanesville area's ceramics, and Dresden's basket business all come to mind.

The best part about the Appalachian Hill Country, something not evident from a glance at the landscape, is that it's far from homogenous. The varying geography, economics, and people of each town make each a different experience. The towns covered in this section—Marietta, Portsmouth, Zanesville, Dresden, Athens, and Chillicothe—have as many differences as they do commonalities.

■ RIVER DANCE

In the most basic sense there are two kinds of town in Ohio's Appalachia—those that are on the Ohio River and those that aren't. Most towns in the region are on *some* river (Chillicothe on the Scioto, Athens on the Hocking, Zanesville on the Muskingum), but the Ohio's scale lends its river towns boasting rights: older settlements, better shipping, more fertile soils, easier trade. There's a proud history in what de Tocqueville called the most beautiful river valley in the world. Before frontiersmen and the military blazed trails through unbroken hardwood forest, the river *was* the path, and it continued as an indispensable conduit for trade and transportation through the end of the steamboat era in the 1870s. Marietta was a bustling jumping-off point for westward excursions and later became an actual port and a shipbuilding center of oceangoing liners. Portsmouth was an important transfer point between barges and steamboats.

To see it now, the Ohio's riverbed is a uniform channel in which glassy waters slide idly by, but for most of the river's existence, its water volume belied its irregularity, tight bends, and general orneriness. Imagine the skill required by old-time riverboat captains to navigate through waters little more than a foot deep. Heavy loads had to be timed with river-swelling spring rains. In the early days of settlement, no craft but canoes could reliably travel the river without running aground.

Indians were known to wait on the banks and ambush parties ensnared by hidden gravel bars and fallen trees.

Even worse for those who settled on the river, the Ohio drains some of the wettest land in the country (including three-quarters of Ohio) and wends through narrow valleys among steep hills. Floods could wipe out a community. Although Franklin D. Roosevelt had signed legislation directing the U.S. Army Corps of Engineers to begin flood protection projects along the Ohio, it took the Flood of 1937, which hit many towns particularly hard, to hasten the construction of flood walls and levees in order to prevent similar disasters in the future. Corps projects since that time have mitigated much of the impact of the Ohio's flooding.

Nine locks and dams along the state's border with the Ohio River maintain a minimum depth of 9 feet for navigation and prompt some to joke that it's really just a series of long lakes. In 1929 the Corps managed to build and maintain a navigable channel for all of the Ohio's 981 miles. Like the statewide system of canals before it, the river's channelization brought improved accessibility shortly before another transportation system diminished its full potential. The lock-and-dam system made possible the passage of enormous commercial loads just as the automo-

The Ohio River flooded Marietta in 1936, but greater damage came in 1937.

Kayaking is sublime on the Scioto River.

bile reduced people's interest in river transit. Highways, then interstates, became the lifeblood of travel.

After World War II heavy industry moved into the valley and, with it, toxins that made the river unappealing for recreation. Less than 1 percent of sewage and industrial wastes discharged into the Ohio was treated. One factor of such reckless pollution was that people naturally became less interested in spending time around the river and so were less vigilant of its blatant misuse. Now that the Ohio was no longer essential for transportation and was disconnected from the public at large, its cultural alienation was complete.

River towns found a measure of protection from flooding in new flood control systems, but like sled-toting children who find they can't keep up with the big kids while wearing snow pants, these towns are constricted and isolated by the structures of the systems that protect them. People coming in from out of town are naturally drawn to the riverfront, which is often the oldest part of town and the social center, but in some towns entering visitors are confronted with flood-walls and levees that interrupt the view of the river and cause a disconnection from the natural surroundings.

Ohio's High Waters

As the largest tributary to the Mississippi, the Ohio River is a powerful, and sometimes devastating, force of nature. This 981-mile-long waterway drains more than 200,000 square miles and forms Ohio's borders with Kentucky and West Virginia. When the rains come, the river floods, and even today's extensive lock-and-dam system can't hold it back. Here's a closer look at five of the state's most destructive floods:

1884: Known as one of the greatest floods of that century, this natural disaster was fueled by melting snow and ice that dumped water into the Ohio. At one point the water level in Portsmouth rose at the rate of 6 inches per hour. Some small towns had only two or three houses left standing when the waters receded.

1913: The beginning of the year brought Ohio residents two serious floods, including the deadliest in the state's history, a mere three months apart. Tributaries to the Ohio River ran over their banks throughout the state. Flooding was so severe in the southeast that every bridge on the Muskingum River between Zanesville and Marietta was destroyed.

1937: It was this great flood that sped up plans by the U.S. Army Corps of Engineers to build flood controls along the Ohio and other rivers. Ninety percent of Ironton was covered in water, and eighteen thousand people in Portsmouth were left homeless. One Marietta business owner reported 6 inches of water in the second story of his building.

1964: Thousands of people were forced to evacuate their homes as flood waters invaded. Waters reached the 66.2-foot mark despite the presence of thirty-nine reservoirs designed to curb flooding. This historic event is often used as a benchmark for modern floods, with "the worst flood since 1964" a popular media catchphrase.

1997: Thousands of people fled their homes in Ohio, Kentucky, and Indiana as waters passed the 60-foot mark in Cincinnati for the first time in thirty-odd years, eventually peaking at just under 64 feet. Damage was so extensive that President Clinton declared nine Ohio counties disaster areas to clear the way for federal aid. More than 130 miles of the river were shut down to boat traffic during the crisis.

Since the 1960s there have been consistent, incremental improvements on the river. Regulation and monitoring have drastically improved water quality. Sport fish, less tolerant of pollution than carp and suckers, are now common. Clean-up campaigns have raised awareness of the river's role in Ohioans' everyday lives, from transportation to recreation to drinking water. Outdoor and environmental organizations sponsor canoe and kayak trips on the river, such as Ohio River Way's Paddlefest, and recognition of the state's riverboat heritage has brought entertainment-oriented riverboats into vogue, notably at Marietta's Sternwheel Festival each September.

Priorities on the river are still unabashedly commercial: the river transports 230 million tons of cargo annually, mostly coal and other energy commodities. But that focus could shift. The Corps, often justly criticized for placing commercial priorities over environmental ones and for devising costly, large-scale projects to justify its own existence, has approval (but no funding) for a $306 million initiative for a comprehensive restoration of the Ohio River ecosystem. Pending federal funding (it has been passed over several times), the project would acknowledge the importance of riverine habitat to wildlife, community health, and the region's growing recreational interests by restoring bottomland hardwood forests, wetlands, islands, and shoreline throughout the river valley. It's too early to know which sites are in line for restoration, but if it proceeds as planned, the initiative would return a small part of the valley to the forces that shaped it.

■ **MARIETTA** *map page 107, B-4*

Affectionately contrary, Marietta didn't get the memo that said towns like this aren't supposed to exist anymore. And they certainly aren't supposed to succeed. The first permanent settlement in the Northwest Territory, Marietta actually lives up to the sorts of claims about historical importance and friendliness that every town's tourism bureau makes and then hopes you forget. People here really do have time to talk, and on the street a pleasant greeting is more common than a blank stare. Asking for directions could yield anything from a hand-drawn map to a personal escort. And then there is the charm: downtown is filled with shops and museums, lovingly maintained behind sturdy brick storefronts with festive white lights, that easily require a weekend. The sheer number and variety make the town feel larger than fifteen thousand.

Enough 19th-century and early-20th-century buildings remain that with a little imagination you can insinuate yourself in a ragtime streetscape. The city maintains more brick streets than anywhere else in Ohio. "We draw a lot of people from Cleveland, Akron, and Canton that come down here and enter a different world, where you don't have to lock your car doors," says Karen Briley of Schafer Leather Store, a fifth-generation family business begun as a harness shop after the Civil War and still at the same location. A local manager in the travel business describes Marietta's relationship with nearby Parkersburg, which promotes tourism regionally and gets matching funds for advertising from the state of West Virginia, as a "sugar daddy arrangement," with Marietta being the pretty girl.

Marietta's success results in part from good timing and from its prime location at the confluence of the Ohio and the Muskingum rivers. Forty-eight settlers led by founder Gen. Rufus Putnam arrived at Marietta in 1788, less than a year after passage of the Northwest Ordinance, which established laws and policies for the Northwest Territory (now Ohio, Indiana, Illinois, Michigan, Wisconsin, and part

Steamboats ply the Ohio in front of the Lafayette Hotel in Marietta.

of Minnesota) that would later serve the entire United States—trial by jury, freedom of religion, and the outlawing of slavery. Marietta was a primary departure and resupply point on the frontier and was well guarded during the Indian Wars (1791–1794) by Campus Martius to the north and Fort Harmar west of the Muskingum. The town was named in honor of the embattled French queen Marie Antoinette to recognize France's aid during the American Revolution.

So auspicious were Marietta's beginnings that George Washington remarked, "If I was a young man, just preparing to begin the world, or if advanced in life and had a family to make a provision for, I know of no country where I should rather fix my habitation." It was the only site west of the Alleghenies that was in the running to be the nation's new capital, and it wasn't really even a town yet so much as frontier hopes in physical form. It's just as well that those grand aspirations didn't come to pass; Marietta's graceful platting would have been trampled in the rush toward progress, and the White House would be red brick.

Practical history in Marietta begins at the **Lafayette Hotel** (101 Front Street; 740-373-5522), about as close as you can get to the confluence of the Muskingum and Ohio without falling in. There has been an inn of some sort on the site since Marietta's founding. Even if you aren't staying here, stop in to get a feel for what hotels, and life, were like in the riverboat era. As you enter, note the 11-foot pilot wheel, taken from the *J. D. Ayres,* suspended from the lobby ceiling. Elegant Victorian-style decor, quirky room layouts, and a what's-your-hurry elevator make the Lafayette feel as much Old World as New. (Most of the exterior dates to 1896, the interior to 1918.) Many of Marietta's attractions are within walking distance of the Lafayette.

The Lafayette is also ground zero, *the* place to be, when the **Sternwheel Festival** rolls around the weekend after Labor Day. The Sternwheel is Marietta's time to shine, with around thirty riverboats, a hundred thousand people, and a fireworks show any other town would roll out on the Fourth of July.

On most other days it's the museums and downtown business owners who roll out the show. The historic area known as **Harmar Village,** which is accessible from downtown via a pedestrian walkway, awaits west of the Muskingum. Small and easily walkable, it is home to the Marietta Soda Museum and the Children's Toy & Doll Museum, which features teddy bears, dolls, games, and dollhouses from the late 19th and early 20th centuries. Harmar Village got its start as Fort Harmar, a presettlement outpost commissioned to run squatters off land in the Ohio Country and protect early surveyors.

Downtown Marietta offers a range of specialty shopping—antiques, jewelry, clothing, furniture, and crafts—that brings people from around the state. Right on the Muskingum and Ohio rivers, this area is especially vulnerable to floods, and many buildings have the high-water marks to prove it. In some stores you'll notice a slight incline in the floor, designed to make post-flood cleanup an easier task. Navigation in town is easy. North–south streets are numbered after Front Street, east–west streets bear the names of Revolutionary War generals, and the rivers take care of the rest.

Part of the town's appeal lies in its easy coexistence with history. The **Campus Martius Museum,** for example, which details the settlement of Marietta and the Northwest Territory, Ohio government, and early life in Marietta, is on the site of the original Campus Martius (Latin for "Field of Mars"). That early Marietta stronghold was surrounded by a stockade and had towers at each corner. Founder Rufus Putnam's house is still on the site, enclosed by the museum and refurbished but unmoved since its construction in 1788. A visitor can walk away with a vivid and entertaining understanding of the Ohio Country's key players, events, and issues. Additional exhibits cover the exodus from rural Ohio during the last half of the 19th century and the 20th century. *601 Second Street; 740-373-3750.*

Enlightened resolutions and thoughtful city platting in Marietta have preserved some of the Adena and Hopewell mounds that were so common here. In other areas settlers and farmers built over them or heedlessly plowed them under. Conus, at **Mound Cemetery** on Fifth Street, is one example of what was saved. It's now a park monument with a staircase to the top, a fine view, and a time capsule to be opened July 4, 2076. The large, conical mound is, oddly, the iconic centerpiece of a cemetery filled with Revolutionary War veterans. The fact that so many settlers passed through here also makes the **Washington County Public Library** (615 Fifth Street; 740-373-1057) a great research destination for those interested in family history. And travelers who go shouldn't be surprised to discover that the library was built on Capitolium, a platform mound. Even mounds long since destroyed get recognition of some sort. Sacra Via, a road running between Third Street and the Muskingum, echoes the sacred Hopewell path that once led from the platform mound Quadranaou to the river.

At just over one hundred years old, the Washington County Courthouse is a relatively new building for Marietta.

The residential streets east of downtown, particularly Fourth and Fifth, have as much to offer as the rest of the city. On the south end of Fourth and Fifth, Marietta College's redbrick buildings fit in seamlessly with adjacent homes. As you stroll down these streets, bronze plaques sprinkled liberally through the neighborhood identify which homes, churches, and museums have historical and architectural value. They lend a patrician class to the scene, but the real marvel here is that nearly every home, big or small, evinces a pride of ownership and sense of community that welcome neighbors and travelers alike. Whether you're on the riverbank watching stern-wheelers or on Harmar Hill overlooking everything, that authentic welcome is what makes Marietta such a joy to visit.

■ **PORTSMOUTH** *map page 107, A-5*

Approaching Portsmouth from nearly any direction, a traveler has to wonder how a place once in the middle of it all became so remote. Portsmouth lies about as far as any town can get from Ohio's interstates, at the mouth of the Scioto River, one of the larger Ohio River tributaries and the same river that has fed Columbus's rapid growth. Empty factories and vacant buildings betray the major industry of years past. Whether you drive in from the west through Shawnee State Forest, from the east through Wayne National Forest, or from the north through the rural Scioto River valley, the feeling of seclusion is much the same. Unlike many Ohio River towns, Portsmouth doesn't have a neighbor on the other bank to counter the sense of isolation. The south bank rises sharply to ragged, wooded ridges.

In the early days of river transport, Portsmouth was an important transfer point for barges and riverboats. In 1832 the Ohio & Erie Canal connected Portsmouth with Cleveland and made the city a prominent player in the transportation business. Portsmouth grew from one thousand to five thousand between 1830 and 1857. One early problem, however, was that the city was *too* much in the middle of things. The southern branch of the Ohio & Erie originally ended in the Scioto, which made the canal prone to flooding and clogging from both rivers. The terminus subsequently moved to the west side of the river, a better spot technically but a poor choice logistically—the town lies on the east bank. In any case, railroads began supplanting canals in the 1850s, and eventually the canals were abandoned altogether.

Portsmouth's Floodwall Murals commemorate local artist Clarence Holbrook Carter (top) and its shoe-making industry.

The era also saw the development of the iron and steel industries in Portsmouth, part of the Hanging Rock Iron Region, which runs from Jackson, in southern Ohio, into northern Kentucky. Small companies sprang up to mine the iron and process it at furnaces for use in the manufacture of finished iron and steel. **Buckeye Furnace** (123 Buckeye Park Road, T-167, near Wellston; 740-384-3537), east of Jackson, is now a 270-acre state historic site that includes two nature trails. It is remote, as these furnaces tended to be, but open to the public year-round. The furnace is a great example of the typical setup used in this area. Visitors can see the reconstructed iron blasting furnace, casting shed, engine house, and company store. The Hanging Rock region's iron business became obsolete when a combination of vertical integration, new iron ore supplies on Lake Superior, and processing improvements unfavorable to Ohio's small-furnace operations shifted the focus of iron ore processing to Pittsburgh and the Lake Erie region.

The name given an early Portsmouth football team, the Shoe-Steels, effectively demonstrates the area's 20th-century economic engine: steel making and shoe making, led by Burgess Steel and Iron Works and such shoe companies as Selby and Williams. Much of the area's prosperity in that time could be attributed to those two industries, and when the last of them shut down between 1977 and 1980, hard times hit Portsmouth. Twenty percent of the city has left in the past twenty-five years. Martings, the local department store and downtown anchor, closed in 2002.

One bright spot has been the commission and completion of the **Portsmouth Floodwall Murals,** on Front Street. In fifty-two scenes Louisiana artist Robert Dafford highlights the people, work, and events that make Portsmouth what it is. There are notorious floods, period cityscapes, and portraits of local legends Branch Rickey, Roy Rogers, and Jim Thorpe (who coached and played for the Shoe-Steels in 1928). Driving south down Court Street, you expect to pass through the artwork's crowded archways to meet revelers at the shoreline, where riverboats await. The murals took ten years to complete (1993–2002). A rallying point for civic pride, they have turned what was isolating riverfront infrastructure into an iconic and popular attraction and have put Portsmouth back on the map.

The success of Portsmouth's murals, which were inspired by a similar project in Steubenville, has inspired other small towns looking for an economic boost to pursue notoriety through public art. Covington, Kentucky, across from Cincinnati, will have eighteen floodwall murals by Dafford completed by fall 2005, and both Chillicothe and Lancaster have taken cues from Portsmouth in creating their own downtown murals.

The **Southern Ohio Museum** is the nexus of Portsmouth's art and culture *indoors*. Most of the museum's space is dedicated to rotating exhibits, cutting across a range of media and often regional in nature, so it feels new every time you return. The permanent collection features the paintings of Clarence Holbrook Carter, a Portsmouth native who spent the first part of his career documenting river life in his hometown. In much of this work Carter peeks through windows, literally or figuratively, into small-town domestic life. One is a portrait of his mother, Hettie May Holbrook, who he says as a teenager would sneak out of the house after her parents were asleep, ride a horse to parties, and dance. Only after the local Methodist minister threatened to kick her out of the church did she drop the habit. *825 Gallia Street; 740-354-5629.*

■ SHAWNEE STATE PARK AND STATE FOREST *map page 107, A-5*
From spring to fall Portsmouth is a hub for outdoors enthusiasts exploring the 62,000 acres of the Shawnee State Park (4404 Route 125; 740-858-6652) and State Forest (13291 U.S. 52; 740-858-6685), the largest contiguous forest in the state. Ohioans generally recognize the Hocking Hills near Logan (also in the Appalachian Hill Country), as the state's best hiking spot, but Shawnee State Forest rivals that area and is usually less crowded. Shawnee combines the toughest backpacking and hiking in the state with comfy, well-appointed Shawnee Lodge. So well known is its reputation for misty hills and fantastic scenery that someone nicknamed it the Little Smokies. Although the area feels remote, the park and forest are two hours from Columbus and Cincinnati and about two and a half hours from Dayton.

In Shawnee State Park there are eighteen holes of golf, 75 miles of bridle trails, tennis courts, a swimming pool, bass fishing at Turkey Creek Lake, and modern campsites with electric hookups, showers, and laundry facilities. Some fishers claim the stretch of the Ohio River that passes through the park has the second-best fishing in the state after Lake Erie. Fall brings some of the state's most vivid color, which usually peaks around the third week of October. About 8,000 acres of this oak-hickory forest is designated wilderness, and rangers say the occasional black bear pops up. Shawnee is, after all, just across the river from eastern Kentucky. If you don't care to hike, fish, or ride, the park is still worth driving through with a pair of binoculars. Both wildflowers and wildlife are common. In November the

(following spread) Fresh snow quiets Conkles Hollow State Nature Preserve.

group QuiltEscape hosts a retreat for quilters at the hilltop Shawnee Lodge, a cozy sanctuary with oversized fireplaces, great views, and fifty guest rooms that might make you decide southern Ohio isn't remote at all. The lodge's comfort and style are a welcome surprise in these rugged hills.

■ ZANESVILLE *map page 107, B-2/3*

Although it is set firmly in the southeastern hill country, Zanesville is a cultural border town, trading on its I-70 accessibility and proximity to Columbus while retaining strong ties to the Arts and Crafts movement that made it famous. More than anything, it's a destination town for pottery. Abundant local clays spurred the ceramics industry in the late 1800s, and the city was once known as the Pottery Capital of the World. Pottery enthusiasts will find such well-known brands as Robinson Ransbottom, Fioriware, Burley, and Hartstone as well as a variety of outlets, retail stores, vintage pottery, museums, and factory tours.

Revolutionary War veteran Col. Ebenezer Zane and John McIntire founded the town in 1799. Zane had struck a deal with the federal government to blaze a trail from Maryland into the western wilderness that would open up the new country to settlers. In exchange he would receive land at three major river crossings on his path, which became known as Zane's Trace, and the right to operate ferries at each for a profit.

Zane depended partly on existing Indian paths and game trails to cut his route. The first part of Zane's Trace came west through Cumberland, Maryland, and Wheeling, West Virginia, to the confluence of the Licking and Muskingum rivers, where Zanesville sprang up. West of the Muskingum, Zane jogged south and west and set up crossings on the Hocking River at Lancaster and on the Scioto River at Chillicothe before finishing the trail on the Ohio at present-day Maysville, Kentucky. Looking at a state map, you can see the crescent-moon shape that towns on his trail form through southeastern Ohio.

The challenge of building a town at the confluence of the Licking and Muskingum rivers has given Zanesville its other claim to fame, the Y-Bridge, the "only bridge in the world where you can cross and still be on the same side of the river." The Licking flows east into the Muskingum, which runs north and south here. Picture the Y lying on its side pointing right: two sections of the bridge serve travelers west of the Muskingum (one north of the Licking and one south of the Licking), and the third meets them in the middle of the Muskingum and runs to

A slice of Zanesville's thriving art and pottery community on Main Street.

the east bank. It's said that early aviators used the Y-Bridge as a navigation aid because of its immediate recognizability. The original bridge was built in 1814, but the current version, the fifth incarnation, was completed in 1984.

■ THE POTTERY SCENE

Not long after settling here, farmers were tapping clay deposits in the area to make low-cost containers of all sorts. By 1880, when Cincinnati's popular Rookwood Pottery opened, the concept of art pottery had developed. The late 1880s saw the rise of the American Arts and Crafts movement, a reaction to the industrial excesses of the period. Emphasizing handcrafting and natural materials, the movement influenced the development of Zanesville's art pottery scene. Rookwood Pottery wasn't able to compete against lower-cost knockoffs and finally went out of business in 1967, yet the Zanesville area's potteries have managed to adapt and prosper in increasingly competitive times.

Zanesville by no means has a monopoly on pottery. Roseville and Crooksville, to the south, boast their own manufacturers and also are major centers in Ohio's pottery region. The **Pottery Lovers Reunion** (740-455-8282), held every July in

Zanesville, is the best time to survey the entire scene. The festival coincides with A Taste of Zanesville and the Crooksville/Roseville Pottery Festival and includes an auction, open houses, tours, demonstrations, and special sales. Both potters and collectors come from around the country to participate, and at least for that week it doesn't appear people are interested in much else.

Every visit to Zanesville should include a stop at the **Zanesville Art Center,** which includes not just significant local ceramics but also art glass, sculpture, American and European paintings, and antique dolls—more than seven thousand pieces in all. A $3 million renovation and expansion in 2003 left the center feeling too comprehensive and well scrubbed to be free, but it is. *620 Military Road; 740-452-0741.*

To linger more on the history of pottery in the area and explore the different types of pottery made, head south to the **National Ceramic Museum and Heritage Center,** which is open seasonally. Comprising five buildings, the center uses a sizable collection to illustrate the course of art pottery here. Most of the area's historic potteries, including such collector favorites as McCoy, Weller, Roseville, and Gonder, are represented. Hocking College now administers the site in conjunction with the Ceramic Pottery Museum Association. *7327 Ceramic Road NE, between Roseville and Crooksville; 740-697-7021.*

■ NATIONAL ROAD

In 1811 construction began on the National Road, now U.S. 40. This was the first major road-building effort to link the lands opening west of the Appalachians with the population centers of the East. The road eventually spanned 600 miles from Cumberland, Maryland, to Vandalia, Illinois. In Ohio it ran through Cambridge, Zanesville, Columbus, and Springfield. Connecting Western agriculture with Eastern markets was a primary goal of the road, but it also fostered a pioneer society along its narrow shoulders, shaping the look of the frontier and the way people lived, much as the interstate highway system has today. Politics, religion, new traditions, and trade came to the frontier on the National Road and fanned out into the wilderness, traveler by traveler.

The **National Road-Zane Grey Museum,** in Norwich, east of Zanesville, reveals the economic and social importance of this westward roadway. Exhibits follow Grey's path to stardom with his personal effects, his novels and manuscripts, and memorabilia. The history of the National Road is illustrated through a detailed diorama and full-scale re-creations of life during the route's early years. Separate dis-

Western author Zane Grey was supported and encouraged by his wife, Dolly.

plays of pottery from Zanesville's famous ceramics companies pay homage to the region's ceramics reputation and include noteworthy examples of Weller, Owens, and Roseville pottery, among others. *8850 East Pike, Norwich; 740-872-3143.*

Hardy laborers, mostly men, received 50 cents to a dollar a day to clear the land, level the ground, and build the bridges that would make up the road. By our standards, it was only a jeep trail, a dusty and rutted path not often wide enough for wagons to pass in both directions. In rainy weather it wasn't uncommon for carts and wagons to get stuck in muddy furrows. Towns formed along the route as inns and taverns set up shop to accommodate travelers, and other businesses moved in nearby. As with the canals, already established settlements wrangled to bring the National Road through town in hopes of tapping into the lively commerce, but the mandate was clear that the road proceed west without regard for towns of any size except state capitals.

After the railroad became the nation's transportation of choice in the 1850s, the road waned in importance and fell into disrepair. It wasn't until cars became popular in the early 20th century that attention again turned to the road as a primary travel route and revived it as a cultural icon. Between 1914 and 1916 the government paved the National Road, and during the 1920s it rose in importance as U.S. 40, the first federal highway in the United States.

ZANE GREY: BIG FISH AND PURPLE SAGE

Zane Grey popularized the Western as a genre in novels laced with crimson sunsets and honorable, chivalrous horsemen. With 17 million copies sold during his lifetime, Grey's novels, combined with the early movies based on his works, *became* the West in the popular imagination. His story is classically American. Fittingly, Grey—born in 1872 Pearl Zane Gray—grew up in Zanesville, the grandson of town founder Ebenezer Zane. He studied dentistry at the University of Pennsylvania to please his father, also a dentist, and played baseball on scholarship. (Grey wrote a handful of baseball novels, including *The Shortstop* and *The Young Pitcher.*)

During a miserable stint as a dentist in New York City, Grey worked on his writing at night and began working on *Betty Zane,* the first book of his Ohio River Trilogy, stories of his ancestors' Revolutionary-era adventures in the Ohio River Valley. Publishers showed little enthusiasm for his work—he self-published *Betty Zane*—and he may well have given up if not for his wife, Dolly, who edited his manuscripts, provided financial and moral support, and later managed his publishing career. More than anything Grey needed outdoor adventures to preserve his enthusiasm for life. Inspired by a trip he had taken to Arizona, *The Heritage of the Desert* was published in 1910. His next Western, *Riders of the Purple Sage,* exploded onto the best-seller lists and allowed him the outdoor immersion he craved. Sailing and fishing in particular became lifelong passions; he set fourteen fishing records and sailed along the West Coast and in the South Pacific on his *Fisherman* and *Fisherman II.*

Critics dismissed his work as naive melodrama, while the public couldn't get enough. Certainly the 2-cent Westerns bearing his name didn't help matters, but Grey was admittedly a hopeless romantic and didn't always counter his reputation for predictable plots and razor-thin characters. "Romance is only another name for idealism," he wrote, "and I contend that life without ideals is not worth living."

It's the rare hack whose novels endure a hundred years after publication and say something about our national character as fascination continues with arguably the harshest and most exotic corner of our country. Harper & Brothers routinely released a new Zane Grey book every year or two for about twenty years after his death in 1939, and many remain in print.

In a city renowned for its ceramics, one of the greatest art sites turns out to be all about bronze. **Alan Cottrill Sculpture Studio & Gallery** provides the unheard-of opportunity not only to view an artist's entire output—all of his sculptures are represented here in some form—but also to talk to him about his work and, if your timing's right, observe him in action. The studio is open to the public free of charge. Cottrill moved his studio to downtown Zanesville from Washington, Pennsylvania, in 2003 and says he's nearly always here. Looking at the work around his gallery, one's inclined to believe it. The collection includes busts and figures of all sizes: miners, soldiers, Indians, historical figures, and dozens of others, part of the largest bronze sculpture exhibit of any living sculptor's work. Cottrill himself is a fascinating study, a cigar-chomping straight talker and former restaurant entrepreneur with a bulldog's physique and determination. Visitors to his studio can draw inspiration from individual sculptures, the entire collection, or the passion with which an artist approaches his life and love. Cottrill also co-owns Coopermill Bronzeworks Ltd., a few miles away, where he casts his creations (and where you might also wrangle a tour with a little notice). *110 South Sixth Street, Zanesville; 740-453-9822.*

At Zane's Landing Park, a Cottrill piece, *The Bicentennial Legacy,* marks the place where Col. Ebenezer Zane and his son-in-law, John McIntire, first came ashore on the Muskingum. It includes figures of McIntire; the Civil War veteran Noah Norris (who was in Ohio's first African-American Civil War regiment); the astronaut and former U.S. senator John Glenn, a New Concord native; and the author Zane Grey. Zane's Landing is also home base for the *Lorena Sternwheeler,* which offers public rides in the summer and fall and dinner cruises in summer.

■ **DRESDEN** *map page 107, B-2*

Art and commerce converge in a big way at Dresden's **Longaberger Basket Company.** The basket-making tradition here harks back to the days when the Dresden Basket Factory produced "ware baskets," used to carry the local pottery. The basket factory didn't survive the Depression, but Longaberger—founded in the 1970s by the son of a Dresden Basket Factory employee—has since made basket making a cultural hallmark for the county, and as Zanesville's largest employer, it has become a dominant economic force. Longaberger sells through independent "sales consultants," much the way Tupperware does, so visitors don't trek here for the holy grail of outlet basket shopping. Instead they come to experience a lifestyle that Longaberger sells as effectively as any product.

The late Dave Longaberger started the company with a handful of weavers working for IOUs in a previously vacant mill in Dresden, but through principled management, a personal approach, and maverick risk taking, he built a robust company. The **Longaberger Homestead** (5563 Raiders Road, Frazeysburg; 740-322-5588) is one of Dave's many successful ideas brought to life. It's a small theme park where guests can eat at one of several restaurants, watch street entertainers and a daily parade, and shop for home accessories. J.W.'s Workshop, the original, relocated building where Dave's father wove baskets on the side to support his twelve sons and daughters, as well as a replica of the family home help relate the Longaberger story. Frequently a member of the Longaberger family is on hand at J.W.'s Workshop to sign baskets and tell tales from childhood. Teas, luncheons, crafts shows, and an array of other events held throughout the year make the homestead a social destination. The nearby manufacturing campus also has tours that include the chance to make a basket with help from one of the basket makers. Shuttle buses take visitors from the homestead to the factory for tours.

Fifteen miles west of the homestead in Newark, the company headquarters (1500 East Main Street)—a seven-story basket complete with handles—illustrates the degree to which Longaberger immerses customers in its idyllic world. The company's unusual approach to business and its unique building have netted a fair amount of publicity, as has Longaberger's record of charitable giving. The Longaberger Foundation has given more than $7 million to charity over seven years, and through its independent sales consultants Longaberger has generated $10 million over nine years for breast cancer research as part of its Horizon of Hope campaign. Since 1996 Longaberger has made *Forbes*'s list of the five hundred largest privately held companies; 2002 revenues approached $1 billion.

■ ATHENS *map page 107, B-4*

Athens may well be the best-known town in a region full of iconic towns. It's debatable whether Portsmouth or Athens is the more isolated among southeast Ohio's large towns, but Athens's hilly topography and thick pine forests make it feel far from everything. Athens has many facets, but the primary draws for visitors are education, arts, and the outdoors.

Like it or not, Ohio University (OU), which celebrated its bicentennial in 2004, runs the show in Athens. From its start as the first university in the Northwest

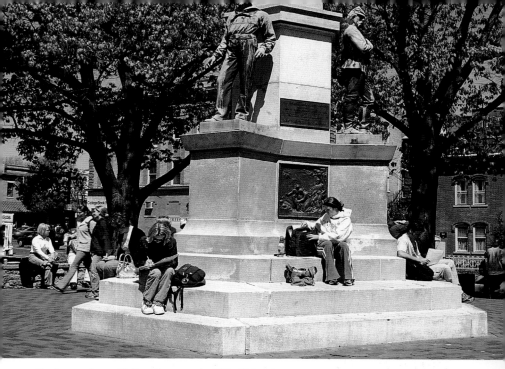

Students gather at College Green on the Ohio University campus.

Territory until after World War II, OU had a modest influence on the town; it was more a counterpoint to the predominant Appalachian flavor of Athens than a cultural driver. Now, the spirit of the school is very much the spirit of the town, and you'll see it everywhere—in mothers and fathers filling the streets during Parents' Weekend, in student craziness on Halloween (is that guy in costume or not?), and even daily as an instructor grabs a veggie burrito on the way to class.

In relation to its setting, OU seems an anomaly. Rarely do universities this remote and surrounded by such rugged natural beauty also have this caliber of academics—or nineteen thousand students enrolled. (The university also has broadened its reach beyond Athens, with eight thousand more students at campuses in Chillicothe, Ironton, Lancaster, St. Clairsville, and Zanesville.) Cultural opportunities surround the university community, and that's good news for travelers. Much of what's available for students is also accessible to those just passing through.

Be sure to check out **The Ridges,** a 700-plus-acre slice of university land across the Hocking River south of campus that is the site of arts centers and a nature preserve. If you think the Victorian Gothic architecture of the primary building perched atop the ridge here, Lin Hall, belongs in a Mary Shelley novel or Alfred

The Bobcat's athletic program includes eight men's sports and ten women's.

Hitchcock film, you're not far off base. The oldest part of the complex of buildings here began as the Athens Lunatic Asylum, although that name changed multiple times over its hundred-plus-year history as both attitudes about mental illness and the services it provided shifted.

The asylum's purpose and imposing appearance have generated a number of campfire stories, mostly apocryphal. One is true. In December 1978 a female patient in her mid-fifties disappeared and was not discovered missing until after curfew. Open-ward patients were permitted to leave the grounds provided they signed out. Staff conducted a three-day search and a series of follow-up searches for another week, all to no avail. But six weeks later a maintenance man found the body of the woman in a vacant ward, which apparently had been temporarily unlocked long enough for her to slip in, then locked after the area was searched. The hospital speculated that the rather reclusive woman had hidden from searchers and then was unable to get out. Her outline, an indelible, yellowish stain, remains on the floor where she lay down to die; it is said to be the result of her decomposing body, exposed to bright sunlight, reacting chemically with the concrete floor.

Navajo rugs and contemporary prints are two reasons to visit the Kennedy Museum of Art.

The **Kennedy Museum of Art,** which now occupies the ground floor of Lin Hall, acts as a hub for educational programming. It includes both traveling and permanent exhibits that often incorporate local artists and themes important to the region. It's especially known for its large collection of Native American art, which includes many Navajo rugs, as well as for its contemporary print collection. *Lin Hall, The Ridges; 740-593-1304.*

Just south of the Kennedy Museum is the **Dairy Barn Southeastern Ohio Cultural Arts Center,** an internationally known premier venue for arts and crafts. The Dairy Barn is the locus for community arts and crafts exhibits, festivals, and educational programs. It hosts two biennial juried exhibitions, Quilt National (in odd years) and Bead International (in even years), that draw visitors and artists from forty countries. At one time this building really *was* a working dairy barn that helped provide food for patients of the asylum. Local arts supporters saved the barn just a few days before its scheduled demolition. The arts center celebrated its twenty-fifth anniversary in 2003. *8000 Dairy Lane; 740-592-4981.*

As you navigate Athens you can't help but be aware of the world outside. Forests press in from all sides, and the hills dictate transportation routes. That's true of the roads, and it's true of the old Hocking Valley Railroad, which has been converted into the **Hockhocking Adena Bikeway.** The 19-mile path loops around Athens and Ohio University and jogs northwest to Nelsonville. Plans call for it eventually to extend east to Strouds Run State Park. You can access Athens's 5-mile stretch of the bikeway by heading for the Hocking River and looking for the path on the side closest to town. In addition to thick forests and rocky ledges, there's a bit of history still left along the path. It was once the towpath for the Hocking Canal, and parts of the canal basin are still visible between Armitage and Chauncey.

Near Mile 7, the path passes the **Eclipse Company Town,** an old coal-mining town of white Monopoly-style houses. The town dates to around 1900 and stands as one of the best examples of the company-town model in Ohio. In other regions these structures are used for historical interpretation, or are simply vacant, if they're even still standing. Here you'll find a bike-path-town-in-progress, consisting of the **Starving Wolf & Yellow Moon Café** (11310 Jackson Drive; 740-797-4443), rental cottages, private residences, and a few alternative medicine centers. Eventually the old company store will house communal space, a museum, and a dash of retail. *To reach the Eclipse Company Town from Athens, take U.S. 33 north to Johnson Road. Turn left on Johnson, then left onto Jackson Drive.*

■ APPALACHIA OUTDOORS

Athens, Nelsonville, and Logan are the gateways to the best overland outdoor opportunities in Ohio. **Hocking Hills,** 20 miles from Nelsonville, is the king of the state park system and a treat for recreationists of all stripes. If you haven't explored the forests of southeastern Ohio before and aren't interested in epic excursions, come here first. (If you have a longer trip in mind, consider seeking out less popular terrain.) The park features a dining lodge, cottages, fishing on trout-stocked Rose Lake, and the most beautiful scenery in the state. Old Man's Cave, a huge recess cave that was once home to a post–Civil War hermit, is probably the most-visited site in the park, and Cedar Falls, actually shrouded by hemlocks, is also popular. The other sites are Ash Cave, Rock House, and Cantwell Cliffs, the outlier and least used among the five. The combination of high hills and deep gorges here often leaves the Hocking Hills area several degrees cooler than western and southern sections of the state, a good fact to keep in mind when looking to escape the summer heat and when packing.

A patchwork of agencies manages tens of thousands of acres in the Hocking Hills region. Strouds Run State Park, Burr Oak State Park, Zaleski State Forest, Conkles Hollow State Nature Preserve, and Wayne National Forest offer a range of landscapes, pursuits, and user rules to suit most any traveler. And since Ohio ranks last among states in percentage of adults who exercise regularly, you can revel in the solitude of the open trail, lake, or parking spot.

If you have grander plans, both the 1,250-mile Buckeye Trail and the North Country Trail pass through the region. The **Buckeye Trail** is the state's own Woodie Guthrie song made manifest, an all-encompassing loop trail that stretches from the Lake Erie shoreline to the southern forests of Portsmouth and hits many of Ohio's natural highlights on the way. The Hocking Hills section (known as the Grandma Gatewood section) might be the best. It passes the top attractions mentioned above—Old Man's Cave, Ash Cave, Cedar Falls, and Conkles Hollow—before hooking up with the Scioto Trace section to the southwest.

The **North Country Trail** runs roughly 4,000 miles from Lake Sakakawea in North Dakota to Lake Champlain in New York; it is the Appalachian Trail Ohio never had and is about twice as long. Practically speaking, this trail mostly borrows the route of the Buckeye Trail, conceived in the late 1950s, but it is still worth noting because Ohio has never had an interstate trail on this scale before. Once all the sections have been completed and certified—a massive undertaking—the trail can begin establishing its own life and legend in earnest.

For a tamer outdoors experience, consider the **Bob Evans Farm** in Rio Grande (that's *rye*-o grand), a versatile and folksy destination that the whole family can enjoy. Visitors can camp and hike on the 1,000-acre property, tour the homestead, and revel in the fact that Bob Evans isn't simply a commercial creation like Betty Crocker and Aunt Jemima. Yes, there really is a Bob Evans, and he and his wife, Jewell, lived here with their children in the 1950s and 1960s when Bob Evans was becoming a household name. Early commercials invited customers to drop by the farm for a visit, and before long too many did. The original home is now the Homestead Museum, which has a free exhibit that chronicles the growth of Evans's sausage business and spin-off restaurant chain. There are now Bob Evans restaurants in twenty-one states.

(following spread) Upper Falls at Old Man's Cave, in Hocking Hills State Park.

The working farm has a crafts barn with items for sale, a Revolutionary War cemetery, an outdoor amphitheater, an Ohio Bicentennial Barn (celebrating Ohio's 200th anniversary, in 2003—there's at least one barn painted with the Ohio bicentennial logo in every Ohio county), a small animal barnyard for the kids, and, of course, a Bob Evans Restaurant. RV camping is available, as are horseback riding and canoeing. The farm does feel a bit commercial, but it's also mellow and lives up to the soothing "down on the farm" tagline. Every October there's a three-day Farm Festival with music, dancing, crafts, and food. *791 Farmview Drive (off Route 588); 800-994-4375.*

For a more exotic escape, check out the **Wilds,** an outdoor zoological park west of Cumberland and southeast of Zanesville. Built on reclaimed mining land, the Wilds is home to some two dozen species from Africa, Asia, and North America—giraffes, rhinos, bison, and some you've never heard of—many of them threatened. Scientists here are working on breeding programs, conservation, and ecological restoration; support staff provide public tours and educational programs. There are even day camps and overnights for children. Open May to October, the park offers a refreshing alternative to traditional zoo habitats. *14000 International Road, Cumberland; 866-444-9453.*

■ CHILLICOTHE *map page 107, A-4*

Chillicothe, just one point on the map, divides two regions. Not far to the north and west, hilly forests yield to fertile plains. To the east and south, the Appalachian plateau rises up in earnest. The Scioto cuts through Chillicothe from the north and separates the old part of town from the new. Paint Creek joins the Scioto just south of town. Compared with other Appalachian towns, Chillicothe is rich with both economic possibility *and* historical importance, and it manages to court both attributes to come out on top.

Chillicothe's founding came early by Ohio settlement standards. Prior to the Treaty of Greenville in 1795, Ohio towns were restricted to the Ohio River corridor to avoid conflicts with Indians. Nathaniel Massie laid out Chillicothe in 1795, and settlement began a year later. Massie, Thomas Worthington, and Edward Tiffin were prominent influences in frontier politics and were instrumental in overruling the territorial governor and paving the way for Ohio's statehood in

The Ross County Courthouse in Chillicothe is on the site of Ohio's first statehouse.

STATEHOOD
DAY

THE GREAT SEAL OF THE STATE OF OHIO

Chillicothe
OHIO'S FIRST
CAPITAL
1803

ACCESS
AT REAR

1803. All were elected to the territorial legislature, and the gregarious Tiffin became Ohio's first governor. Worthington, however, is the bigger name; he was Ohio's first U.S. senator, its sixth governor, and the "Father of Ohio Statehood." It was Worthington who led the campaign for statehood and hand-delivered the Ohio Constitution to Congress in Washington, D.C.

More important in Chillicothe today, he built a mansion in 1807 that is now preserved as part of the 320-acre **Adena State Memorial.** Worthington's sandstone Italian-villa–style home sits atop a hill northwest of town. Its setting and building style are said to have been inspired by Jefferson's Monticello. Indian mounds were discovered on the property, so the ancient peoples who built them became known as the Adena.

Chillicothe was the first capital of the Northwest Territory and the first capital of Ohio. It benefited from the canal boom and a stable papermaking industry, and it is now a commercial hub of southern Ohio and host to a booming string of national retailers on Bridge Street on the north side of town. The outstanding outdoor drama *Tecumseh!* is performed in Chillicothe, and the Hopewell Culture National Historical Park, one of the best sites in the country to explore ancient indigenous cultures, is here.

The well-kept, architecturally significant downtown includes an array of beautiful, unique buildings. Water and Paint streets form the backbone of one of the state's most diverse and impressive historic districts. Examples of Greek Revival, Italianate, Victorian Revival, Federal, and Romanesque architecture are common throughout downtown and add authenticity to this viable and respectable commercial quarter. Remarkably, there are no breaks in the facade left by demolished buildings and no boarded-up windows, and the newer structures generally blend with the period buildings.

Chillicothe's centerpiece is the **Ross County Courthouse,** an imposing limestone structure built in 1858 on the site of the first county courthouse, which also served as the original Ohio statehouse. The Ohio Constitution was signed on this site in 1802. (Visitors interested in the original 1801 courthouse should head to the offices of the *Chillicothe Gazette* at 50 West Main Street. The *Gazette*—the "oldest paper west of the Alleghenies"—built its offices as a replica of the original courthouse-statehouse in the early 1940s.) The current courthouse's clock tower, which is wood painted to look like stone, has plenty of company: towers rise from buildings all along downtown's streets and make Chillicothe immediately recognizable in photographs. *2 North Paint Street; 740-773-2330.*

A tidy bed-and-breakfast exemplifies the beauty of Chillicothe's historic downtown.

Paint and Water streets form a T at the head of Yoctangee Park and are downtown's widest streets, thanks to an 1852 fire that destroyed essentially everything in a two-block-square area. After the fire, buildings were reconstructed farther back from the road to allow more room for traffic. Many of the replacement buildings along Water Street were designed in the Greek Revival style. Water Street, incidentally, was named not for the canal or Yoctangee Park Lake but for the Scioto River, which once ran adjacent to the street but shifted its course in the mid-1800s. The lake follows part of the river's former path. When the Ohio & Erie Canal came here in 1832, it ran right along Water Street, above the Scioto but underneath today's wider Water Street.

Older Chillicothe neighborhoods display the same grandeur seen downtown. **Tanglewood** (177 Belleview Avenue), a privately owned Greek Revival gem on Belleview Hill that was part of the Underground Railroad, and the **Willis/Cook/Biggs House** (now Blair House Bed & Breakfast, 58 West Fifth Street; 740-774-3140), the oldest, rear section of which the founder of the *Scioto Gazette* built in 1805, are just two of the treasures that reveal Chillicothe's deep historical roots.

Take a stroll or drive down West Fourth and Fifth streets to get a sense of the remarkable variety of older houses, many of which are still private residences. The **Ross County Historical Society Museum** (45 West Fifth Street; 740-772-1936), which itself dates to 1838, is a great place to learn about the history of the area and view historical artifacts, including the table on which Ohio's Constitution was signed.

Be sure to wander past the **Mountain House** (8 Highland Avenue), the onetime home of Dard Hunter, whose front yard offers a great view of downtown. Hunter was a pioneer in the American Arts and Crafts movement and was influential in reviving 16th-century techniques of papermaking and bookbinding. He wrote twenty books on the art of papermaking, eight of them hand-printed on handmade paper. Mountain House served as his studio. If you take a close look at the exterior, you'll notice that the many long, narrow windows are shaped like wine bottles. German immigrant vintners built the house in the 1850s to overlook their vineyard and used the stone vaults below the house to store wine. Dard Hunter III now lives in the house.

■ HOPEWELL CULTURE NATIONAL HISTORICAL PARK
map page 107, A-4

Between fifteen hundred and twenty-two hundred years ago, the lands around Chillicothe and Newark, 60 miles to the northeast, were major centers of a Hopewell culture that ranged from present-day New York and Wisconsin to the Gulf of Mexico. The Hopewell name comes from a Chillicothe resident, Mordecai Hopewell, on whose farm mounds were discovered. So important were the lands of Chillicothe and Newark to these ancient people that Columbus-based archaeologist Bradley T. Lepper has discovered evidence of an ancient path, the Great Hopewell Road, running in a straight line between the two towns.

Hopewell Culture National Historical Park encompasses five sites: Mound City, just north of Chillicothe along the west bank of the Scioto River; Hopewell Mound Group, west of Chillicothe, the site once owned by the Hopewell people's namesake, Mordecai Hopewell; Seip Earthworks, east of Bainbridge; High Bank Works; and Hopeton Earthworks. Only the first two sites are open to the public.

The park's flagship site, **Mound City** has a visitors center and some two dozen mounds enclosed by a low, squarish earthworks, augmented by explanatory plaques. The visitors center is modern, pleasant, and especially helpful in making the story of the Hopewell tangible. On-site rangers have substantial knowledge of Hopewell culture and the site's significance. An exhibit at the center contains jewelry, crafts, and other artifacts that increase curiosity about and respect for the mounds and their builders. *16062 Route 104; 740-774-1126.*

The Hopewell built their earthworks near streams and rivers, often in intermediate riparian zones that offered both packable, durable soils and a degree of protection from floods. The mounds are mostly cone-shaped and vary in size, from small rises a few feet high to tent-sized and parachute-sized mounds. Aside from being two thousand years old and unusually resilient, they are unremarkable. What is remarkable is the story the mounds and artifacts tell about the Hopewell culture.

Hopewell mounds were built over dome-shaped ceremonial lodges thought to be used for cremation and burial of their dead, although they could have had other purposes as well. Archaeologists have discovered a number of artifacts in these burial mounds and in other mounds: carved stone pipes, sharks' teeth, spear points and other stone tools, pottery, and headdresses. From the presence of numerous materials in these mounds that were not locally available at the time, archaeologists know that the Hopewell had an elaborate trade network stretching from the Rocky Mountains to the Atlantic Coast.

Ephraim Squier and Edwin Davis, both residents of Chillicothe in the 1840s, undertook the first serious excavations and documentation of the mounds in Ohio and around the eastern woodlands. Squier was the editor of the *Scioto Gazette* and Davis a physician. They coauthored the groundbreaking *Ancient Monuments of the Mississippi Valley,* published in 1848, and chronicled the existence of many of these mounds before the mounds were lost to settlement and agriculture.

■ Travel Basics

Getting Around: Southeast Ohio is nothing more than one big scenic drive. With no sizable cities, public transportation is limited. A car is one alternative for sightseeing; even better are the riverboats that ply the Ohio and Muskingum. If you drive, get a detailed map and head off the beaten path. A good choice for an afternoon drive is to take Route 26 east from Marietta until it ends in Woodsfield. It's a hilly route through gorgeous Wayne National Forest and takes you near several covered bridges. Highway 32 also runs through pretty country, and the roads around the Hocking Hills can't be beat for natural beauty.

Climate: The hills and valleys come alive with fall foliage around mid-October, when temperatures are typically mild. Spring temperatures range from 40 to 70 degrees Fahrenheit, while summer is hot and humid. The average winter temperature is around 25 degrees Fahrenheit.

CENTRAL OHIO

Central Ohio includes Franklin County, home to Columbus, and a rough square of nine surrounding counties: Delaware, Morrow, Marion, Union, Madison, Pickaway, Fairfield, Licking, and Knox, as well as the southern portion of Ashland and Richland counties. Columbus wields an ever-growing influence over its surrounding communities. This is dramatically evident northwest of Columbus in Dublin, which has experienced a population explosion during the past thirty years. Lancaster and the Mohican Country around Loudonville, also covered here, are more insulated from the capital city's outward rush.

Many people think of central Ohio as being white-bread, but that view comes more from old immigration patterns than from a present-day reality. Fittingly, new arrivals in northeast Ohio tended to have roots in the Northeast; southern Ohio drew from Virginia and the southern Appalachians; and central Ohio saw immigrants from Pennsylvania and the mid-Atlantic states, mainly Germans and English. African-Americans have long had a significant presence in Columbus, and they now make up 24 percent of the population. A 2002 Black Entertainment Television study named Columbus the number-one city in the country for black families. In the past few decades the city has seen large increases in many smaller ethnic groups from around the world, due mostly to the strong university presence. Among other things, Columbus has the second-largest Somalian population in the country.

■ COLUMBUS *map page 148*

The landscape in central Ohio is measured in miles to, or away from, Columbus, a fast-growing city that fans out in all directions. Most roads in the state lead here, so it's easy enough for folks in nearby Lancaster, Delaware, and Marysville to commute or make weekend forays into the city and just as easy for city dwellers to move to the suburbs without sacrificing urban convenience. A glance at an interstate map reveals that east–west I-70 and southwest–northeast I-71 cross in Columbus, but so do four-lane U.S. 23 and U.S. 33. Combined with the I-270 outer belt, the four make Columbus look like the axle of a ragged Ohio wheel.

Access has been a crucial factor in central Ohio's development. Lacking the geographic advantages of Lake Erie and the Ohio River inherent in the state's other

Columbus skyscrapers surpass the Ohio Statehouse in height but not grandeur.

big cities, Columbus came of age with the advent of the Interstate Highway System. A strong network of roads enabled the city to support the rapid growth that soon came. Columbus's population grew 89 percent between 1950 and 2000. Part of the city's growth is rooted in a policy of aggressive annexation; it has absorbed numerous towns and villages, many of which were in need of city services. As a result, Columbus has more land area than any other Ohio city, about two and a half times that of Cleveland, Cincinnati, or Toledo.

Years ago, in an essay on his hometown of Des Moines, Iowa, humorist Bill Bryson described how the city had a way of sucking people in, how motorists venturing off the interstate for gas and Big Macs would get lost and end up living there for thirty years. Although there are few other comparisons to be made between the two cities, Columbus does have a Des Moines–like way of sneaking up on you. Often the process begins in the colleges and universities, the farm teams of Columbus residency: Capital University, Columbus State, Columbus College of Art & Design, Franklin University, and, of course, the Ohio State University (the second largest university in the country), which pulls students from Ohio and all over the world. Students graduate, land a job in town while pondering their options, and find themselves living here, content and serene, five years later.

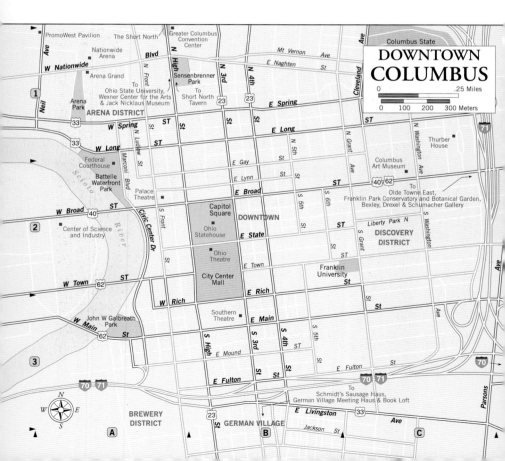

The same happens with professionals, who see an energetic business environment and near-bulletproof economy and soon decide they don't want to be anywhere else. The steady hands of government and education have helped protect the Columbus economy, while its central location has fostered a balanced business mix that includes manufacturing, banking, insurance, finance, and warehousing. Residents-to-be have been wandering into town since World War II, but unlike other cities in the northeast, Columbus continued to benefit from migration throughout the seventies, eighties, and nineties, making it the envy of Ohio, the only city in the state to grow during that period. Many assume that Cleveland, or maybe Cincinnati, is Ohio's largest city, but with 711,470 people Columbus takes that distinction too (although Cleveland has a larger overall metro area, with 3 million people). Robust population growth—26 percent over twenty years—has

These young women attended a leadership workshop at Capital University in 1951.

Columbus was growing along the Scioto River in 1868.

brought Columbus dependable prosperity and prompted vigorous private investment. In addition, because of widespread annexation and geographical parity, the city feels more unified than Cleveland and Cincinnati.

The assumption that Columbus is a small town could stem partly from the fact that it is a capital city, and conventional wisdom says capital cities are otherwise ineffectual hamlets, the recipients of political bones. Important cities also are supposed to have major league sports teams. Cleveland has them. Cincinnati has them. But until the National Hockey League Blue Jackets arrived in 2000, Columbus was the largest market in the country without a pro team in one of the four major sports: football, baseball, basketball, and hockey. It now also has the Arena Football League Destroyers, formerly of Buffalo, New York.

The most pernicious argument against Columbus is that it is *placeless.* Certainly a major city of national importance should somehow register in the collective conscious—a prominent building, a geographic feature, an economic staple . . . ? Drawing a blank? Some would mention Buckeye football, but otherwise Columbus is out of luck.

It's about time that America discovered Columbus—"Klumbus" if you're a local. Lying at the confluence of the Scioto and Olentangy (oh-luhn-*tan*-jee) rivers, Columbus has the highest percentage of residents with college degrees of any city in the state. It is served by a half dozen colleges and universities, and several others, including Denison University in Granville and Ohio Wesleyan in Delaware, are nearby. Columbus is a white-collar town but still down-home, the birthplace of hamburger chains Wendy's, White Castle, and Max & Erma's.

And yet, the city's identity has been hurt by its cavalier attitude toward preservation during decades of tremendous growth. This created grounds for the charge of placelessness. New developments vanquished such landmarks as the Old Franklin County Courthouse and Union Station train depot, whose destruction raised a broad-based hue and cry in 1976. Only one of Union Station's arches was saved; today it stands at the head of Arch Park in the Arena District.

To an extent the city has atoned for its sins. Preservationists saved ailing German Village from demolition in the 1960s and 1970s with a heroic restoration effort. The entire district is now on the National Register of Historic Places and remains the largest such area created with private funds; it is a highly desirable middle-class neighborhood. In the 1980s artists and urban pioneers revitalized the decaying Short North—a strip of High Street between downtown and the OSU campus— which is now probably the hippest and most vital place in the city. Successes have multiplied, but threats to historic neighborhoods and architecture continue to challenge preservationists' efforts and resources.

■ **DOWNTOWN** *map page 148*

Columbus began as a planned community, chosen as the new capital in 1812 for its central location in the young state (although it didn't succeed Chillicothe as capital until 1816). Other than its equal proximity to prominent settlements, there was little to recommend the place. It did offer shipping access via the Scioto, but the area was marshy, unpleasant, and sparsely settled. The state legislature met here for the first time in 1816, after the War of 1812, and an extension to the Ohio & Erie Canal built in the 1830s boosted trade in the city.

You wouldn't know that Columbus used to be swampy to look at it, but town platters created downtown on the higher east bank of the Scioto, appropriately called the High Bank, to avoid flooding. High Street is the main north–south

(following spread) Downtown Columbus glistens on the high bank of the Scioto River.

Citizens gathered for the Columbus centennial celebration at the Ohio Statehouse in 1912.

street and Broad Street the main east–west street. Both run the course of the city. High Street becomes U.S. 23; Broad Street becomes U.S. 40.

While downtown is not without its redeeming qualities, many of the blocks are occupied by the mainstays of government and business. It's clear from looking at the center of this grid of high-rises and seats of government (bordered roughly by the Scioto River on the west, I-70/71 on the south, Grant Avenue on the east, and Spring Street on the north) that historically it has anchored the city. It is also clear that in order to succeed, the city's most dynamic areas, such as the Arena District and German Village, must reject the downtown label. Many of Columbus's superb cultural and social opportunities lie at the edges of downtown. One of the first steps in generating a buzz for a section of downtown is to affix a name to it—the Discovery District, the Arena District, the Brewery District. When business owners south and east of the Arena District (the entertainment venues around Nationwide Arena) were struggling for an identity, they formed the Uptown District, a label with more panache than dreary old downtown.

More than likely, every downtown neighborhood eventually will have its own name, but the practice of subdividing doesn't change the fact that the **Ohio**

Statehouse (Capitol Square; 888-644-4123) is the dominant downtown landmark. The iconic capitol building is unusual for its use of Greek Revival architecture, as well as its protracted construction schedule. Groundbreaking began in 1839, and by the time the Statehouse was completed in 1861, Greek Revival seemed charmingly retro. To those of us with an untutored eye, the cupola appears to be missing its round dome. The original design indeed called for a round dome, but subsequent architects scratched those plans to retain classical authenticity.

Directly south of the Statehouse, the **Ohio Theatre** (39 East State Street; 614-469-0939) represents another architectural triumph. Home to the Columbus Symphony Orchestra, the former movie house is known for its intricate Spanish-Baroque interior. But it's not the only show downtown. The corridor along High Street, directly west of the Ohio Theatre, also includes the **Palace Theatre** (34 West Broad Street; 614-469-9850) and the **Southern Theatre** (21 East Main Street; 614-340-9698). All have been restored to their former glory, although there is now talk of additional renovations for the Ohio and the Palace to address structural limitations of the two landmarks, including stage room and acoustics. Still, these theaters host a range of performing groups, from Opera Columbus to Broadway in Columbus and Ballet Met.

On the west side of the Scioto, the **Center of Science and Industry (COSI) Columbus** is the perfect rainy-day or cold-weather destination. Adults will appreciate the interactive, educational exhibits covering such topics as space exploration, human life, and the ocean, but the convention-center–sized exhibit halls are aimed at kids. In the space exhibit, for example, children can use remote-controlled robots to pick up and move objects, launch a plastic bottle into "space" using air pressure, and witness footage from space expeditions. The highlight of the museum is the high-wire unicycle, believed to be the only one of its kind in the world, that visitors can ride right over the lobby. *333 West Broad Street; 888-819-2674.*

In addition to supporting stable public and civic institutions, officials have struggled to facilitate a strong mix of housing and unique retail outlets that could return the southern end of downtown to prominence. City Center, the introverted downtown mall, has continually shed stores and seems destined for some sort of overhaul or redevelopment. Retailers want to see more residents to justify urban investment, while potential residents need good reasons, and everyday services, to make moving worthwhile. This is a familiar dilemma for cities around the country, but it's easy to forget that even robust Columbus plays by the same rules.

The Columbus Symphony Orchestra performs more than a hundred concerts each year.

Building a new ballpark in the Arena District or River South District (near City Center) could cue a turnaround. The AAA Columbus Clippers currently play in seventy-year-old Cooper Stadium, a county-owned venue isolated near the I-70/71 interchange. The construction of a new stadium, probably built with a combination of public and private funds, presents its own challenges, but it holds the appeal of a proven formula that has worked with downtown ballparks in Akron, Dayton, and Toledo.

■ **ARENA DISTRICT** *map page 148, A-1*
On the north edge of downtown, the Arena District, the district that almost didn't happen, is the next big thing in Columbus. The wildly popular Columbus Blue Jackets were lured to the city in 2000 with the construction of **Nationwide Arena** (200 West Nationwide Boulevard; 614-246-2000). The expansion National

Hockey League team now plays here to capacity crowds. Surrounding the arena is a growing roster of restaurants, shops, housing, office space, and entertainment outlets that developers and city officials expect to be *the* downtown destination for years to come. Nationwide Insurance has space here, of course, but so do law firms, marketing firms, and a growing number of small companies. **PromoWest Pavilion** (405 Neil Avenue; 614-461-5483), an outdoor, club-size concert venue in the area, is complemented by the **Arena Grand** (175 West Nationwide Boulevard; 614-470-9900 for show times; 614-469-5000 for reserved seating), a movie theater with personality, leather seats in the balcony, and a café serving liquor. Activity in the Arena District should only increase as more people move into its residential developments.

Before the Blue Jackets came to town, the blocks now composing the Arena District were dominated by parking lots and the Ohio Penitentiary. The area, bordered by High Street on the east, Vine Street on the north, Spring Street on the south, and the Olentangy River on the west, wallowed in an abyss too far from either the downtown government anchors or the convention center and Short North to get any help. In 1997 Columbus voters, known for their dislike of publicly funded developments, rejected a proposal for a three-year sales tax that would have financed an arena-stadium complex. In the wake of that decision, with city officials contemplating next steps, Nationwide Insurance stepped up and offered to build not only the arena but also all the accompanying developments, with some help from the Dispatch Printing Company. The vacant penitentiary has come down, and the city's largest private employer has a branded playground in its own backyard. No muss, no fuss.

The Arena District is now a key link in the corridor between downtown and Ohio State, and it is within walking distance of the convention center, Short North, hotels, the riverfront, and more downtown clubs. Strengthening that link is "the Cap," a new High Street bridge that has extended platforms for retail shops over I-670. Heading over the Cap (modeled after the old Union Station, which was torn down to build the convention center), surrounded by storefronts on both sides, you might not even realize you're on a bridge.

■ THE SHORT NORTH *map page 148, A-1*
One of those places that were destined to be cool, the Short North has early-20th-century architecture, a prime location between downtown and the Ohio State campus, a large queer community, and a catchy name. Columbus's own Greenwich

Village is filled with the highest concentration of galleries in the city—high-end, low-end, specific mediums, specific cultures, and crafts. The first Saturday every month brings a Gallery Hop, with exhibit openings, receptions, and live perform-ances. The area also hosts a wide variety of restaurants, designer furniture stores, and shops of all kinds. The **Short North Tavern** (674 North High Street; 614-221-2432) has been a neighborhood standard for twenty-five years; it features live music on the weekends and a prime view of the action on High Street.

The neighborhood, really a strip of North High Street between the Greater Columbus Convention Center and Ohio State, feels like it's in the middle of every-thing. Rows of two- and three-story buildings, a consciously cultivated streetscape, and bleed-through from its former life as urban wasteland lend it an edge. Downtown rises up just to the south. (The name Short North came from police working the area in the 1960s and 1970s, when the district had a reputation for crime, drugs, and prostitution.)

In 2003 the city and the Short North Improvement District installed new steel, lighted street arches from I-670 up to Fifth Avenue. These are reminiscent of those the district had in the late 1800s and early 1900s. The core of the district, along High Street from I-670 to Ohio State, has been an anchor for a range of urban improvements, especially the development of the Arena District and the northern edges of downtown.

High Street is also the dividing line for Victorian Village and Italian Village. **Victorian Village,** west of High Street between Fifth Avenue and Goodale, has been both a beneficiary and a catalyst of the Short North renaissance. Like the Short North, Victorian Village drew inspiration from the successful restorations in German Village; roughly 80 percent of the buildings have been renovated as part of the Victorian Village Historic District. Despite what the name implies, not all the homes here were built in Victorian style, although many date to the Victorian era. To get a taste of the neighborhood, venture down to the south end around Goodale Park, one of the district's most beautiful spots.

Italian Village, east of High Street, was one of Columbus's first suburbs and was annexed by the city in the 1860s. Redevelopment in the village has been slower than along High Street. The long-awaited Jeffrey Place development, east of Fourth Street and south of First Avenue, will make over more than a dozen blocks of an old industrial site with a mix of town houses, apartments, traditional single-family homes, condos, and retail outlets. The community, when completed, will fill formerly less-desirable space along I-670.

Muralists Steve Galgas and Mike Altman turned American Gothic *on its head with this piece in the Short North.*

■ **DISCOVERY DISTRICT** *map page 148, C-2*
In a less vital city, the downtown area farthest from the river would be forgettable. In Columbus it's another notable spot. The Discovery District, the long, eastern slice of downtown, runs the entire grid between Fifth Street and the north–south jog of I-71. Columbus State and Columbus College of Art & Design keep pedestrian and car traffic high here. In an earlier time the district included a desirable, trendy east-side neighborhood where James Thurber's family rented a home on Jefferson during his college years at Ohio State. Thurber, who later was well known for his cartoons and such popular short stories as "The Secret Life of Walter Mitty" and "The Catbird Seat," also worked as a reporter at the *Columbus Dispatch.*

That old Victorian rental home was renovated and opened to the public in 1984 as the **Thurber House,** a combined literary center and Thurber museum. The Ohio State library is the central repository for Thurber's material, but the Thurber House sponsors a number of readings each year and has brought in many great humor writers, among them David Sedaris, Ian Frazier, and Garrison Keillor. *77 Jefferson Avenue; 614-464-1032.*

JAMES THURBER: COLUMBUS'S NEW YORKER

Why do cities and states always exalt the celebrities and impresarios that abandon them for bigger things? If there's a hope for glory in proximity to greatness, then Columbus has a better shot at it with James Thurber than most do with their departed favorite sons and daughters. Thurber made a name for himself at *The New Yorker*, but incidents and themes from his years in Columbus continually found their way into his writing. "Many of my books prove that I am never far away from Ohio in my thoughts, and that the clocks that strike in my dreams are often the clocks of Columbus," he wrote.

The Thurber family rented houses on Bryden Road and Parsons Avenue during James's childhood, although it was their place on Jefferson Avenue, now the Thurber House museum and literary center, that figures most prominently in the Thurber canon. Some of his reminiscences in *My Life and Hard Times* take place in the Thurber home, such as the stories "The Night the Bed Fell" and "The Dog That Bit People." Thurber had a fondness for dogs, even dogs that bit people, and they turned up frequently in his cartoons, such as one classic *New Yorker* cover (February 9, 1946), a monochromatic montage of dogs, alternately irritable-looking and noble. Thurber said that his worst dog, the title character in "The Dog That Bit People," "always acted as if he thought I wasn't one of the family. There was a slight advantage in being one of the family, for he didn't bite the family as often as he bit strangers. Still, in the years that we had him he bit everybody but mother, and he made a pass at her once but missed."

A childhood bow-and-arrow accident left Thurber blind in one eye and, combined with his slight and distinctly nonathletic stature, shaped his introspective path, one capitalizing on his dramatic flair, dark moods, and unerring ear for language. He could compose and edit up to two thousand words in his head and then dictate this—fortunate because his eyesight worsened throughout his lifetime until, at forty-five, he was legally blind. But that doesn't entirely account for his inimitable style of drawing, a spare and seemingly tentative, childlike approach. One of Thurber's favorite pieces of reader mail came from a seven-year-old girl: "Dear Mr. Thurber—I can draw better than you." Amazingly, he was able to continue drawing despite his failing sight.

Many of Thurber's stories, and cartoons, turn on male-female relationships—especially the formidable wife and the meek husband—as in his first book, *Is Sex Necessary?* (coauthored by E. B. White), and in *Thurber Country: A Collection of Pieces About Males and Females, Mainly of Our Species*. If there was any doubt that his work would become classic, the enduring themes he used eliminated it. He and his first wife, Althea Adams, a forceful beauty from Ohio State, divorced in 1935. That same year he married Helen Wismer, who would become his partner in life and all his writing. Thurber scholars credit Helen with enabling the prolific output of his later years as he battled a thyroid condition and general poor health. In a 1960 *Life* magazine article about Thurber, he contemplated the idea of love: "We think it is a push-button solution, or instant cure for discontent and a sure road to happiness, whatever it is. . . . A lady of 47 who has been married 27 years and has six children knows what love really is and once described it for me like this: 'Love is what you've been through with somebody.' "

In dozens of books and thirty-plus years, Thurber readers certainly lived through a lot with him.

Thurber the iconoclast at age 60.

Just around the corner from Thurber's old haunt is the **Columbus Art Museum.**
The museum stands among residents' favorites in a city filled with cultural institutions. It houses a mix of standard greats from the late 19th and early 20th centuries—Matisse, Monet, Renoir—as well as such home-grown talents as folk artist
Elijah Pierce and painter George Bellows. *480 East Broad Street; 614-221-6801.*

In 2001 the museum acquired the Photo League, a powerful photographic collection documenting urban life nationwide from the Depression era to the early
1950s. The collection takes its name from the New York–based cadre of photographers intent on exposing social problems through their images. The league had
some of the best-known names in 20th-century photography, including Lewis
Hine, Aaron Siskind, and Berenice Abbott, but was subject to scrutiny from the
House Un-American Activities Committee and broke up in 1951. Interestingly,
James Thurber also butted heads with the committee and declined an honorary
degree from Ohio State in 1951 to protest academic censorship.

■ GERMAN VILLAGE AND THE BREWERY DISTRICT
map page 148, A/B-3

Fifty years ago the area now known as **German Village** was hurting. Urban
renewal had required the demolition of the northern end of the district, and industry was encroaching on the southern end. Absentee landlords in what was known
as the Old South End were neglecting properties badly needing some TLC. Many
families had given up and headed for more promising neighborhoods.

In 1949, however, Frank Fetch, a city administrator, bought a house here with
an eye toward turning the area around. Fetch, himself possessing some German
ancestry, spearheaded an effort to designate the neighborhood a historic district
and founded the German Village Commission to establish review authority over
exterior design changes. By relabeling the neighborhood German Village, defin-
ing its boundaries, working to have it rezoned from manufacturing and commercial to high-density residential, and investing in his own restorations, Fetch
encouraged additional private restoration of homes. Step by step, over twenty
years, he and a few hundred members of the German Village Society made
German Village one of the most desirable places in the city to live. (Some charter
members, perhaps a few dozen, are still active with the society.) Since 1960 individuals and groups have restored sixteen hundred buildings in an area covering
more than 230 acres. The district is the largest privately restored area ever on the
National Register of Historic Places, and it continues to help stabilize the down-

Though not extravagant, the restored German Village homes are undeniably appealing.

town core even as trendier districts to the north snare the headlines. The **German Village Meeting Haus** (588 South Third Street; 614-221-8888) serves as a neighborhood visitors center with information on the village's transformation and attractions.

The homes of German Village are not extravagant, but the charm and sturdiness of their brickwork are undeniably appealing, as are the details of the neighborhood—brick-paved streets, narrow alleys, and assiduously maintained gardens—mostly absent from newer areas. Some of the district's grandest homes line Deshler Avenue, along the south edge of Schiller Park, at the southern end of the village. During December's **Luminaria,** residents light candle lanterns around their cottages and in the park, which provides a visual breather from the tightly spaced homes and is beautiful any time of year.

The ever-popular **German Village Oktoberfest,** the neighborhood's signature event, has been going strong for forty years and has earned a national reputation for its selection of bands, authentic German food, and laid-back atmosphere. German food can be found year-round at **Schmidt's Sausage Haus** (240 East Kossuth Street; 614-444-6808), which opened its doors in 1886 and serves fantastic schnitzel, spaetzel, knockwurst, and potato pancakes as part of a full traditional menu. Another highlight of German Village is the **Book Loft** (631 South Third Street; 614-464-1774), a block-long bookstore divvied up into dozens of rooms and carrying more than one hundred thousand new books.

Directly to the west of German Village, the **Brewery District** was home to as many as six breweries in the 1870s. It is really an extension of the village, with apartments and new commercial construction that blends with the traditional brick structures. Although it is more commercial and less intact than German Village, the Brewery District retains some of the same character in its historic structures. The everyday chain businesses along High Street, however, make it feel more contemporary. A popular dining and entertainment destination in Columbus for almost ten years, the Brewery District continues to get better as brewpubs and nightspots keep moving in.

■ EAST SIDE *map page 148, C-2*
The east side of Columbus comprises architecturally rich Olde Towne East, beautifully green Franklin Park, and tony Bexley. Just east of downtown, **Olde Towne East** has a grand history and a lot of well-preserved late-19th- and early-20th-century architecture, as you'd expect from its dignified name. One of the first neighborhoods in the city, this is a diverse area with a strong African-American population (which goes for the east and northeast parts of town in general) and a wide range of people, including young couples, families, retirees, professionals, artists, students, and laborers. At the turn of the 20th century the neighborhood was dubbed the Silk Stocking District because of its wealthy residents. The Olde Towne East Neighborhood Association sponsors house tours in spring and winter, but attractive homes and gardens reward the walker most anytime.

Just to the east of Olde Towne East, the **Franklin Park Conservatory and Botanical Garden** (1777 East Broad Street; 614-645-8733) draws visitors from all over the city. The conservatory, modeled after the Glass Palace at Chicago's 1893 Columbian Expedition, includes flora from the tropical rain forest, desert, Himalayan mountains, and Pacific islands as well as a bonsai courtyard. Beautiful Franklin Park actually predates the conservatory, and for ten years in the 1870s and 1880s it was the site of the Ohio State Fair. The Civil War hero and general William T. Sherman uttered perhaps his most famous line here while addressing a group of Civil War veterans amid pouring rain: "There is many a boy here today who looks on war as all glory, but boys, it is all hell."

Continuing east down Broad Street, you enter **Bexley,** the first suburb east of downtown. Bexley seems a rarity: a vibrant, growing, inner-ring suburb with excellent schools and generous amounts of green space. It's entirely surrounded by Columbus yet retains its own identity, that of an elegant enclave, and it succeeds unquestionably in providing a livable community both convenient and established. The neighborhoods are gorgeous and walkable, the businesses thrive, and the location is tough to beat. Venture off Broad Street to discover homes opulent enough to be mistaken for churches and large enough to sit on estates rather than lots. North of Broad Street, the French-inspired Norman Revival homes of Sessions Village offer more community than the stand-alone mansion. Downtown, the **Drexel** (2256 East Main Street; 614-231-9512 for show times; 614-231-1050 for office) is a Bexley institution and the best movie theater in Columbus for art-house fare. Be sure to check out the **Schumacher Gallery** (2199 East Main Street; 614-236-6319) at Capital University; it features 16th- to 19th-century paintings, Inuit art, an Asian Gallery, and other collections as well as special exhibitions.

School kids learn about flora from across the globe at the Franklin Park Conservatory.

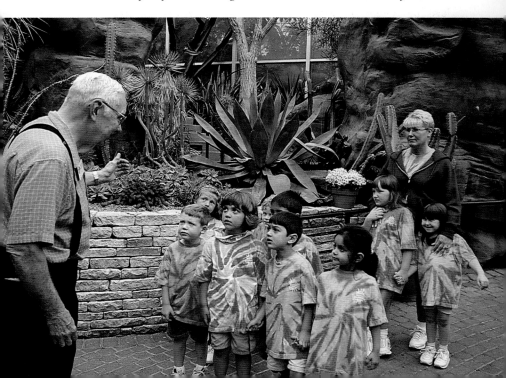

Students trek across the Oval, the heart of the Ohio State campus.

■ **The Ohio State University** *map page 148, A-1*
The soul of Columbus and one of its most popular attractions is the Ohio State University (OSU), which is second home to fifty thousand students and second in employment only to the state of Ohio. Its eminence is clear: the capital of Ohio's educational system, a perennial economic boon, and the bias in the city's cultural fabric. To many around the country, OSU and Columbus are one and the same.

For a state university east of the Mississippi, Ohio State came to the game rather late. Classes didn't begin until 1873, nearly seventy years after the founding of Ohio University, the state's first college. Although the board of trustees early on established a broad educational focus, many campaigned for an institution teaching only agriculture and mechanics, which were considered the most useful disciplines at the time. Indeed, the school's first name was the Ohio Agricultural and Mechanical College. Nevertheless, agriculture was far and away the most important program offered. Students and professors over the years have joked about the university's generous funding of the agriculture school at the expense of the liberal arts, no doubt contributing to Columbus's Cowtown nickname.

The rest of the country knows the school and the city for their winning football teams. When broadcasters hover over the **Horseshoe** (aka Ohio Stadium, or simply "the Shoe"), packed with scarlet-clad fans, football aficionados nationwide can glance at the TV and tell you who's playing. The magic that a football Saturday in Columbus generates is palpable and contagious—a combination of a storied program, top recruits, enthusiastic alumni and students, and the Best Damn Band in the Land, the Ohio State University Marching Band. Fans get nearly as excited about the halftime show as they do about the game. Year after year, marching band alumni return for the first home game—and the necessary practices prior to it—to march and play with the current band. The band's trademark is the "script Ohio" formation, which looks just what it sounds like: a cursive *Ohio* "written" on-field. Seating capacity seems to expand annually, and attendance expands with it, or vice versa. OSU completed a $187 million stadium renovation in 2001 that expanded the press box, increased the number of bathroom facilities, and added permanent seats to the south end zone, a sort of heel on the Horseshoe.

The most revered figure in Buckeye lore, and the one every visitor must know to avoid harsh words and affronted hosts, is Woody Hayes. In twenty-eight seasons as Ohio State head coach, "the Old Man" went 205-61-10, with five national titles and thirteen Big Ten titles. Hayes favored a traditional running game he called "three yards and a cloud of dust," which reflected his philosophy of

OHIO STATE VS. MICHIGAN

Okay, let's dispense with the conditional phrases and admit that Ohio State–Michigan is the best rivalry in college sports. Ten good reasons are the Woody Hayes–Bo Schembechler coaching battles from 1969 to 1978, the end of Hayes's career at Ohio State and the beginning of Schembechler's at Michigan. In that span one of the teams won or shared the Big Ten title nine times, and the other finished second eight times. In seven of those years, one or both teams entered the matchup undefeated. So legendary is their mutual hatred that the stretch is known as the Ten-Year War. To add a little more drama, Schembechler was a former assistant coach to Hayes at Ohio State. Here's a rundown of the matchup games in the Ten-Year War:

1969: Michigan 24, Ohio State 12
Undefeated in twenty-two straight games, No. 1 OSU loses to No. 12 Michigan in the game that begins the Woody–Bo era. (Some say Ohio State had the best college football team ever that year.)

1970: Ohio State 20, Michigan 9
No. 5 Ohio State comes away with the Big Ten title, a Rose Bowl bid, and sweet satisfaction.

1971: Michigan 10, Ohio State 7
Michigan is ranked No. 3; Ohio State is unranked.

1972: Ohio State 14, Michigan 11
No. 9 Ohio State hangs tough on defense and makes it to the Rose Bowl.

1973: Ohio State 10, Michigan 10
Ohio State has three of the top five vote-getters for the Heisman Trophy. The two schools split the Big Ten title, but athletic directors vote Ohio State into the Rose Bowl.

1974: Ohio State 12, Michigan 10
The No. 4 Buckeyes edge No. 3 Michigan to again split the Big Ten title and play in the Rose Bowl. Running back Archie Griffin wins his first of two Heismans.

1975: Ohio State 21, Michigan 14
The No. 3 Buckeyes again handle No. 5 Michigan to claim a fourth straight Rose Bowl bid.

1976: Michigan 22, Ohio State 0
No. 4 Michigan avenges the No. 8 Buckeyes' series winning streak and heads to the Rose Bowl.

1977: Michigan 14, Ohio State 6
No. 5 Michigan shares the Big Ten title after victory over the fourth-ranked Buckeyes.

1978: Michigan 14, Ohio State 3
The Wolverines, No. 6 in the country, dispatch No. 16 Ohio State, share the Big Ten title with Michigan State, and go to the Rose Bowl.

The Wexner Center for the Arts serves as Ohio State's cultural catch-all.

outworking opponents rather than outsmarting them. One of his greatest legacies is the legion of successful coaches he bred, assistants at Ohio State who went on to become legends in their own right: Earle Bruce, Lou Holtz, Bill Mallory, and Bo Schembechler. Famous for his kindness but infamous for his temper, Hayes saw his career end quickly after the 1978 Gator Bowl, in which he punched a Clemson player.

On the other side of campus, the **Wexner Center for the Arts** is the kind of premier arts facility that any university would be fortunate to have. Wexner's multi-disciplinary scope accommodates theater performances, music, the visual arts (including film and video), and other contemporary arts. Although it's been open now for more than fifteen years, the facility still feels fresh and modern, a tribute to architect Peter Eisenman's design. On the south side of the building, Maya Lin's exterior installation *Groundswell* consists of shattered glass shaped into an undulating landscape, a form she based partially on the ancient Indian mounds in southern Ohio. The center holds 12,000 square feet of galleries, a bookshop, and a café and regularly brings in high-profile exhibits and performances from all over the world. *1871 North High Street; 614-292-3535.*

The **Jack Nicklaus Museum,** in the Ohio State University sports complex, counters the international flavor of the Wexner Center with a tribute to a hometown celebrity and veteran of the Ohio State golf team. Nicklaus is one of the greatest golfers to play the game, the only person ever to win all four major championships—the U.S. Open, the British Open, the Masters, and the PGA Championship—on both the PGA Tour and the Senior Tour. The museum, opened in 2002, displays most of the clubs Nicklaus used to win his twenty championships, assorted memorabilia, trophies, and personal items such as letters and report cards. It also takes a look at the game's development and traditions. *2355 Olentangy River Road; 614-247-5959.*

■ **DUBLIN** *map page 173, B-2*

For die-hard golfers, a trip to the British Isles and a few rounds on the classic courses would be a dream vacation, but there's a much closer, domestic version northwest of Columbus. Just outside the I-270 beltway lies Dublin, a growing Ohio city of thirty-two thousand that is home to golf legend Jack "Golden Bear" Nicklaus and his prestigious Memorial Tournament, a PGA Tour event held in June at Dublin's Muirfield Village Golf Club. The tournament benefits a variety of central Ohio charities, in particular Columbus Children's Hospital.

For most of its existence Dublin was a stand-alone settlement on the banks of the Scioto, a pleasant village that Irish surveyor John Shields named after his old country's capital city. It too was in line to be a capital, selected by a commission to succeed Chillicothe as the capital of Ohio, but political deal-making secured that distinction for Columbus. It's just as well. Eventually most everyone moved here from Columbus anyway. As recently as 1970 Dublin had fewer than seven hundred residents. The land rush started when companies began relocating headquarters in Dublin and Jack Nicklaus developed the private Muirfield Village Golf Club in the mid-1970s. (*Golf Digest* has ranked Muirfield one of the best courses in the country.)

The game was on. In 1999 Arnold Palmer completed a residential golf club called Tartan Fields with eighteen holes of championship golf directly north of Nicklaus's Muirfield. The private course is home to the LPGA's Wendy's Championship for Children. Even newer is the **Golf Club of Dublin** (5805 Eiterman Road; 614-792-3825), a public course opened in 2002 with British Isles–style links and a clubhouse that's right out of Ireland. Area courses outside of

Dublin include Darby Creek (Marysville), Indian Springs (Mechanicsburg), Bent Tree (Sunbury), Royal American (Galena), Mill Creek (Ostrander), and the Columbus Zoo–owned Safari Golf Club. Dublin, interestingly, could have heightened its stature as golf mecca with the Jack Nicklaus Museum but declined the project due to traffic concerns.

If you expect a city called Dublin to hold a huge Irish festival of some sort, you're exactly right. The **Dublin Irish Festival,** held each August, celebrates all things Irish with traditional dances, music, food, storytelling, craftspeople, specialists in Irish genealogy, and interpretive history. Sunday morning offers a traditional mass in Gaelic and an Irish breakfast. Dublin also hosts a St. Patty's Day bash on a Saturday in mid-March with a parade, pancake breakfast, music, and the usual celebratory shenanigans.

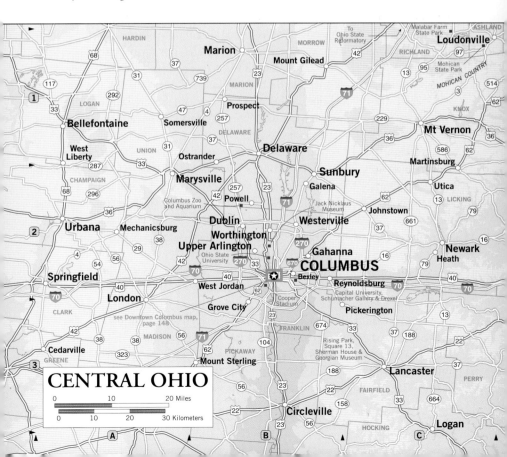

East of Dublin, Powell is home to the **Columbus Zoo and Aquarium.** Much of the credit for the zoo's lofty international reputation goes to director emeritus Jack Hanna, known for his show *Jack Hanna's Animal Adventures* and his regular appearances on *Good Morning America* and the talk show circuit. Hanna started with the zoo in the late 1970s and moved it from a cage-based facility to a network of realistic habitats. He helped increase attendance fourfold over fifteen years. The zoo is recognized for its successful breeding programs and has one of the largest reptile collections in the world. But "Jungle Jack" hasn't done it alone; along with dedicated staff, the zoo has a docent program with more than three hundred volunteers. In 1999 the zoo added a Manatee Coast exhibit, one of a handful of manatee facilities outside of Florida. *9990 Riverside Drive; 614-645-3550.*

■ **LANCASTER** *map page 173, C-3*

Like Chillicothe, Lancaster is a border city, situated on the same glaciated plateau that snakes through the central portion of the state. The town shares a past with Chillicothe as well as with Zanesville. All three are on major rivers in the southeast leading to the Ohio: Zanesville on the Muskingum, Lancaster on the Hocking, and Chillicothe on the Scioto. When Col. Ebenezer Zane blazed Zane's Trace from Wheeling, West Virginia, to Maysville, Kentucky, in 1796, he set up ferry crossings at each of these points and marked his lands there.

Chillicothe's and Lancaster's geographies naturally make them gateways to the Appalachian hills; Zanesville's position on the National Road and now I-70 sets it up as a jumping-off point too. Today, as the closest major town to the Hocking Hills, Lancaster works equally well as a gateway to the southeast's natural gems and, if you happen to be traveling from Logan or Nelsonville, as a gateway to Columbus. Mount Pleasant, a 250-foot sandstone outcropping in **Rising Park,** offers an impressive view of the surrounding countryside.

Lancaster is centrally located, so immigrants came here from both the northeast and the southeast, but early on the town was known as New Lancaster because so many of its arrivals had come from Lancaster, Pennsylvania. Thus, the name is properly pronounced *Lank*-aster and had a heavy German influence. The first newspaper was written in German, and the first school taught in German. Even before Lancaster got hooked up with the Ohio & Erie Canal in 1836, it aspired to importance. In the wheeling and dealing that settled on Columbus as the young state's final capital, Lancaster came up just one vote short.

Lancaster has a rich history evident in its outstanding architecture. Architecturally significant buildings crowd into four historic districts, the most noteworthy collection of which is in **Square 13,** bounded by Mulberry, High, Chestnut, and Broad streets. Ebenezer Zane laid out the block; it contains the birthplace and boyhood home of William Tecumseh Sherman, the Civil War general and hero (or villain, if you're from the South) who sieged Atlanta before his ruthless March to the Sea, and his brother John Sherman, a U.S. senator, secretary of state, and secretary of the treasury. The **Sherman House** (137 East Main Street; 740-687-5891) re-creates the Sherman era with family heirlooms and the Victorian era in the later Victorian-style addition on the front of the house. It also includes Civil War memorabilia. General Sherman is one of the most popular figures in military history, a complicated man with Southern sympathies, a dislike for war, and an indomitable will and sense of duty. A statue in Zane Square, at the corner of Main and Broad, commemorates him.

One block to the north is the can't-miss **Georgian Museum,** furnished to the period and incorporating many items belonging to the Maccracken family, who originally owned the home. Samuel Maccracken had the house built in 1830 after a trip to England that spurred his enthusiasm for the country houses there. The Federal-style home is something of an anchor for Square 13. The Fairfield Heritage Association, which also owns the Sherman House, runs the museum. *105 East Wheeling Street; 740-654-9923.*

■ **MOHICAN COUNTRY** *map page 173, C-1*

For being "outstate" Ohio, the countryside around Loudonville and Mohican State Park offers a pleasing variety of activities for visitors. Midway between Columbus and Cleveland, it has long been a reliable destination for outdoors people from Columbus and northeast Ohio seeking a nearby getaway. Just to the east in Holmes and Wayne counties lies Amish Country, which is covered in the Yankee Ohio section of this book. River rats know Loudonville for the **Mohican River,** the best place in Ohio to hit the water for canoeing and float trips.

Three tributaries join south of Loudonville to form the Mohican: the Clearfork, Blackfork, and Lakefork. The Clearfork is attractive and relatively wild, shrouded in white pine and hemlock. The Blackfork, also known as the Muddyfork, is more commercial but still enjoyable. Many of the state's streams can be frustrating or impossible to float come August or September because of low water, but the

The Ohio State Reformatory north of Mansfield has been home to thousands of convicts, a handful of movie crews, and at least a few ghosts. Many recognize it as the setting for The Shawshank Redemption.

Blackfork has the advantage of being floatable year-round. The Lakefork, though also scenic, is a less popular option. It is more isolated than the Blackfork and floatable only during the summer season.

The Mohican is unusual, and beautiful, because of a geologic quirk that has it flowing through plains into gorges amid higher ground to the south. During the last Ice Age, the Wisconsin ice sheet blocked the north-flowing river and forced it to carve a new, southerly path. Three-hundred-foot-deep Clearfork Gorge, in **Mohican State Park** (3116 Route 3; 419-994-5125), is one result. Canoeists and kayakers who float the Clearfork get a bass's-eye view.

An entirely different experience awaits at **Malabar Farm State Park** (4050 Bromfield Road; 419-892-2784), which isn't so much a state park as a literary excursion and a country retreat rolled into one. From 1938 until his death in 1956, Ohio author Louis Bromfield owned Malabar and ran it as an experimental, conservation-conscious farm. Bromfield was one of the original staff members at *Time* magazine; he was also the author of *Pleasant Valley* and *Early Autumn*, for which he won the Pulitzer Prize, as well as many other books. It was at Malabar Farm that he put his philosophies about man's ties to the land into practice with soil restoration, improvement of biodiversity, and reduction of chemicals and pesticides. Although now part of the state park system, the farm continues its mission. This is where Jefferson's agrarian ideal meets the Ohio frontiersman's dream of upward mobility.

Bromfield lived a glamorous life; one of the farm's claims to fame was Humphrey Bogart and Lauren Bacall's wedding in the thirty-two-room mansion in 1945. Alas, events here today are more pedestrian but still absolutely worthwhile. Nearly anything you'd want to do on a private farm is fair game: primitive camping, hiking, horseback riding, fishing, sledding, cross-country skiing, and picnicking. The park offers house tours year-round and a number of special events, such as March's Maple Syrup Festival and Candlelight Christmas at Malabar Farm. Two other pluses: Malabar Farm Market, which offers seasonal farm-grown produce, and Malabar Farm's Youth Hostel, which is in an old Sears catalog house and is another lodging option for the young and semi-indigent.

Curiously enough, the **Ohio State Reformatory** (100 Reformatory Road; 419-522-2644) north of Mansfield also has Hollywood connections. The late-19th-century prison, at once grand and austere, has been a popular filming location and was used in *The Shawshank Redemption* and *Air Force One*. The atmosphere during construction appears to have been every bit as Hollywood as in its later film-set years. Mansfield residents were grateful to win the facility and turned out en masse for the ceremonial laying of the cornerstone, which Senator John Sherman and former president Rutherford B. Hayes attended. In Columbus some in the crowds handed cigars to prisoners being transported to Mansfield. For their part, the Columbus prisoners seemed enthusiastic about moving to such an impressive facility and joked and smiled on the way. The Mansfield Correctional Institution supplanted the facility in 1990.

Getting people in the door these days is a bit more difficult. The Mansfield Reformatory Preservation Society maintains the structure and offers frequent public events, but upkeep costs for a building this age and size (250,000 square feet) are enormous. Restoration has proceeded slowly. One of the most popular events at the old prison now is the Ghost Hunt, held about a dozen times throughout the year. Short of an old mental hospital, what setting would be more ideal? Visitors tour the building at night with flashlights, cameras, and tape recorders in hopes of encountering the paranormal—and more than a few say they have.

■ TRAVEL BASICS

Getting Around: Ohio's largest city, Columbus experiences heavy rush-hour traffic. Be warned that the I-70/71 split downtown is considered one of the most congested and dangerous spots in the state. The good news is that you can see a lot of the city on foot or by public bus. A good choice is the Downtown Link, a bus running up and down High Street that makes it easy to get from German Village to the Short North.

The outlying areas of the city are easily navigated by car. Roads tend to run in a spoke style out from Columbus, so even when you're outside the city, it often makes sense to head there first and use I-270 toward your intended destination. Lancaster is a thirty-five-minute drive from Columbus down U.S. 33, which continues southeast into the Hocking Hills. Loudonville and Mohican State Park are farther off the beaten path, reachable from Columbus by taking I-71 north to U.S. 30 (Exit 176) east and Route 60 south to Loudonville or I-71 north to Route 97 (Exit 165) east to Mohican.

Climate: Here you'll find four seasons and a generally moderate climate. In Columbus the average annual temperature is 53 degrees Fahrenheit, with a January average of 28 and a July average of 75. There's enough winter snowfall—about 28 inches a year—to cause the occasional backup on the roads.

MIAMI RIVER VALLEYS

Once upon a time, long before South Beach vacations, Gloria Estefan, and Elián González, Ohio's Miami took precedence over its Southern brother. There was the Miami Tribe that inhabited the area before the Treaty of Greenville in 1795 cleared the way for white settlement. There were the Little Miami River and the Great Miami River, the latter responsible for how much of southwestern Ohio looks today. And there was Miami University, the seventh-oldest state-assisted university in the country. If the notoriety of the Miami Valley has waned, the shift is at least more in keeping with its people's modest, hard-working nature.

Hamilton, Middletown, and Dayton sit on the Great Miami like bobbers on a line, while Cincinnati, the big fish, lurks nearby. Interstate 75 follows the river as far north as Sidney. The Little Miami roughly divides the Miami region into two areas with distinct identities: industry and the populace to the north and west, rambling rural hill country to the south and east. Although this hill country in places is Appalachian in character, it has always had important commercial ties to the Miami corridor's cities, and those ties are more prominent than ever. Cincinnati and Dayton are where big shopping gets done, where the jobs are, and, more and more, where the folks who own neighboring land used to live.

The inattentive traveler will miss the area's "ah-ha" moments, which tend to occur unexpectedly and on a smaller scale than those on Lake Erie or in the track-less backcountry of the southeast. These moments include a glimpse of Amish schoolchildren whispering outside a barn; the first step into the Wright brothers' bicycle shop; and a jaunt across a tidy village that looks to have been hibernating for fifty years when you arrive and will continue on for fifty more after you leave. There is an earnestness that permeates the creeks and soils, reinforced by the legacies of presidents who spent their youth in the Miami Valley's good graces.

■ **APPALACHIAN FOOTHILLS** *map page 182, B/C-2/3*

Somewhere south and west of Chillicothe, you get the sense that the most rugged parts of Ohio's Appalachia, the pines and the mines, are behind you. Up ahead the sometimes sharply rolling hills hold more and more farms, and the pastures and

The Wright brothers worked the bugs out of their Wright Flyer II *at Huffman Prairie.*

cropland look less like cleared forest than they do God-given abundance. By the time you reach Clermont County, Cincinnatians who have edged into eastern bedroom communities snap a traveler out of the pastoral. But in between, there are fertile hills, just enough farmhouses and small towns to give texture to the scene, and the occasional buggy creeping along a side road.

It's not just that time moves more slowly here, as it does in many rural areas. It's that change has imposed itself less forcefully. A longtime Seaman resident who grew up in New Jersey puts it this way: "When I moved to Cincinnati, I thought I had gone back in time fifty years. When I moved here, I thought I had gone back one hundred." Even as real estate pressures and agricultural struggles change the economic and cultural makeup, some traditions continue.

MIAMI RIVER VALLEYS

■ WINERIES

One of the best such traditions is viticulture. Ohio ranks sixth among U.S. states in wine production. The earliest wineries in the state flourished along the banks of the Ohio thanks to the guidance and insight of Cincinnati's Nicholas Longworth, the Father of Ohio Wine, and his discovery of the Catawba grape for wine making. Longworth provided cuttings for many landowners in the area to begin growing their own grapes, and his Catawba wine prompted Henry Wadsworth Longfellow, possibly after consuming liberal amounts of it, to carry on at length about the virtues of the Catawba and Cincinnati in general.

Southwestern Ohio isn't the most popular region for wineries anymore—that honor goes to the Lake Erie shoreline—but several wineries continue the tradition and produce excellent regional wines derived from the Catawba and a range of European grapes. Look for them in Ripley, Manchester, Bethel, Versailles, and, primarily, Cincinnati. There's nothing better than spending a morning antiquing or walking the historic district of an old river town and the afternoon sampling a range of wines while overlooking the vineyards that produced them.

Kinkead Ridge Vineyard & Winery, whose vines occupy a ridge high above the Ohio River, is one of the newer additions to the Ohio viticulture scene. Owners Robert Barrett and Nancy Bentley moved here from Oregon in 1997 and produced their first vintage in 2001. Intent on establishing a world-class reputation, they focus on premium estate wines, including cabernet franc, cabernet sauvignon, and Riesling, made only from vinifera grapes (an Old World European species). Kinkead Ridge wines have received enthusiastic early reviews. Hours are limited, so call ahead. *904 Hamburg Street, Ripley; 937-392-6077.*

With a restaurant on site and regular winery hours, **Moyer Vineyards Winery & Restaurant** offers an experience different from that at Kinkead's. Ken and Mary Moyer opened the winery in the 1970s, though they've since sold the business. The entire operation sits right on the Ohio west of Manchester, and the back deck overlooking the river is a great place to relax, sample the wines, and watch the river traffic. Wines, including red, white, blush, and fruit, start at about $6 per bottle. The food is fair but convenient if you're visiting the winery. *3859 U.S. 52; 937-549-2957.*

Kinkead Ridge produces its premium wines in the cradle of Ohio viticulture.

■ **AMISH COUNTRY** *map page 182, B-3*

About 60 miles east of Cincinnati, Adams County's Amish settlements lack the commercial draw of their larger and better-known counterparts in Holmes County, so if you're seeking a day of peace and simplicity among the Amish, Adams County is a refreshing change of pace. RVs and tour buses aren't an issue, but you might run across tractor-trailers hauling bird feeders and other Amish-made cedar products, a cash cow for families here. (Historically cedars have lacked the commercial value of such hardwoods as oak and walnut and are sometimes considered a nuisance for their speedy colonization of prairies and deforested land. They grow especially well in southwestern Ohio, where the Amish have put them to good use.)

The Amish settlements began to take shape in the hills south of Route 32, the Appalachian Highway, in the late 1970s, when families moved here for the wide-open spaces, views, and reasonably priced land. While the area is less commercial than Millersburg or Berlin, you won't be disappointed if you come hoping to find Amish-made crafts, furniture, baked goods, or seasonal produce stands. **Miller's Bakery and Furniture** (960 Wheat Ridge Road; 937-544-8524) is a hub of activity for both locals and travelers, and it is a good place to begin sampling what the area offers. Driving along Wheat Ridge Road, Tater Ridge Road, and Unity Road will give you a good sense of the landscape and the farms it holds. As you might expect for an area that produces so many cedar products, Adams County has several Amish-owned cedar mills. Consider bringing bikes, parking at one of the general stores, and cycling to farms and other shops in the area. (You can return later with a car to pick up any purchases.) And remember that you won't find any businesses open on Sunday.

■ EARLY INDIGENOUS CULTURES

As were many points along the Midwest's waterways, southwest Ohio was the domain of indigenous societies that designed elaborate earthworks from 750 B.C. into the Middle Ages. The Adena (1000 B.C.–A.D. 100), Hopewell (200 B.C.–A.D. 500), and Fort Ancient (A.D. 900–1500) are examples of early cultures known in Ohio. Many southern Ohio towns can claim ancient Indian mounds, from Portsmouth to Marietta. Chillicothe, in Ross County, and Newark, east of Columbus in Licking County, are especially notable.

Still, the most famous mound is in the southwest, in Adams County, several miles north of Peebles on Route 73. From ground level **Serpent Mound** (3850 Route 73; 937-587-2796) is a winding, pleasingly sculpted embankment, lush and fastidiously maintained. Add a few sand traps and a green, and the mound area, wedged as it is around a bend in Brush Creek, would appear to be the start of a challenging golf course. The well-worn metal observation tower will give you a better look at the mound, at 1,348 feet long one of the largest effigy mounds in the world. Its builders incorporated numerous astronomical alignments in the writhing form: an imaginary line drawn through the rearmost point of the triangular shape that forms the serpent's head to the center of the egg shape in its mouth marks the sunset on the summer solstice. If you're here for the solstice, you'll gain a greater appreciation for the dedication and precision with which the mound was constructed, and you'll no doubt have some company. Other alignments based on the serpent's curves correspond with a variety of lunar events.

There is still uncertainty about which culture was responsible for the mound. Popular opinion, based on carbon dating of charcoal from the mound, attributes it to the Fort Ancients, who had a village south of here. Construction has been pegged at A.D. 1030. The site also contains three burial mounds, one thought to be Fort Ancient and two others identified as Adena.

Fort Ancient State Memorial, like Serpent Mound, is one of the great historic treasures of Ohio. The memorial lies 35 miles northeast of Cincinnati, near Oregonia, a few miles south of where I-71 crosses the Little Miami River, one of the finest interstate views you'll find in Ohio. Fort Ancient isn't bad either. The earthworks were built atop a bluff about 240 feet above the Little Miami and are more than 3 miles long, comprising a "north fort," "middle fort," and "south fort." Modern archaeologists believe that the site wasn't used for defense but possibly for religious ceremonies. It has many of the same traits as Serpent Mound as far as astronomical alignments go and may have served as a calendar for its builders. Despite its name, the earthworks is of Hopewell origin; the people known as the Fort Ancient lived on the site later, between A.D. 900 and 1500. *6123 Route 350; 513-932-4421.*

Fort Ancient makes a fine day trip for people in Cincinnati, Dayton, and Columbus. The museum offers exhibits and displays not just on the Fort Ancient culture but also on all of the indigenous peoples of the Ohio Valley for more than fifteen thousand years. The nearby Little Miami Scenic Trail, about 70 miles long, is a paved path that's perfect for cycling; it runs from Springfield, northeast of Dayton, to Milford, east of Cincinnati. And canoe liveries serve the Fort Ancient area of the Little Miami, a National Scenic River best floated in the spring.

Serpent Mound and Fort Ancient are not the only mounds in Ohio, or even in southwest Ohio. There are still hundreds, if not thousands, of mounds around the state, and they turn up in the most unlikely places, recognized and unrecognized, urban and rural. *Ancient Monuments of the Mississippi Valley,* by Ephraim Squier and Edwin Davis, is the benchmark work on mounds in the eastern United States and has much to say about Ohio's. Both authors lived in Chillicothe. Because the book was published in 1848, it has both technical inaccuracies and a great deal of insight into the era's prevailing views on the mounds and indigenous cultures.

■ OHIO RIVER

In contrast to sections of the Ohio upriver, where the presence of heavy industry is more apparent, many sections of the Ohio west of Portsmouth look natural. Shawnee State Forest follows close to the river for 20 miles. Maysville, Kentucky (population 9,000), is the biggest town between Portsmouth and Cincinnati, possibly because there aren't any major tributaries to the Ohio in that span.

Because this stretch of river has no cities, few tributaries, and little in the way of public land (aside from Shawnee), one might begin to wonder why it is important. The answer is that the Ohio serves as a cultural and political boundary. As shallow as it is, the Ohio clearly and cleanly divides north and south. Before and during the Civil War, crossing the Ohio was the difference between freedom and bondage. In *Democracy in America,* de Tocqueville wrote, "The traveler who floats down the current of the Ohio . . . may be said to sail between liberty and servitude, and a transient inspection of surrounding objects will convince him which of the two is more favorable to mankind." Southerners also helped slaves, but before the crossing especially, runaways risked harsh laws, false allies, and an increased chance that violent pro-slavery forces would root out their Underground Railroad conductors. These dramas played out elsewhere on the river and around the country, but the area around Ripley on the Ohio side and Maysville on the Kentucky side in particular produced spectacular fireworks in the antebellum era.

The Freedom Stairway in Ripley led runaway slaves to John Rankin's home.

■ **RIPLEY** *map page 182, B-3*

No one knows for sure, but it is said that the term Underground Railroad originated in Ripley, which has become known nationally and internationally as the capital of the underground system used by slaves to escape bondage. John Parker, a slave of mixed parentage, bought his freedom and settled here about 1849. He is said to have always walked down the middle of these streets. His behavior might not have been out of place in Tombstone, Arizona, but in Ripley it was an oddity necessary for survival. Parker's help of runaways on the Underground Railroad made him a marked man in town, and, were he to use the sidewalks, he could never be sure who might step out of a dark, narrow alley to make him pay.

Frank M. Gregg, a journalist, interviewed Parker in the 1880s and wrote a manuscript based on those interviews that W. W. Norton published as *His Promised Land* in 1996. In the introduction of the book, Gregg describes Parker: "A fearless man, quick witted, and resourceful time and again he went into the county of the 'Enemy,' as he designated it, read the posters for his reward captured dead or alive, then went on to round up his runaways. . . . "

Parker wasn't just tough; he was shrewd. He owned his own foundry in Ripley and was one of the few African-Americans to get a patent in the 1800s. In fact, he had several patents for his inventions, including one for the Parker Pulverizer (a tobacco screw press). The **Parker House** (300 Front Street; 937-392-4188), where it is believed Parker lived from the time of his arrival in Ripley around 1849 until his death in 1900, is a handsomely renovated brick structure standing alone at the far west end of Front Street. It is now a museum dedicated to bringing Parker's adventures to life through artifacts and storytelling.

An abundance of plaques and historical markers around town attests that this is a city that knows its own rich history, and if Ripley is stuck in the past, that can be a good thing for the town's economy. Tobacco, the government's favorite whipping boy, is big business here—Ohio growers earn about $55 million a year from tobacco—but no one knows how long this will last. The small size, hilly topography, and poorer soils of farms in this part of southern Ohio just aren't suited for many other crops. And when Ripley's largest employer, the U.S. Shoe factory, closed in 1993, the area lost four hundred jobs. Rather than run from the past, res-

(following spread) Doreen Kinley portrays Eliza, a character in Uncle Tom's Cabin, *at the Rankin House in Ripley.*

idents have embraced it in the form of history-oriented tourism. They expect the opening of the National Underground Railroad Freedom Center in Cincinnati to bring in even more travelers as museumgoers follow the Ohio River to explore the front lines of the old battles over slavery.

Although it does not concentrate on the Underground Railroad, the **Ripley Museum** (219 North Second Street; 937-392-4660) helps bring the town's important history into focus with period furnishings, several hundred historical items, and a genealogical library in an 1850s-era home. The **John Rankin House** (6152 Rankin Road; 937-392-1627), home to the town's famous Presbyterian minister who vied with Cincinnati's Levi Coffin for abolitionist acclaim, is a must-see for any curious traveler. If you have no interest in history, go for the view. The house is atop Liberty Hill, an almost-too-perfect symbol of hope for escaping slaves that is easily visible from across the river. In *Uncle Tom's Cabin,* Harriet Beecher Stowe wrote of Eliza, a slave woman who escaped with her child from bounty hunters on thawing ice in the Ohio River; it is a true story of a woman Rankin helped.

If you don't mind the humidity, Ripley makes a good summer jaunt, when you can ramble idly through antiques shops, sample wine at **Kinkead Ridge Vineyard & Winery** (*see* "Wineries"), and take in the **Ohio Tobacco Festival,** held every year since 1982. You don't have to smoke to enjoy the town's flagship event. The August festival has parades, a queen pageant, a flea market, a tobacco worm race, and an antique car show. November is another good time for a visit—for holiday shopping and, for a different taste of Ripley's tobacco culture, the auctions at Ohio-Kentucky Tobacco Warehouse.

■ GRANT COUNTRY *map page 182, A/B-3*

Towns from Georgetown to New Richmond have developed a cottage industry based on the legacy of Ulysses S. Grant: "Grant was born in this cottage," "Grant stayed at this cottage during school," "Grant sneezed in this cottage". . . . But really, Grant's legacy does factor heavily in the history and culture of the area. The lore begins in Point Pleasant at **Grant's birthplace** (U.S. 52 at Route 232; 513-553-4911), a small three-room frame cottage filled with Grant memorabilia. It is run by the Ohio Historical Society. Point Pleasant has a few other period houses, a store catering to visitors, and not much else. The Grant house is small enough to have traveled more widely than many mobile homes. In the late 1800s some entrepreneurs took the house on a barge tour around the country and charged visitors

Ulysses S. Grant's birthplace toured the country on a barge in the late 1800s.

to see it. Later, it was disassembled and reconstructed for an appearance at the Ohio State Fair in Columbus.

Grant's story continues in Georgetown, 30 miles east of Point Pleasant, where his father moved the family in 1823 and where Grant grew up. As a child he was named Hiram Ulysses Grant. Only later, after a congressman's clerical mistake in his appointment to West Point, did he adopt Ulysses S. Grant. The **Grant Boyhood Home** (219 East Grant Avenue; 937-378-4222) and the **Grant Schoolhouse** (508 South Water Street; 937-378-4222) are the major sites here. Both are furnished in the style Grant would have known in the early 1800s, although few items are original. Grant attended this school from the age of six until he was thirteen. The large Georgetown home better illustrates the Grant family's relative affluence. Ulysses' father, Jesse, was a successful tanner who secured a private-school education and admission to West Point for his son and later served as the mayor of Georgetown and the first mayor of Bethel. (Grant also attended the Presbyterian Academy in Ripley for a time.)

Despite the fact that Grant graduated from West Point, his adult life prior to the Civil War was mostly undistinguished. During the Civil War as the colonel of a volunteer infantry in Illinois, Grant quickly rose through the ranks with major victories at Shiloh in 1862 and Gettysburg and Vicksburg in 1863 to become one of the greatest generals of all time. It's sometimes forgotten that he was also an enormously popular two-term president, although his military skills far outshined his political skills. He would have been wise to draw the line as another Civil War hero, Lancaster's William T. Sherman, did. Sherman declined the Republican nomination in 1884: "I will not accept if nominated and will not serve if elected."

Thus, you'll find many reenactments of Grant's Civil War victories but none rehashing the scandals of his administration. In April Georgetown celebrates Grant's birthday, April 27, with **Grant Days,** which include a Civil War Grand Ball, carriage rides, living-history demonstrations, and, of course, battle reenactments. Civil War buffs in the market for period military or civilian dress can order custom-made, sharp-looking clothes at **General Lee's Closet** (619 North Columbus; 937-378-9188) in Russellville.

■ CINCINNATI *map page 195*

If you drive north on I-71/75 through Kentucky, you'll descend into the Ohio River basin, round a cut in the hill in Covington, and watch in awe as Cincinnati unfolds before your eyes. After you have driven past bluegrass countryside and outlying villages, the city appears impossibly metropolitan. This is one of the grandest entrances you can make into an American city—and not without its stage magic. Downtown's tallest, most impressive-looking buildings, on Fourth Street, form a set piece, hovering over the riverfront stadiums and masking the shorter structures beyond that sit amid an easy-to-navigate, walkable downtown.

Geography has had the greatest influence on Cincinnati and is its greatest asset. The Midwest isn't supposed to be this hilly, and the names of many of the inner-ring neighborhoods—Price Hill, Mount Auburn, Fairview, and so on—celebrate that dissonance. Early settlers clustered in the only flat area north of the Ohio, now the downtown basin, and the steep hills on the remaining three sides made Cincinnati the most densely populated city in the country in the mid-1800s, even more so than Manhattan. Soon after, incline railways helped people escape the river basin into the hills beyond, and Cincinnati's new, outlying streets were forced to negotiate those contours.

Heading across town can take you twice as long going east to west as it can traveling north to south, because valleys run north and south toward the Ohio River. You might as well be in the Appalachians. If you plan on driving while you're here, be sure to carry good maps—and bring along a native if you can. Downtown east–west streets are numbered. You can remember the north–south streets with the acrostic "Big strong men will very rarely eat pork chops." From east to west, that stands for Broadway, Sycamore, Main, Walnut, Vine, Race, Elm, Plum, and Central. If you can survive the roads, the topography redeems itself with stunning views, some very desirable hillside homes, and a wealth of gorgeous urban parks— Eden Park, Mount Airy Forest, Mount Storm Park, Ault Park, and Mount Echo Park among them—that contribute greatly to the city's storied livability.

The most notable cultural icon in Cincinnati is the flying pig, a reference to the city's hog-butchering prominence in the mid-19th century and the civic progress it

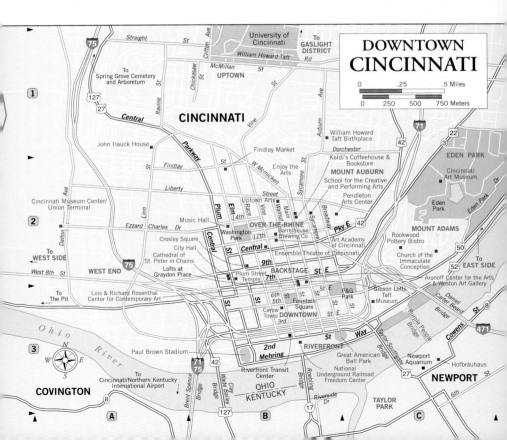

This view of Cincinnati in 1900 shows the city's trademark basin and hills.

has made since then. Cincinnati is full of other paradoxes. It's a Northern city with a Southern gentility, a hilly enclave in the Midwest, and an arts town that worships at the altar of sports. Out-of-towners frequently describe it as insular, but that doesn't stop Cincinnatians from fretting about their place in the national pecking order. Most unmercifully, the country's major news outlets tend to pick up here the sorts of cringe-inducing headlines—Larry Flynt, Robert Mapplethorpe, Marge Schott, Pete Rose, the 2001 riots—that leave city officials, public relations firms, and convention and visitors bureaus with a lot of polishing to do.

More recently Cincinnati has enjoyed the high-profile positive coverage that it had coming. The universally lauded Contemporary Arts Center, museum expansions, riverfront development, popular festivals such as Tall Stacks, and waves of residents returning to live in renovated spaces in the downtown core all play to the city's strong suits and represent major civic victories that any city would envy. Just as approaching downtown from the south makes Cincinnati appear bigger than it really is, the arts here offer the big-city experience at small-town prices. The existence and support of the Fine Arts Fund and the generosity of such Fortune 500 companies as Procter & Gamble, Kroger, Fifth Third Bank, Federated Department Stores, and General Electric translate into a multitude of cultural choices every night of the week.

■ **RIVERFRONT** *map page 195, B-3*
The Ohio River feels more personable and intimate than the sweeping Mississippi, and this character extends to the city of Cincinnati itself. Despite its cargo-hauling duties and its numerous locks and dams, the river has a grace and art in its meandering that make it more than a liquid railroad. Unfortunately, for too long downtown turned its back on the river, the very asset that allowed the city to flourish in the first place. One area that stemmed the tide is Sawyer Point, a park on the eastern edge of downtown that has riverfront paths, a concert venue, and athletic facilities. Still, until 2000 there was a real sense that Cincinnati's heyday on the Ohio had come and gone.

A change in this view began with the reconfiguration of Fort Washington Way, the stretch of I-71 that cuts between downtown and the riverfront. The road was altered to allow Cincinnatians greater access to the river. The old L&N railroad bridge, dubbed the Purple People Bridge, was painted purple and converted in 2003 to a pedestrian walkway that connects Cincinnati with ambitious northern Kentucky developments such as the Newport Aquarium and Newport on the

The Contemporary Arts Center of Cincinnati displays plenty of cutting edges.

Levee. Ferries serve the crowds that flock to the river for festivals and sporting events, and a new Riverfront Transit Center under Second Street makes the district an important bus hub.

Most important, Cincinnati is at work on the **Banks,** its own planned riverfront development anchored by the **National Underground Railroad Freedom Center** (50 East Freedom Way; 513-333-7500), the premier institution of its kind in the country, which opened in the summer of 2004. Before the Civil War, activists such as Lyman Beecher, president of Lane Theological Seminary in Walnut Hills and father of Harriet Beecher Stowe, and Levi Coffin, a Quaker who was called the president of the Underground Railroad for his prominent role in its operation, made Cincinnati a rallying point for abolition and a beacon for enslaved African-Americans. Coffin and his wife helped an estimated two thousand slaves escape to the North.

With slaveholding states Kentucky and what was then Virginia just across the river, southern Ohio towns, from Ripley and Ironton to Marietta and Gallipolis, served as important crossing points for former slaves. Historians estimate that as many as 40 percent of escaped slaves crossed the Ohio River in their journeys northward. The museum not only chronicles the figures and beliefs behind the Underground Railroad but also addresses their implications today. In addition, it covers contemporary movements for freedom among oppressed peoples worldwide.

Two other mainstays at the Banks come courtesy of Hamilton County taxpayers: the Cincinnati Reds' **Great American Ball Park** (100 Main Street; 513-765-7000) and the Bengals' **Paul Brown Stadium** (1 Paul Brown Stadium; 513-621-8383). Great American borrows much from the now-familiar line of cozy retro ballparks that focus on the game instead of the seats, but its greatest achievement is connecting the park with the city. A long shot to right could end up in the Ohio. Fans in the upper deck can see the river and Civil War–era homes on Covington's Riverside Drive. A slice in the facade on the third-base side permits a peek inside from Sycamore Street. It's a worthy venue for a venerable franchise, the first professional baseball team, and its fans, who remember its history and its stars well.

Paul Brown Stadium is the first football-only facility the Bengals have had since the franchise began in Cincinnati in 1968 as an AFL expansion team. The $450 million stadium marked the initial phase of the Banks development and with its

(left) Cincinnati's Tall Stacks festival celebrates the river and history in equal parts. (following spread) Tall Stacks draws dozens of riverboats from around the Midwest and South.

THE CROSSING

Just when she thought he was taking her back to Kentucky, he turned the flathead and crossed the Ohio like a shot. There he helped her up the steep bank, while the boy without a jacket carried the baby who wore it. The man led her to a brush-covered hutch with a beaten floor.

"Wait here. Somebody be here directly. Don't move. They'll find you."

"Thank you," she said. "I wish I knew your name so I could remember you right."

"Name's Stamp," he said. "Stamp Paid. Watch out for that there baby, you hear?"

"I hear. I hear," she said, but she didn't. Hours later a woman was right up on her before she heard a thing. A short woman, young, with a croaker sack, greeted her.

"Saw that sign a while ago," she said. "But I couldn't get here no quicker."

"What sign?" asked Sethe.

"Stamp leaves the old sty open when there's a crossing. Knots a white rag on the post if it's a child too."

She knelt and emptied the sack. "My name's Ella," she said, taking a wool blanket, cotton cloth, two baked sweet potatoes and a pair of men's shoes from the sack. "My husband, John, is out yonder a ways. Where you heading?"

Sethe told her about Baby Suggs where she had sent her three children.

Ella wrapped a cloth strip tight around the baby's navel as she listened for the holes—the things the fugitives did not say; the questions they did not ask. Listened too for the unnamed, unmentioned people left behind. She shook gravel from the men's shoes and tried to force Sethe's feet into them. They would not go. Sadly, they split them down the heel, sorry indeed to ruin so valuable an item. Sethe put on the boy's jacket, not daring to ask whether there was any word of the children.

"They made it," said Ella. "Stamp ferried some of that party. Left them on Bluestone. It ain't too far."

Sethe couldn't think of anything to do, so grateful was she, so she peeled a potato, ate it, spit it up and ate more in quiet celebration.

"They be glad to see you," said Ella. "When was this one born?"

"Yesterday," said Sethe, wiping sweat from under her chin. "I hope she makes it."

Ella looked at the tiny, dirty face poking out of the wool blanket and shook her head. "Hard to say," she said. "If anybody was to ask me I'd say, 'Don't love nothing.' " Then, as if to take the edge off her pronouncement, she smiled at Sethe. "You had that baby by yourself?"

"No. Whitegirl helped."

"Then we better make tracks."

—Toni Morrison, *Beloved*, 1987

sleek, modern design stands in sharp contrast to Great American Ball Park. Paul Brown's sight lines and amenities are also a vast improvement over those of Riverfront Stadium, the Bengals' previous home.

Plans for the Banks also call for a number of shops, boutiques, and condominiums to flank the museum and a 40-acre park, but a time line for completion has not yet been established. It should make the riverfront an all-day destination, with added value from the shops and attractions on the Kentucky side.

■ **DOWNTOWN** *map page 195, B-3*
Cincinnati's spiritual heart lies on **Fountain Square** (Fifth and Vine streets), so named for the fountain that Henry Probasco gave to the city in 1871 in honor of his brother-in-law, Tyler Davidson. The figure atop the Tyler Davidson Fountain is the Genius of Water, acknowledging water's importance to the development of Cincinnati. If Fourth Street is the city's office, Fifth is the Cincinnati of postcards and leisure. Several of the downtown hotels line up here, all bound together through a skywalk system, which connects the convention center on Elm with shops and upscale restaurants, both on ground level and above, between Fourth

(above) In 1900, Fountain Square had a place for streetcars. (following spread) Today a pedestrian mall surrounds the Tyler Davidson Fountain at Fifth and Vine.

and Sixth streets. **Carew Tower** (Fifth and Vine streets; 513-241-5888) is hooked into the skywalk system and contains one of downtown's main retail shopping destinations, Tower Place. Still the tallest building in the city, the art deco masterpiece was finished in 1930, the first full year of the Depression.

Even if you're not staying at the Hilton Netherland Plaza Hotel inside Carew, it's worth ducking in for a glimpse at the Palm Court restaurant and bar to see its lavish marbled interior. The Carew Tower observation deck (513-241-3888) might be the cheapest date in the city; admission is $2.

The **Taft Museum,** previously known as the Baum-Longworth-Taft House, is old-school Cincinnati. The house's history rivals that of its contents. Dating to 1820, it was at one time the finest house in the city, and it is perhaps Cincinnati's best example of Federal-style architecture.

Nicholas Longworth, Cincinnati's first millionaire, lived here from 1830 into the 1860s. One of the city's earliest arts supporters, Longworth was also a vintner who championed domestic grape growing and wine making in Cincinnati. He settled on the native Catawba grape to deal with Ohio's relatively short growing

The Taft Museum collection includes James Abbott McNeill Whistler's At the Piano.

season and helped propagate southern Ohio vineyards with his cuttings. From his back door, Longworth reportedly could survey his vineyard on what became Mount Adams. Charles Taft, the publisher of the *Cincinnati Times-Star*, later lived here with his wife, Anna, and in 1927 they bequeathed the house and their private art collection to the Cincinnati Institute of Fine Arts, an institution they created and endowed.

The collection is among the best of small museums' throughout the country. The nearly seven hundred pieces include European and American paintings, Chinese ceramics, French enamels and watches, and American furniture. The Taft underwent a $22.8 million renovation and expansion from 2001 through 2004 that nearly doubled its size and added an enlarged special exhibitions gallery, class-room space, and café. *316 Pike Street; 513-241-0343.*

■ **BACKSTAGE DISTRICT** *map page 195, B-2*
Inside of ten years, the Backstage District has become downtown's premier cultural destination. The **Aronoff Center for the Arts** (650 Walnut Street; 513-721-3344) regularly brings in top performers for theater, ballet, opera, and symphonies from around the country and is the primary venue for the Cincinnati Ballet. The **Weston Art Gallery** (513-977-4165), next door in the same building, is one of Cincinnati's best exhibition spaces and features the region's top artists in sculpture, painting, film, photography, and more.

Across the street, the groundbreaking new home of the **Lois & Richard Rosenthal Center for Contemporary Art** (CAC; Sixth and Walnut; 513-345-8400) has reinvigorated the city's arts scene. This Zaha Hadid–designed structure, which Herbert Muschamp of the *New York Times* called the most important build-ing completed since the end of the Cold War, is the first freestanding American museum ever designed by a woman. All the exhibits rotate regularly; there is no permanent collection.

This tremendous investment in the arts has helped build business for the sur-rounding restaurants, cafés, and shops and has also prompted two upscale residen-tial loft developments (among many others in the city)—the Lofts at Graydon Place, next to the CAC, and the Gibson Lofts, across from the Aronoff. These, in turn, are encouraging more commercial investment.

The Aronoff Center draws the best in theater, ballet, opera, and symphonies.

■ CROSLEY SQUARE *map page 195, B-2*
Between 1934 and 1939 Cincinnati's WLW radio became known as the Nation's Station for its unprecedented 500,000-watt broadcast power, which garnered listeners around the country for such shows as *Moon River* and the comedy-variety program *Crosley's Follies.* The spirit behind the innovative station was the entrepreneur and industrialist Powel Crosley. Aside from being a businessman, Crosley was a tireless tinkerer who essentially fell into radio, and by the time WLW had to reduce its output to 50,000 watts, he had started TV broadcasting in Cincinnati.

In 1942 Crosley bought an Elks Temple at the corner of Ninth and Elm, and it quickly became the cultural epicenter of the Midwest. Renamed Crosley Square, it first held radio studios, but as television programming developed, WLWT broadcast from here too. Crosley Square brought the biggest names in show business and politics through Cincinnati on TV shows such as *The 50-50 Club, The Paul Dixon Show,* and *Midwestern Hayride,* which were picked up by NBC affiliates nationwide. And if a VIP—Duke Ellington, Jerry Lewis, Roy Rogers—came in from out of town, he was apt to turn up at Crosley Square. (Former Cincinnati mayor Jerry Springer broadcast the first season of his talk show from the building in 1991.) In 1999 the Hearst-Argyle-owned TV station WLWT, which had been using the building for news broadcasts, moved to contemporary offices in Mount Auburn. The Crosley Square building is now part of the Cincinnati Hills Christian Academy and is closed to the public.

For anyone who grew up in the thirties and forties, the Crosley name might conjure a variety of images, among them Crosley cars, refrigerators, washing machines, and radios. Nostalgia buffs can buy 21st-century replicas of the old Crosley radios in department stores, at specialty retailers, and by mail through the Crosley company (866-276-7539).

In Cincinnati, Crosley means baseball as much as it does radio. The Reds

---

WHAT ABOUT CINCINNATI'S OTHER FAMOUS RADIO STATION?

People of a certain age who have never been to Cincinnati and know little else about it still recall *WKRP in Cincinnati*, the cult TV show that ran for CBS in the late 1970s and early 1980s. Gordon Jump, later beloved as the Maytag repairman, played Arthur Carlson, a station manager attempting to convert his mother's failing radio station to a rock format in hopes of turning a profit. The show was known for a strong ensemble cast that included Richard Sanders as Les Nessman, Loni Anderson as Jennifer Marlowe, and Tim Reid as Gordon "Venus Flytrap" Simms.

Sadly, there is no real WKRP in Cincinnati, but thanks to syndication the station is better known today than local giant WLW Radio. *WKRP in Cincinnati* creator Hugh Wilson based the show at least partially on his experiences in advertising with the Atlanta radio station WQXI. But there is some of Cincinnati in the show, which still airs in syndication. Fountain Square and the old *Enquirer* building show up in the intro, and the WKRP radio tower does have a WLW connection. The tower in the show is at 2222 Chickasaw Street, north of downtown. When *WKRP* first aired in 1978, the NBC TV affiliate WLWT, sister station to WLW, used it.

It's amazing Cincinnati gets as much notoriety for the show as it does. CBS canceled it after four years of frequent time slot changes; only in syndication did it develop a broad following, which prompted *WKRP* actors to joke that viewers finally knew where to find it.

(above) An 1894 scorebook previews the Reds' entire season. (right) The Findlay ... het Opening Day Parad. tradition dates to 1920.

played at Crosley Field (known as Redland Field until 1934) from 1912 to 1970, and Powel Crosley owned the team until 1961. It was his enterprise that led the Reds to play the first ballgame under lights and ushered in the era of night baseball. If you're in the tristate area, you can listen to WLW broadcasts—and Reds baseball games—at 700 on the AM dial.

■ **PLUM STREET** *map page 195, B-2/3*

The usually serene little Plum Street is home to the Cathedral of St. Peter in Chains, Plum Street Temple, and City Hall, all at Eighth and Plum. At its dedication in 1845, the Greek Revival **St. Peter in Chains** was called "the finest building in the west, and the most imposing in appearance of any cathedral in the United States." The interior features a large mosaic of Christ giving keys to St. Peter and includes many striking Greek details, such as those in the stations of the cross, in keeping with the exterior design. The cathedral serves the Catholic Archdiocese of Cincinnati and is open to visitors, although the hours are sporadic.

Cincinnati is the seat of Reform Judaism and thus has a larger Jewish population than one would expect of a mid-size Midwestern city. Although the Jewish community has more recently centered in Roselawn, Amberley Village, and Blue Ash, one of its greatest temples is on Plum Street. The **Plum Street Temple** (513-793-2256) was built at the direction of Isaac M. Wise, the founder of American Reform Judaism and of Hebrew Union College (which later merged with the Jewish Institute of Religion) in Clifton. The exterior combines Gothic and Moorish influences, but it's the interior that makes the building priceless: dazzling hand-stenciled walls and ceilings aglow with stained-glass light. The temple is not open for regular tours, but you may call ahead to observe a service.

Compared with St. Peter in Chains and Plum Street Temple, **City Hall** (513-352-3000) looks brooding and authoritative, just as a city hall should. Noted architect Samuel Hannaford (whose other credits include Music Hall and the Cincinnati Observatory) designed it in the Romanesque style with a soaring clock tower on the southeast corner, two courtyards, and, appropriately, access on all four sides. Unfortunately, as is true in many government buildings, the interior doesn't measure up to the exterior. On the occasions when Plum Street isn't serene, it often has something to do with a gathering or demonstration on the building's steps.

The clock tower at Cincinnati City Hall is the building's most striking feature.

■ **WEST END** *map page 195, A-2*

The West End has been home to some of the toughest and most colorful neighborhoods in Cincinnati. Although immediately adjacent to downtown, it retains a more or less distinct identity through its departure from the strict grid of city blocks and with I-75 slicing right through its middle. The highway's construction in the 1950s displaced many of its residents, a saving grace considering that many of the poorest migrated to Over-the-Rhine and prevented the more historic buildings there from being razed.

New town houses on the blocks east of I-75 and south of Liberty have brought people back to the central city to live. These sturdy brick homes offer more peace and quiet than homes downtown but have easy access to Music Hall, the West End's nearby parks, and shops and boutiques throughout downtown.

West of I-75 the West End turns commercial and industrial. The street grid is so broken by the interstate, various viaducts, rail lines, and dead-end streets that finding anything you're looking for is simply good fortune. But it's worth venturing here anyway, because the western edge of the West End holds Cincinnati's greatest attraction.

You can see it from almost a mile away, straight west down Ezzard Charles Drive. The windowed, ten-story half dome of **Union Terminal** (1301 Western Avenue) looks like it could be an amphitheater. What it is is arguably the best example of art deco architecture in the country, the one site every visitor to Cincinnati must see, and a case of civic decision making done right, three times over.

Before the nation flew, train stations held the community-in-a-box status now accorded airports—but with more style and romance. Union Terminal featured clothing shops, newsstands, restaurants, lounges, a shoe shine, a barbershop, and a toy store in what must have seemed extravagant surroundings when it was completed in 1933: a 100-foot-tall dome adorned with silver strips, walls of red and yellow Verona marble, and two glass mosaic murals on the north and south walls of the rotunda. It was as practical as it was attractive. Union Terminal simplified a muddled infrastructure of five train stations and seven lines into one centrally located stop. It's only a shame that visitors don't step off trains here anymore.

Today Union Terminal houses the **Cincinnati Museum Center** (513-287-7000), a large village in its own right that comprises the Cincinnati History Museum, the Museum of Natural History & Science, the Children's Museum, an Omnimax Theatre, and the Cincinnati Historical Society. A visitor can come away from the Museum Center with a solid understanding of the city's settlement, progress, and culture without even having seen the rest of Cincinnati.

It's a minor miracle that the station is still here at all. The city bought the station in the mid-1970s and, after some desperate attempts at luring commercial investment, used a major bond issue and restoration

Union Terminal is a case of civic decision making done right.

grants to open the current complex in 1990. If you fly into Cincinnati/Northern Kentucky International Airport, look for the fourteen Winold Reiss murals displayed throughout the airport. These hung in the main concourse at Union Terminal until 1973, when demolition loomed and concerned citizens raised funds to save them.

■ OVER-THE-RHINE *map page 195, B-2*

Downtown changes identities faster than a superhero once you cross Central Parkway, the east–west artery built in the 1920s over the old Miami & Erie Canal (then known as the Rhine). South of Central Parkway is the business district, the eateries that cater to it, and the Cincinnati of travel agency brochures. Crossing Central Parkway puts you in Over-the-Rhine (OTR), once the epicenter of German-American life and now an embattled urban core doing triple duty as a haven for technology companies, the arts, and entertainment.

It's easier to imagine the Cincinnati of old here than it is farther south, because Over-the-Rhine has the largest number and most intact examples of Italianate architecture in the country. Many buildings are in fair to poor condition, tarnished by barred windows and in need of a face-lift (Steven Soderberg filmed a number of scenes for *Traffic* here), but the neighborhood has proved more resilient than a passerby fifteen years ago might have expected. Drawn by attractive prices, plentiful entertainment options, and numerous residential loft developments, young urbanites are moving here on an impressive scale.

The arts carry the day in OTR, particularly in the area around Walnut and 12th. **Music Hall** (1243 Elm Street; 513-381-3300), home of the Cincinnati Symphony Orchestra; the **Ensemble Theatre of Cincinnati** (1127 Vine Street; 513-421-3555); the **Pendleton Arts Center** (1310 Pendleton Street; 513-559-3958 ext. 1257); **Uptown Arts** (123 East Liberty Street; 513-651-1500), an arts education center for children; the **School for the Creative and Performing Arts** (1310 Sycamore Street; 513-363-8000); the **Art Academy of Cincinnati** (1212 Jackson Street; 513-562-8777); and art galleries and specialty shops make the area a perfect case study for *Rise of the Creative Class* author Richard Florida. Expect urban planners to hail OTR as a success story in urban redevelopment in the future.

The best way to take in the OTR arts scene is to walk it. The local organization Enjoy the Arts hosts Final Friday gallery walks, which are informal tours of the gal-

Music Hall overlooks nineteenth-century Italianate homes in Over-the-Rhine.

Music Hall was even more ornate when it opened in 1878.

leries and shops around North Main Street, on the last Friday of each month. More than two dozen businesses stay open evenings from 6 to 10, and the artists are often present. There's no set path, but participants can start at the **Enjoy the Arts** building (1338 Main Street; 513-621-4700) for refreshments, mingle with other arts walkers and get a map that highlights participating galleries.

Final Fridays make for the ideal segue—mere steps—to OTR's bar scene. Main Street has the greatest concentration of bars, clubs, and coffeehouses in the city, and the offerings spill over onto nearby 12th, Sycamore, and Walnut streets. The district has something for nearly every taste, from indie dance spots to cigar bars and campy chain nightclubs, but it also has a harder edge that's absent from tony Mount Adams and the average neighborhood pub.

Along with the uptown spots near the University of Cincinnati, OTR is your best bet for live music. **Kaldi's Coffeehouse & Bookstore** (1204 Main Street; 513-241-3070) is a great example of the variety available here—in this case all in one place. Old paperbacks lining the walls make Kaldi's look more like an absentminded professor's study than a destination bookstore. On any given night you can hear jazz, bluegrass, or acoustic guitar while enjoying coffee, tea, wine, beer, or a mixed drink. And it has one of the best vegetarian menus around for lunch and dinner.

Another local favorite, **Barrelhouse Brewing Company** (22 East 12th Street; 513-421-2337) is a great place to kick back with pub food and live music. It is also one of the last torchbearers of Cincinnati's mostly forgotten reputation for great beer. Barrelhouse pours fresh lagers, ales, stouts, and bocks and has a tasty soup-salad-sandwich menu. The real draw is its monthly "beer dinner," when the pub's brew experts teach customers about a different type of beer. Tastings and a buffet dinner are included. If you don't make it to the brewpub, you can taste Barrelhouse beers at one of the countless restaurants around the city that serve it.

It's worth mentioning that a more recent addition to the region's beer tradition, the **Hofbräuhaus,** is across the river in Newport, Kentucky (Third Street and Saratoga; 859-491-7200). The Hofbräuhaus is a satellite of the original beer hall in Munich, Germany, and the first Hofbräuhaus in America.

Over-the-Rhine's longest-running attraction is also the best reason to visit. **Findlay Market** is an immersion experience like nothing else. It's also one of the few viable places for neighborhood residents to buy groceries. On market days (all sections are open on Wednesday, Friday, and Saturday), shoppers from all over the city come to buy—and smell and sample—fresh produce, seafood, meats, cheeses, breads, and desserts. The people-watching is unparalleled. The hundred-and-fifty-year-old marketplace now has a visitors center and improved vendor space. Renovating the surrounding market-rate housing and commercial space is an ongoing effort. Like the arts destinations on the eastern edge of the neighborhood, Findlay Market should encourage renewal and investment for years to come. *Elder between Elm and Race; 513-665-4839.*

The market itself sits like an upside-down T between Elm and Race streets and stretches up to Findlay Street at its northernmost point. This is the northern edge of Over-the-Rhine, and the area feels worlds away from downtown and certainly the riverfront. Spiritually, however, it's next door. Every April since 1920, on the Reds' Opening Day (always the first among major league teams), the market is the starting point for the **Findlay Market Opening Day Parade.** Tractors, fire trucks, horse-drawn wagons, and thousands of optimistic fans jam the downtown streets for what might as well be a city holiday. Plan on joining the fun, because if your route takes you through downtown, you won't get wherever you're going anyway.

(following spread) Churches rank among the grandest landmarks in Over-the-Rhine.

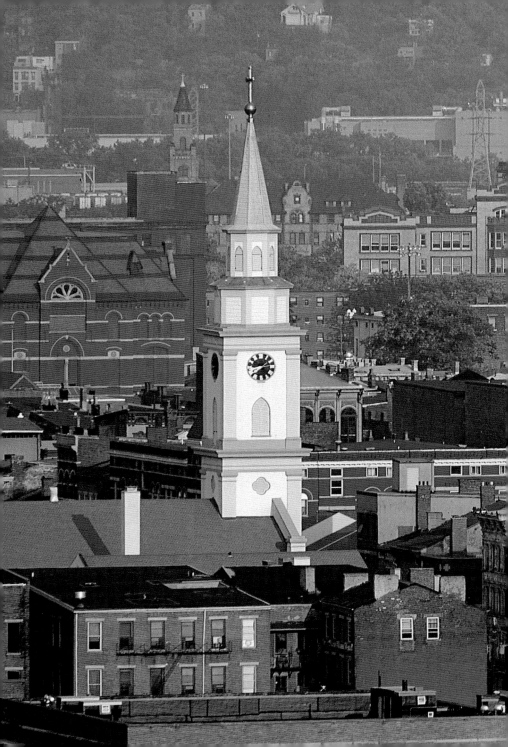

TROUBLE BREWING

An intrepid drinker in 1880 Cincinnati could weave through the streets and pick from almost two thousand saloons in a town of two hundred and fifty-five thousand—enough competition to ensure a 5-cent draft beer and a free sausage to go with it. In those days a traveler's first impression of a place often came from a glass of the local brew, and Cincinnati has stood at the fore. "There is something about the waters of the Ohio River that gives a flavor to beer made in Cincinnati that can not be obtained in any other city not convenient to that river," George E. Stevens wrote during that era, as told in Timothy J. Holian's *Over the Barrel*, Volume One. New York, Milwaukee, and Chicago produced more beer, but no city produced more, or probably consumed more, in proportion to its population.

Beer was a rallying point for German immigrants, simultaneously a source of ethnic pride and a connector to the larger population, which, for the most part, readily celebrated the tradition. Brewing overshadowed even Cincinnati's almighty pig; names such as Christian Moerlein, John Hauck, and Ludwig Hudepohl commanded an unmatched reverence. So prodigious was Cincinnati's consumption that brewers here never really embraced the national and international markets available to them. This left them hard-pressed to counter rivals such as Pabst and Anheuser-Busch in the post-Prohibition brewing era, when cash and marketing trumped craft and tradition. Hudepohl-Schoenling was the last local brewer to close down, in 1996. It owned many of the old-time brands, some of which are still brewed by other companies on contract arrangement, including Little Kings and Christian Moerlein.

Still, Cincinnati's brewing history remains. A number of facilities stand today as testaments to the city's best-loved industry, although their condition doesn't do justice to their earlier greatness. All are closed to the public, and most are in no shape to enter. The old Hudepohl brewery (later Hudepohl-Schoenling), with its prominent chimney bearing the company name, survives at Sixth and Gest streets in the West End. The Clyffside Brewing Company buildings remain along McMicken, Stonewall, and Mohawk, and the old bottling works of the John Hauck Brewing Company stand on Central Avenue near Dayton Street. The building displays a sign for Red Top, a brewer that later bought the facility. The John Hauck House (812 Dayton Street; 513-721-3570), built in 1870, will give you a taste of how beer barons lived at the end of the 19th century; it is open for tours.

(right) Christian Moerlein was one of Cincinnati's foremost brewers.

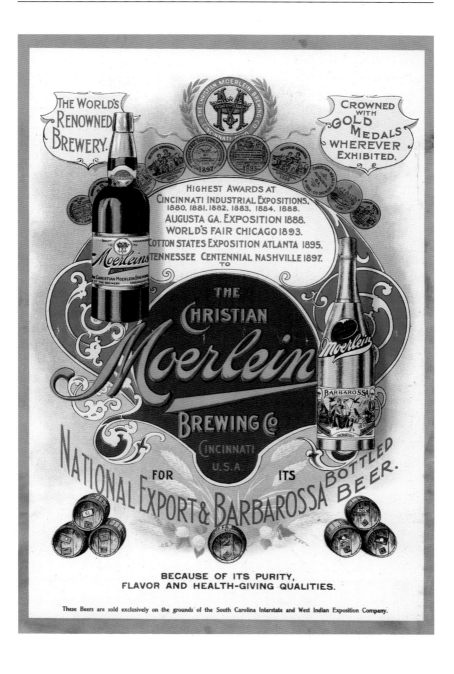

Symphony fans will hardly agree that Findlay Market is the best reason to visit Over-the-Rhine. The truth is that **Music Hall** (1243 Elm Street; 513-381-3300), home to Paavo Jarvi's Cincinnati Symphony Orchestra and Erich Kunzel's Cincinnati Pops, is equally remarkable, more visually impressive, and, at more than a hundred and twenty-five years old, nearly as enduring. Architect Samuel Hannaford (who also designed City Hall) built his reputation with this design when he won the contract over the better-known competitors. It was a High Victorian Gothic–style multiuse center that, at the time, combined music in a central theater with horticulture exhibits in the south wing and mechanical exhibits in the north wing. Music Hall is one of Hannaford's greatest achievements. If you survey Over-the-Rhine from the lookouts of Mount Adams, you'll see that it dominates even the cavernous churches around it and retains its heft from a mile away.

■ MOUNT ADAMS AND EDEN PARK *map page 195, C-1/2*
For residents who rarely see the need to come down, it's known simply as the Hill. And once you go up, you'll see why they rarely leave. Mount Adams packs an obscene amount of charm into a handful of city blocks while gracefully negotiating its dual identities: high-priced roost for professionals and sophisticated entertainment destination for everyone else. Throwback pubs and modern clubs mingle with some of the best restaurants in the city, all under tangles of lights that twinkle from the tree branches year-round. The only exceptions to the charm are parking hassles and late-night disturbances, if you happen to live next door to a dance hall.

The location is unrivaled. The neighborhood's front porch has a panoramic view of the Ohio River and northern Kentucky that wouldn't look out of place above a mantle. Mount Adams has Eden Park for a backyard, and to the west is one of the better views of downtown, a five-minute drive, or bike ride, away.

It's amazing that Mount Adams remained undeveloped for as long as it did. As Cincinnati erupted with buildings and people in the 1830s, the hill, then known as Mount Ida, was part of Nicholas Longworth's vineyard, but the vines died off in the early 1860s. John Quincy Adams's 1843 visit to lay the cornerstone for the Cincinnati Observatory here gave the hill its present name, and not long after, Irish and German immigrant families began arriving in larger numbers, bringing with them a heavy Catholic influence. The inclined railway completed in 1876 opened Mount Adams to the curiosity seekers, but the neighborhood retained a certain solitude that exists to this day.

TOURING CINCINNATI STEP BY STEP

Spend more than a few days in Cincinnati, and you'll begin to notice the steps. Grand stairways. Flights leading up to unseen homes. Furtive pathways winding into leafy obscurity. Naturally, a city with so many hills must have the means to surmount them.

There are so many sets of public steps in Cincinnati—hundreds—that many remain a secret even to natives. And the surprise is what makes them compelling. These aren't marked recreational trails or fixed loops but rather a loose network of stairs and sidewalks that predate the automobile era. A number have existed in some form since city dwellers first began venturing up the hillsides in the first half of the 19th century. There are sets of stairs so disconnected from the contemporary street layout that they could be portals, leading you to places you didn't realize were accessible from your starting point and that you approach from unexpected directions.

The most famous steps in Cincinnati are those leading to Holy Cross-Immaculata Church in Mount Adams. Every year on Good Friday, starting as early as midnight, about ten thousand come to pray on these blessed steps. As the tradition goes, pilgrims say a prayer on each of the eighty-five steps between St. Gregory Street and the church, although some begin at one of the lower streets, Celestial, or even Eggleston. The roots of the Good Friday pilgrimage date to 1860 with the Cincinnati archbishop John Purcell's call for parishioners to pray for the church's completion; the first pilgrimage took place in 1861, several months after the dedication.

Other neighborhood stairways are more mysterious but less mystical: You might find steps that you could have sworn led somewhere else previously, like something out of *Harry Potter*. Other steps change their appearance entirely with the seasons, as the bushes they tunnel through flourish and die. The people change too: runners and dog walkers in summer, kids hauling sleds in the winter. Essentially any neighborhood with a "mount" or a "hill" in the name has staircases to climb, but others do as well. Mount Auburn, Mount Adams, Price Hill, Walnut Hills, and Mount Lookout all offer great paths, a chance to explore, and brisk exercise. (One city dweller says he swore he'd never move another piece of furniture after helping his girlfriend, now his wife, move all her belongings down the endless steps in front of her Mount Adams apartment. Now he lives in mercifully flat Forest Park.)

After you ramble through downtown and along the river, a walk on Cincinnati's hillier paths is a fine way to delve deeper into the city, its parks, and its history. Most, but not all, of the public stairs are well kept and safe, with handrails to assist, and most invariably reward walkers with outstanding views. Mary Anna DuSablon's *Walking the Steps of Cincinnati* is an excellent guide to getting started. You never know where the stairs might lead.

It has an almost monastic feel that *could* stem in part from its lofty elevation (818 feet)—or perhaps the Holy Cross Monastery at the top of the hill. The monastery has been here since the 1860s, along with **Holy Cross Church** (the Irish parish; 30 Guido Street) and the **Church of the Immaculate Conception** (the German parish; 30 Guido Street). The two churches later combined as the Holy Cross-Immaculata Church. Even when the churches aren't visible, the street names—Monastery Drive, St. Gregory, and Celestial, to name a few—tell the story.

Mount Adams is just the beginning of an arts island that extends into Eden Park and whose best-known legacy is the Rookwood Pottery Company. Started in 1880 by Maria Longworth Nichols (granddaughter of Nicholas Longworth) and moved to Mount Adams in 1892, Rookwood gained international acclaim for its flawless designs, dazzling glazes, and unique pieces—every one marked by artist and date. Advances in ceramics production, and the rise of cheap knockoffs that came with them, drove Rookwood to ruin by the early 1940s, but its international reputation lives on in homes around the city. Pick up a copy of the Sunday *Enquirer*'s real estate classifieds, and you'll run across ads boasting about the houses' Rookwood fireplaces, tiles, and accents, prized features you won't find on this scale in nearly any other city.

The Rookwood kilns remain at the old site where Nichols and her artists fired their pottery, now the **Rookwood Pottery Bistro** (1077 Celestial Street; 513-721-5456), but the place to take in the pottery that made the company famous is the **Cincinnati Art Museum** (953 Eden Park Drive; 513-721-5204), which opened in 1886. The museum's airy Cincinnati Wing features paintings by Frank Duveneck and John Twachtman along with a range of other artists and media, including sculpture, furniture, and some fine examples of Rookwood pottery. The wing opened in 2003 and flaunts its high-tech status with multimedia presentations and computer workstations offering more background on the art and artists. The rest of the museum, one of the oldest visual-arts museums in the country, is also worth checking out, and it's all free all the time.

Holy Cross-Immaculata Church occupies the highest point on Mount Adams.

Cincinnati's Eden Park offers something for just about everybody.

■ **UPTOWN** *map page 195, B-1*

Uptown encompasses the neighborhoods immediately north of downtown and Over-the-Rhine that surround the University of Cincinnati campus: Mount Auburn, Corryville, Fairview, Clifton Heights, and Clifton.

Just up the hill from the hustle and bustle of downtown (and down the street from William Howard Taft Road) is the **William Howard Taft National Historic Site** (2038 Auburn Avenue; 513-684-3262), one of the few remnants of Taft's legacy still preserved in Cincinnati. The Greek Revival design was popular when the house was built in the 1840s but today looks out of place in Mount Auburn, now a modest, lower-income neighborhood. Forest-green shutters adorn the pale yellow facade, encircled by a low iron fence.

Taft's father, Alphonso, was a respected attorney and judge who entertained many prominent Cincinnatians, including, on one occasion, President James Garfield. William was born here and lived in the house until he left for Yale in 1874. He eventually graduated second in his class and went on to earn a law degree from the University of Cincinnati. (Taft is the only president in history also to have served as chief justice of the Supreme Court.) For the most part the house is lean on actual Taft heirlooms; the National Park Service bought the house in 1969 and furnished much of it with 1850s–1870s period pieces in a $3 million renovation, which is very well done. The house Taft resided in as an adult is privately owned but still stands not far away, on MacMillan Street.

The hills north of downtown are the suburbs of a hundred and fifty years ago. There were magnificent beer gardens, grand estates, and a sense among the elites who lived here that an ideal society might be built in the wooded, parklike setting. At one time there was an ideal society, and some of the most ornate and exclusive homes in the city remain on these hills to prove it. Clifton is particularly blessed. Its historic Gaslight District, north of the University of Cincinnati, is a leafy enclave for professionals, professors, and lucky students and well worth a walk or drive. It's close to Mount Storm Park, one of Cincinnati's most beautiful parks.

■ **WEST SIDE** *map page 195, A-2*

Cincinnati, as tight-knit as it is, is actually a city divided—the West Side and the East Side. The West Side—not to be confused with the smaller West End—comprises the neighborhoods and towns west of I-75; historically it has been more blue-collar and tradition-bound than the East Side. Kids attend the same high schools their folks went to and settle down to raise kids in the same neighborhoods where they grew up. "The homes might be small, but they're paid for," one West Sider observes. And if the rest of the city is challenging your navigational skills, don't set foot here without a few days' rations. The standard-issue Cincinnati hills reach a higher plain on the West Side, and on the southern end of the East–West divide, Mill Creek and the railways that run alongside it keep the two worlds at arm's length.

The East Side isn't the West's opposite necessarily, but it is generally more affluent and a bit more transient: couples settle down to raise kids in the same neighborhoods they grew up in, but *their* parents moved into town twenty years ago. That hasn't stopped either side from perpetuating an occasionally unfriendly rivalry over which is better, particularly when it comes to high school sports. The Catholic Archdiocese has the largest school system in the area and runs seventeen secondary schools in Greater Cincinnati, including such athletic powerhouses as Moeller (East Side) and Elder (West Side). Elder's football stadium, the **Pit** (3900 Vincent Avenue; 513-921-3744), has a reputation for rabid and boisterous fans

(following spread) Humanity, God, and nature come together at the Spring Grove Cemetery and Arboretum.

that would make Texans jealous. Home games consistently draw crowds of ten thousand. Elder won back-to-back state championships in 2002 and 2003, something not seen from a Division I Cincinnati school since Moeller did it in 1979 and 1980. One former West Sider calls it the "best place in the country to watch a high school football game, if you can make it back to your car alive and don't mind being physically threatened, spit on, and cursed at." Take that with a grain of salt, wear purple, and go anyway.

One of Cincinnati's most ingeniously planned and enduring architectural beauties isn't a building. It's **Spring Grove Cemetery and Arboretum,** at 733 acres among the largest cemeteries in the United States. What might seem like a Victorian anachronism now was a welcome idea in 1845: a lush park where families could socialize, celebrate the dead, and reflect in peace on the interplay of humanity, God, and nature. The cemetery relieved the increasingly overcrowded urban burial plots, which monopolized valuable downtown real estate. The names in Spring Grove are the names of Cincinnati history: Supreme Court Justice Salmon P. Chase, William Procter, James Gamble, Bernard Kroger, Charles Taft, beer baron Christian Moerlein, abolitionist Levi Coffin, and Congressman Nicholas Longworth. Jacob Burnet, the author of Ohio's first constitution, is here, as are thirty-seven Civil War generals and ten state governors. Spring Grove remains the first burial choice for many prominent Cincinnatians. The city's most celebrated architects took turns building chapels, mausoleums, and assorted monuments at Spring Grove, and these can serve as a lengthy architectural tour. Make it a point to look for James Strader's Gothic-style chapel, the Norman Chapel (designed by Samuel Hannaford), and the Dexter Chapel (designed by James Keys Wilson), which recalls the Sainte Chapelle in Paris. Even if you have no interest in the city's history, the grounds alone make it worth the trip. Frederick Law Olmstead, the architect who designed New York's Central Park, called the landscaping the finest in the country.

The land here has much the same feel as it did a hundred and fifty years ago, and in some cases the same trees: roughly twenty state and national champion trees grow here. Spring Grove draws its largest crowds in the spring for the blooming season, which is an ideal time to come because of the weather, range of flowers, and stout, soaring branches on the oldest trees still visible behind budding leaves. Self-guided tours and some formal tours are available. *4521 Spring Grove Avenue; 513-681-7526.*

■ **EAST SIDE** *map page 195, C-2*

Many East Side neighborhoods—Hyde Park, Mount Lookout, Mariemont, Madeira—have everything you'd look for in a place to settle down, or a low-key getaway: convenient access to unique shops; excellent restaurants; charming, mature neighborhoods; well-designed parks; and an active lifestyle. **Hyde Park Square** serves as something of a hub for the area, drawing people from miles around for its shopping opportunities and gourmet Graeter's ice cream. Dog walkers, runners, and families with strollers fill the sidewalks and green space.

Not far away, to the east, lies **Ault Park,** site of innumerable weddings. The park caters to most any taste without compromising aesthetics. There's a soccer field, hiking trails, a quad perfect for flying kites and playing Frisbee, elegant flower gardens, and a hilltop pavilion in the Italian Renaissance style affording a princely view.

To turn your gaze a bit farther, stop by the **Cincinnati Observatory Center** in Mount Lookout, between Hyde Park Square and Ault Park. Its predecessor on Mount Adams was the first observatory in the United States, and when operations moved here in 1873 to escape the heat and pollution of the city, the original telescope came too. Visitors who come for viewing today can search the sky through the same hundred-and-fifty-year-old-plus telescope, and a newer 16-inch model. Don't expect an ivory tower: the Observatory Center's mission is now mostly educational rather than research-oriented, and the center welcomes the public for tours, classes, and stargazing. Call in advance for reservations. *3489 Observatory Place; 513-321-5186.*

■ **NORTHERN SUBURBS** *map page 182, A-2*

Farther north, Cincinnati devolves into the neither-here-nor-there mishmash you find everywhere in American suburbia, but there's at least one place that breaks out from the norm. **Jungle Jim's,** in Fairfield, is no white-bread market. Instead it combines the most stunning selection of international foods you've ever seen with kid-entrancing camp. If Disney ran a grocery store, this is what it would look like. And in some cases, it's the only place in Cincinnati where immigrants can buy the traditional foods of their native countries. Gourmet or gourmand, you can't pass up a place that carries eight thousand wines and nearly a thousand brands of hot sauce. It's not for the indecisive. *5440 Dixie Highway (Route 4); 513-674-6000.*

On the northeast side of town, in Loveland, the story behind **Loveland Castle,** also known as Chateau Larouche, could be a Tim Burton screenplay. Impressed by

Miami University created the town of Oxford.

the medieval castles he saw in Europe during World War I, Harry Andrews spent more than fifty years building his own one-fifth-scale castle using sandstone he harvested from the Little Miami River, which the castle overlooks. He lived here as a bachelor until his death in 1981, leaving the knights' wing of the castle unfinished. It isn't *Edward Scissorhands,* but it is a humbling accomplishment for one man, especially when you consider the extensive terraces and gardens he built to complement his home. If you come in October, the nonprofit caretakers, the Knights of the Golden Trail, run a haunted house that puts a macabre spin on what's already an unusual place. Keep your eyes open for the skeleton in the root cellar. *12025 Shore Road; 513-683-4686.*

■ **OXFORD** *map page 182, A-2*

On the far west side of Butler County, near the Indiana border, Oxford remains somewhat insulated from the explosive growth elsewhere in the county. Calling it a college town is technically accurate, if a bit misleading. Miami University doesn't just influence Oxford—it created it. The university essentially arose out of unsettled woodlands, to the dismay of Dayton, Lebanon, and especially Cincinnati, which spent years trying to get the university moved there. Nearly everyone in town, it seems, either goes to school at Miami, works there, or lives with someone who does. Just west of campus, shops in the uptown area, along brick-paved High Street, cater mostly to students but are well worth exploring if you spend any time here.

Miami really is one of the prettiest campuses in the country, thanks to the consistent, widespread use of Georgian architecture, which gives the impression the entire campus sprang up overnight. The university's name stems from the Miami Tribe, the *Myaamia,* whose ancestral lands, pre-1800s, stretched from the Scioto River to eastern Illinois and from the Great Lakes to the Ohio. It's not a hollow connection. Since the early 1970s, the university and tribe have collaborated to mutual benefit. Qualified Miami Tribe members can attend the university on scholarship, and university students travel to Miami, Oklahoma, to work with the tribe through independent study and formal programs on projects ranging from documenting plants traditionally used by the tribe to compiling a Miami language book for children.

Students kissing under Upham Arch at midnight are destined to marry—a "Miami merger."

MIAMI SPEECH

The Miami language is a central Algonquian language that was historically spoken throughout what are now western Ohio, Indiana, Illinois, and lower Michigan and Wisconsin. Miami words are constructed of smaller parts of meaning. This means that a single Miami word is able to convey the meaning of an entire English sentence. For example, the Miami word *ninkihkeelimaahsoo* literally means in English "I do not know him." The Miami word contains the following meaningful parts: nin- ("I"), kihkeelim- ("know"), -aa ("him"), and -hsoo ("not"). Below are some common words.

ahsenisiipi (äs se´ ni see´ pi)—Great Miami River (literally, "Stone River")

ateehimini (ə tā´ hi mi´ ni)—strawberry (literally, "heart berry")

cecaahkwa (che´ chä kkwa)—sandhill crane

kaanseenseepiiwi (kän zän´ zä pee´ wi)—Ohio River (literally, "Pecan River")

kihcikami (ki chi ka´ mi)—Lake Michigan (literally, "Great Waters")

mahkomishi (mä kko mi´ zhi)—sumac (literally, "bear bush")

mahkwa (mä kkwa´)—bear

miincipi (meen ji´ pi)—corn

moohswa (moó sswa)—deer

oonsaalamooni (oon zä la´ moo ni)—bloodroot plant (literally, "yellow paint")

pileewa (pi lā´ wə)—turkey

šikaahkonki (shi kä kkōngi)—Chicago (literally, "Skunk Place")

taawaawa siipiiwi (ta wa´ wa see pee´ wi)—Maumee River (literally, "Ottawa River")

—Adapted from *myaamia mahsinaakani kaloosiona,*
a Miami dictionary, by Daryl Baldwin, 2004

In the 1990s the two entities began a deeper relationship built on documenting and preserving the Miami culture and language, an unusual move considering that historically academia has been fundamentally at odds with native culture. (The Treaty of Greenville, for example, pushed the tribe out of Ohio, paving the way for a university in the "college lands" northwest of Cincinnati.)

Native speakers had stopped conversationally speaking the Miami language, known today as Miami-Peoria, in the early 1960s, so Daryl Baldwin, a tribe member and linguistics researcher at Miami University, began working on the Myaamia Project with Dr. David Costa, a language specialist from the University of California-

Berkeley who has worked extensively with the Miami Tribe of Oklahoma and the Miami Nation of Indiana. With Baldwin as director, the innovative collaborative project has brought resources to the tribe for cultural preservation and increased cultural understanding to members of the Oxford community. Fortunately, the Miami-Peoria language has been documented over the course of three hundred years and bears many similarities to others in the Algonquian language family. A major component of the linguistic portion of the project is teaching the language to children, with an ultimate goal of widespread fluency in the tribe. "As a result of this work, some in the younger generation can now speak a functional version of the language," Baldwin says, and his own children are among them.

The university now serves as a central repository for tribe-related research, including cultural resources—documents, artwork, maps, photographs—much of which comes through the Myaamia Project but also some from the tribe itself and researchers around the country. The Miami University Art Museum maintains tribal artwork and cultural objects.

While you're on campus, both the **McGuffey Museum** (410 East Spring Street; 513-529-8380) and the **Miami University Art Museum** (801 South Patterson Avenue; 513-529-2232) are worth a look. The McGuffey Museum is the brick house that William Holmes McGuffey, creator of the popular McGuffey Readers, built and lived in with his family during his teaching days at Miami. The university invested a great deal in its restoration and reopened the museum in 2002. Visitors can flip through copies of vintage readers, the most popular book in American history after the Bible, while standing next to McGuffey's signature octagonal desk, where he worked on the books. The art museum, east of campus, houses a permanent collection of roughly sixteen thousand works, including artwork of the Miami Tribe, but also features rotating exhibits and frequent films, lectures, and educational programs.

Just north of town at Hueston Woods State Park, the **Pioneer Farm and Museum** (Brown Road at Doty Road; 513-523-8005) ushers visitors back to the 1830s with period furnishings at the old Doty Homestead. The barn has an excellent collection of farming artifacts from the period, although they aren't original to the farm. In October the Oxford Museum Association hosts its AppleButter Festival, and December brings the Country Christmas Open House, when the farm house is beautifully decorated for the season. The association is also working on restoring the pioneer cemetery across Brown Road.

■ DAYTON *map page 182, A-1*

Boosters sometimes call Dayton the Cradle of Creativity, but that gives the city too little credit. We aren't talking community art classes and woodworking here. Dayton is best known as the city where hometown boys Orville and Wilbur Wright conceived and refined their flying machine, achieving controlled, powered, heavier-than-air flight for the first time, in 1903 (prompting the city's other nickname, Birthplace of Aviation). Less known today are Charles Kettering, a prolific automotive inventor; Leland Clark, who invented the heart-lung machine; and John Morton who, curse him, invented parking meters. Cash registers, ATMs, parachutes, and frost-free refrigerators also were developed in Dayton, among myriad other inventions, earning Dayton yet another nickname: Tinkertown. The city still boasts the most patents per capita of any city in the country.

"Cradle of Creativity" could speak for the city's thriving arts scene as well as the string of well-known writers and performers: the humorist Erma Bombeck; the poet and writer Paul Laurence Dunbar; the novelist John Jakes; and Nancy Cartwright, voice of Bart Simpson, to start. Humor is definitely a theme among

Daytonians love their Dragons, who play single-A baseball at Fifth Third Field.

Daytonians who have risen to prominence. For some reason black-and-white photos of the grim-faced Wright brothers staring out from under their bowlers have given people the impression that Dayton is a serious place. Not true—at least not in a bad way—so in this case two Wrights have made a wrong. Laughter is the great equalizer, and Dayton is nothing if not of the people, friendly and welcoming.

Visitors to Dayton shouldn't take its vibrance for granted. Residents weathered some forgettable years in the seventies and eighties, and a rebound was long in coming. The best place to begin soaking up the city's culture and renewed energy is **RiverScape MetroPark,** which sits alongside the Great Miami River. RiverScape's centerpiece is the Five Rivers Fountain, an ongoing spectacle equivalent to Fourth of July fireworks. One of the largest fountains in the world, it shoots jets of water 200 feet in the air that form a fine backdrop for nighttime laser light shows. And RiverScape is much more than a one-trick pony: there's ice-skating in winter, HydroBike rentals in summer, relaxing landscaped gardens, a food pavilion, and "invention stations" showcasing some of Dayton's most popular innovations. *111 East Monument Avenue; 937-274-0126.*

Just a block or two away is another major downtown landmark, **Fifth Third Field,** not to be confused with the Toledo Mud Hens' Fifth Third Field. The Dayton ballpark is home to the Dayton Dragons, the Cincinnati Reds' single-A affiliate in the Midwest League. It has classic redbrick construction, an approachable scale, and great sight lines for the fans. There's a lot to like here, including minor-league ticket and concession prices. The Dragons have brought pro baseball back to Dayton for the first time since 1951, and their fans pack downtown Dayton on a regular basis during the season. *220 North Patterson Boulevard; 937-228-2287.*

A few blocks south of RiverScape and Fifth Third Field, the **Oregon Historic District** is Dayton's oldest neighborhood and a premier example of the city's urban revitalization. Bordered by Fifth Street on the north, Wayne Avenue on the east, Route 35 on the south, and Patterson Boulevard on the west, the twelve-block district has been on the upswing since the Oregon Historic District Society first met in 1973. In addition to restored and well-maintained homes—the oldest of which date to 1839 and are along Tecumseh Street—Oregon has great live music, including jazz at **Pacchia's Jazz Room** (406 East Fifth Street; 937-341-5050). There are vintage-clothing stores, several boutique restaurants, and comfortable neighborhood meeting spots such as the **Oregon Emporium** (410 East Fifth Street; 937-341-5011), a coffee shop that also has wine, draft beer, and pastries.

(top) Inside a hangar at the Air Force Museum. (above) A Boeing CIM-10A Bomarc accents the Air Force Museum entrance. (right) Kids try out a Sikorsky CH-124 Sea King at the Dayton Air Show.

Appropriately, given the invention that made it famous, Dayton is a headquarters for aviation and aerospace technology, with more than twenty thousand people employed in the industry, mainly because of Wright-Patterson Air Force Base. The city is also the southern extension of an automotive beltway that originates in Motown and runs through Toledo. Industry, you might scoff, doesn't tend to draw the tourists—unless you happen to have the world's largest military aviation museum and one of the world's largest air shows to go with it.

The **Air Force Museum** at Wright-Patt is the best place in the city to grasp what the Wrights' invention created and to follow the course of aviation history, from the *Wright Flyer* and a World War I–era Sopwith F-1 Camel to the SR-71 Blackbird and everything in between. And it's free. The museum has three hangars full of planes and is working on a fourth, and the interpretive exhibits and displays put the planes and flight in context in a way that textbooks never could. Naturally,

DAYTON PEACE ACCORDS

In the past ten years, two events have brought Dayton national attention. One was the 2003 centennial celebration of the Wright brothers' first flight. The other was the Dayton Peace Accords, which ended the Bosnia conflict in 1995. Even as many Americans now would be unable to pick out Bosnia-Herzegovina on a map, the agreements reached at Dayton among presidents Alija Izetbegovic of Bosnia-Herzegovina, Franjo Tudjman of Croatia, and Slobodan Milosevic of Yugoslavia have with international oversight helped establish a tentatively stable state.

President Clinton selected Dayton to host the talks because of Wright-Patterson Air Force Base and his desire to keep the leaders focused on the difficult work of drafting a peace agreement. Dayton proved up to the challenge. It also provided amply for the presidents' dining and entertainment pleasure, something Clinton and Milosevic might not have expected. "What, you are going to keep me locked up in Dayton, Ohio? I am not a priest, you know!" Milosevic said at the time. Izetbegovic, Tudjman, and Milosevic initialed the agreement at Dayton on November 21, 1995.

While the war in the Balkans had nothing to do with Dayton as a city, the historic event has made Dayton synonymous with peace. The legacy of the accords carries on with the Dayton Peace Prize, an international prize awarded annually on the anniversary of the Dayton agreement through the Dayton Peace Accords Project at the University of Dayton.

Wilbur Wright pilots the brothers' 1902 Wright Glider.

the **Dayton Air Show** is the aviation museum's ideal complement. The two-day air show, held in July near Dayton International Airport, is the city's major summer event. Expect a lot of heat, plenty of food, and the best air show you've ever seen. The event can draw a hundred thousand over two days to see stunt planes, barnstormers, precision flight formations, and jump teams. *1100 Spaatz Street; 937-255-3286.*

Another flight-related must-see is the **Wright Cycle Company** (22 South Williams Street; 937-225-7705), now part of the Dayton Aviation Heritage National Historical Park. Orville and Wilbur had always been mechanically inclined, first in the printing business (where they built their own printing press) and then with their bicycle shops (where they developed innovations they later applied to the problem of powered flight). This shop is actually the Wright's third bike shop, and the only one remaining in Dayton. (In 1937 Henry Ford moved the Wright home and a later Wright cycle shop, originally at 1127 West Third

(left) The Wright
Cycle Company,
part of the Dayton
Aviation Heritage
National Historical
Park, is the only
Wright bike shop
remaining in
Dayton. (inset)
Wilbur all decked
out at work in the
bicycle shop.

Street, to Greenfield Village, a sort of historic Disneyland in Dearborn, Michigan.) Aside from sales and repair, the brothers also designed bicycles, such as the VanCleve and St. Clair models. The serious sprocket-head and/or Wright historian should stop by **Cycles Gaansari** (1106 Brown Street; 937-222-8862), a local shop selling its own, modern replicas of Orville and Wilbur's designs as well as contemporary bikes.

For one-stop shopping, it's tough to beat **Carillon Park.** The iconic historical park is home to Deeds Carillon, the bell tower that gives the park its name, and the **John W. Berry, Sr. Wright Brothers Aviation Center.** The park's centerpiece, in the Wright Brothers Aviation Center, is the 1905 *Wright Flyer III,* the world's first practical airplane, which was restored in the 1940s based mostly on Orville's memories of it from forty years previous. The aviation center has one of the best collections in the country of Wright artifacts and historical materials. (In winter, it is open to the public by appointment only.) Like Greenfield Village in Dearborn, Michigan, Carillon Park brings together historically significant buildings and inventions into one easily traversed commons, capped by the **Kettering Family Education Center,** a good base of operations that has an overview video of the park, rotating educational exhibits, and concessions. *1000 Carillon Boulevard; 937-293-2841.*

■ **DAYTON ARTS**

The Dayton Aviation Heritage National Historical Park comprises four noncontiguous sites that recognize Dayton's most prominent historical figures. It thus unites the Wright brothers with another famous Daytonian who befriended the Wrights but found success on his own terms. The writer Paul Laurence Dunbar received wide critical acclaim in the 1890s while still in his twenties, an especially notable achievement because he was black and at that time no black poet had ever been recognized at such a level. Frederick Douglass met Dunbar at the 1893 World's Fair and called him "the most promising young colored man in America." White tastemakers in the United States and England hailed his work and fueled a career that eventually included twelve volumes of poetry and several novels and short story collections. The restored **Paul Laurence Dunbar House** (219 Paul Laurence Dunbar Street; 937-224-7061) is an example of a home at the turn of the 20th century. It includes many of Dunbar's original furnishings and possessions, such as his typewriter and a bike he bought from the Wrights.

Some of Dayton's cultural assets have come to light only with present-day research and documentation. The past fifteen years have brought heightened awareness of the importance of historical landscape design, and Daytonians have learned that the city has numerous Olmsted Brothers–designed landscape projects if not as many as New York and Boston. This is primarily because of John Patterson, the founder of the National Cash Register Company (now NCR Corporation). The Olmsteds were the country's premier landscape architects in the early 20th century, the son and nephew (who later became stepbrothers) of Frederick Law Olmsted Sr., who co-designed Central Park and is considered the father of American landscape architecture. Patterson commissioned the Olmsted Brothers firm to design **Hills and Dales Park** (2800 Patterson Boulevard; no phone) on NCR property; then he turned the park over to the city in 1918. Much of the Olmsteds' work in the park is preserved as a golf course, and some of what was the park became southwest Oakwood. Ridgeway Road in Oakwood, for example, was originally intended to be a park bridle trail. Other Olmsted-designed parks in Dayton include Carillon Park, Triangle Park, and the grounds surrounding the former Patterson home.

When a community's landscaping is fine art, you have to expect good things in the traditional realm too. Stewards of the **Dayton Art Institute** take great pride in managing a museum that is truly a public institution. General admission is free, and the institute makes it a point to reach out to underserved audiences. The building itself is something to be proud of, a tile-roofed Renaissance Revival beauty overlooking the Great Miami River from a hill northwest of downtown. As the Dayton area's only fine art museum, it offers a strong and eclectic mix of works, including contemporary American art, Asian art, and European art from the 1600s through the 1800s, as well as African and pre-Columbian art. *456 Belmonte Park North; 937-223-5277.*

SunWatch Indian Village/Archaeological Park represents a unique chance to participate in the research conducted at an active archaeological site. Right on the Great Miami, it might have made the ideal village site for the Fort Ancient Indians in the 1200s, but its position now on the southwest side of Dayton makes for odd company. There's a wastewater treatment plant to the north. To the west and south are city dumps. In the early seventies SunWatch was scheduled for a similar fate—to become a sewage treatment plant—before emergency excavations established it as a rare find, a site undisturbed following the Fort Ancient period and with almost everything remaining intact.

(above) Dayton's SunWatch Indian Village reconstructs the lives of the Fort Ancient Indians. (following spread) Cyclists on the Little Miami Scenic Trail whiz past Young's Jersey Dairy in Yellow Springs.

Public archaeology is an important force here. Two amateur archaeologists who excavated SunWatch in the mid-sixties had already documented its cultural value when development threatened. Dozens of volunteers came to help with the emergency excavations. And in its programs the park continues to focus on community partnership and educational outreach to explain how archaeological research works and to gain public support. It really is a village, not simply a site, reconstructed from the findings here and brought to life by site interpreters. A solar alignment pole marks the center of the village, and every part of the community—plaza, burial ground, ceremonial houses—radiates from that point. As with other Fort Ancient sites, astronomical alignment was important, whether for agricultural or religious reasons. Each year SunWatch hosts a sleepover for the winter solstice with nighttime tours, stories, and crafts. *2301 West River Road; 937-268-8199.*

■ YELLOW SPRINGS *map page 182, B-1*

Towns like Yellow Springs are supposed to be on the beach north of L.A., on Cape Cod, or paired with resorts in Colorado. When a town attains that rare combination of education, cultural appreciation, and a rebellious adherence to its individual character, the tourists, real estate brokers, and siding salesmen can't be far behind. Before long there's a docent stationed at the edge of town to take your admission and tell you how genuine the place used to be. So why spill the beans? Well, it hasn't been fed to the promotion machine yet, but it isn't exactly a secret either. A visitor from New York once commented, "Yellow Springs sort of reminds me of a theme park, only I can't figure out what the theme is." Anyway, anyone who hasn't been here wouldn't believe this is in Ohio. Shhh.

The first thing you notice about the village is its blessed community layout and natural resources. The Little Miami Scenic Trail, the converted railroad corridor that runs past Fort Ancient State Memorial, also passes through downtown Yellow Springs and continues north to Springfield. But you don't have to put your bike back on the roof rack once you're off the trail. The entire community is determinedly bike-friendly, with bike lanes, marked crossings, kiosks, and a development policy that's mindful of cyclists. If you don't ride, most everything's within walking distance anyway. Downtown, around Corry Street, Xenia Avenue, and Dayton Street, packs in old-school mom-and-pop stores, offbeat independent eateries, and professional services—including bookbinding and a range of alternative health services—all in a town of forty-six hundred. The shops and restaurants alone draw visitors from across the region.

Two miles east of town is **John Bryan State Park**, a 750-acre slice of the Miami River valley with the best views of any state park in southwest Ohio. Although older and smaller than many others in the state park system, John Bryan park is great for tent campers and usually less crowded than the other parks. Trails lead visitors to overlooks of the Little Miami River and Clifton Gorge, and to Clifton Mill, one of the largest water-powered gristmills in the world still in operation. John Bryan's plant diversity makes the Clifton Gorge State Nature Preserve (also part of the park) an important area for geological and botanical study. As with the Scioto River valley and Hocking Hills, you'll find plant species ordinarily common hundreds of miles north. *3790 Route 370; 513-767-1274.*

Glen Helen Nature Preserve is the biggest reason Yellow Springs feels close to nature and is the natural heart of the town. Immediately east of town and adjacent

to John Bryan State Park, the 1,000-acre preserve is home to forested hills, the iron-rich springs that gave the village its name, and the Glen Helen Ecology Institute, an education center dedicated to environmental awareness and stewardship, particularly for school-age children. (Like Glen Helen itself, the institute is owned by Antioch College.) The Raptor Center at Glen Helen rehabilitates birds for reintroduction to the wild and cares for permanently disabled birds, which are used in the center's educational efforts. In the 1800s Glen Helen's mineral springs were the basis for Yellow Springs' booming resort business. Visitors were drawn by the springs' palliative effects; today these visitors would be wearing ionic bracelets. *405 Corry Street; 937-767-7375.*

But Yellow Springs isn't just an environmental sanctuary. It's serious about art. Almost twenty galleries and studios dot the village and bring patrons in for the **Yellow Springs Street Fair** in June and October. **Chamber Music Yellow Springs,** a nonprofit that presents a premier concert series each year, grew out of residents' knowledge of and appreciation for chamber music and has developed an international reputation. Musicians enjoy not just large, enthusiastic audiences but also a private dinner and lodging with a host family during their stay. Antioch-affiliated radio station WYSO brings nuanced culture and music to town while also serving Dayton and Springfield.

Antioch, a celebrated liberal arts college and home to the prestigious Antioch Writers' Workshop, matches the town's funkiness step for step. Students at the mostly female college dream up the world they want to live in, and often the results are unlike anything else you'll find in the state. Independent thinking, social justice, and personal expression are top priorities. With those characteristics, however, comes what Antioch may be best known for nationally: its student-created Sexual Offense Prevention Policy. New students and visitors must sign a contract acknowledging they have read and understand the policy. In place since the early 1990s, it states, in part, "In order for 'consent' to be valid, all parties must have unimpaired judgment and a shared understanding of the nature of the act to which they are consenting including safer sex practices. The person who initiates sexual conduct is responsible for verbally asking for the 'consent' of the individual(s) involved. 'Consent' must be obtained with each new level of sexual conduct. . . . ." Depending on how participants approach an encounter, the policy could either work as verbal Viagra or emotional handcuffs, but it does illustrate a certain sensitivity and respect for boundaries that Antioch students value. (Word has it that a proposal allowing the initiator to secure consent using baseball metaphors failed.)

Fortunately, that respect for boundaries also extends to preservation of community identity, which should protect Yellow Springs' progressive culture and sustain outside fascination with a village that's simultaneously inclusive and exclusive.

■ TRAVEL BASICS

Getting Around: The two major thoroughfares in southwestern Ohio are I-71 and I-75. The latter runs from Cincinnati through Dayton and on north to Toledo and Detroit. Interstate 71 jogs northeast from Cincinnati to Columbus.

If you're exploring downtown Cincinnati, you'll find that many attractions are within easy walking distance of one another. The city's public bus system is easy to use, thoroughly covers the city, and typically offers reduced summer fares. Many outlying suburbs also have bus service, but these routes more commonly cater to commuters.

The Greater Dayton RTA provides comprehensive service in Dayton and Montgomery County, including some electric trolley buses, which only a handful of other U.S. cities have.

Tackling the rest of the region is best done by car. Yellow Springs is just east of Dayton off the I-675 loop on Dayton-Yellow Spring Road. Interstate 75 is notorious for snarling traffic and should be avoided when possible, especially during rush hour, but really any time. Outside the city, you'll find plenty of uncrowded country highways that make it easy to take in the rural charm.

Oxford is reachable from Cincinnati via U.S. 27. From north Dayton, take I-70 west to U.S. 127 south to Route 73 west; from south Dayton, take I-75 south to Route 73 west. No interstates serve the counties east of Cincinnati. Your best bet for reaching Clermont, Brown, Adams, and Highland counties is the Appalachian Highway—Route 32—or, for a scenic river drive, U.S. 52.

Climate: Be prepared to experience every season in full force. Spring brings abundant rain, and summer temperatures reach 100 degrees Fahrenheit for at least a few days each year, usually with high humidity. Smog warnings are a fixture in Cincinnati during the hottest days of summer. Winter temperatures are often below freezing, and there's a fair amount of snowfall that comes along with the cold. The beauty of the changing leaves and moderate temperatures make fall a perfect time to visit.

OLD NORTHWEST

The northwest corner of Ohio represents your best chance of finding wide-open spaces and unobstructed views, whether on the open plains or on Lake Erie, which laps at the region's northeastern shoulder. This was Ohio's last frontier, some of it pioneer country into the 1840s and 1850s, and it retains memories of epic struggles between Indians and the settlers and the British and the settlers. The Battle of Fallen Timbers, St. Clair's Defeat, and the Battle of Lake Erie all took place here.

Despite early military victories, the area remained sparsely settled for several reasons. Under the Treaty of Greenville, signed in 1795, this quarter of Ohio was reserved for Indians, and only later, when the tribes were relocated to reservations in the prairie states, did the land become available for pioneer farming and settlement. In addition, the land farthest north and west, along the Maumee River, was part of the reviled Black Swamp; it not only had to be cleared of trees but also had to be drained.

Things changed with the advent of machine-made drainage tiles in the 1850s, which made it easier to drain the land. More settlers came to take advantage of the incredibly fertile, virgin black soil. (Among other crops, the region leads the state in production of soybeans and wheat.) The good land attracted large numbers of Germans, and to this day northwest Ohio has a heavier German influence than most anywhere else in the state.

Even in the northwest, among the least densely populated and most agricultural of Ohio's regions, generalizations don't work. Farming is indeed big, but so is industry. The proximity of Detroit has resulted in a fair number of parts factories in such cities as Bowling Green and Defiance. Toledo is known as the Glass City for its decorative-glass and window-glass manufacturing. It is also an important shipping port.

The Lake Erie islands are Ohio's playground. Long a resort area, it has become increasingly popular with natives and visitors alike. They come for such one-of-a-kind attractions as Cedar Point Amusement Park, Put-in-Bay, and the world-class walleye fishing. Other parts of the Old Northwest bring pioneer history to life in re-created sites such as Sauder Village, Fort Recovery, and AuGlaize Village and at the Hayes Presidential Center.

The array of cities and towns here appears somewhat scattershot. The reasons for Toledo's location, the site of old strategic military forts at the western end of

(above) Put-in-Bay is recreation central on Lake Erie. (following spread) The village of Put-in-Bay touts a well-established tourism industry.

Lake Erie and on a major river and harbor, are easy enough to figure out, but what about Lima or Findlay? What are they doing out here all by themselves? Both began as agricultural centers and got extra boosts from an area oil boom in the late 1800s. Later, bigger wells in Oklahoma, Texas, and elsewhere foreshortened Ohio's importance in oil production. In addition, Findlay grew irrationally exuberant in the 1880s over the discovery of natural gas, but that supply lasted only about twenty years.

Some towns followed the transportation lines of old. Piqua and Troy, for example, are on the upper stretches of the Great Miami River and the old Miami & Erie Canal route, which cut north to Defiance, far west of I-75, and followed the Maumee River down to Toledo.

Other towns grew from frontier forts and garrisons, including Fort Stephenson (Fremont), Fort Green Ville (Greenville), and Fort Defiance (Defiance). Sandusky, the site of an old British fort, arguably has the greatest location in the northwest: it's on a beautiful natural bay, just across the way from the Lake Erie islands. At a glance it would appear a more attractive location than either Toledo or Cleveland,

and yet it's many times smaller than either city. In 1825 canal legislation made Sandusky the unfortunate loser in a battle for the northern terminus of the Ohio & Erie Canal. Survey teams had determined that the Sandusky River watershed didn't have enough water to sustain a canal route, and Sandusky suffered.

Not that Sandusky didn't recover well from that slight of a hundred and eighty years ago. It's making up for the loss with a steady diet of vacationing millions every year and probably thumbing its collective nose at the flash-in-the-pan canal towns that stole its glory. Those are the breaks in a land of bounty and caprice that holds Ohio's marshiest lowlands and the state's highest point, Campbell Hill. This place, the Old Northwest, expects you to roll with the punches, but it also does its best to provide soft landings.

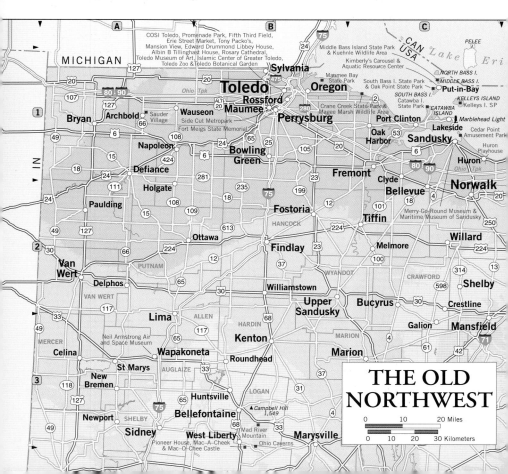

THE OLD NORTHWEST

■ **LAKE ERIE ISLANDS** *map page 258, C-1*

A coast dweller from California, Massachusetts, or Florida might scoff about the merits of an Ohio beach, but the Lake Erie islands—Catawba, South Bass, Middle Bass, North Bass, and Kelleys—are great examples of what the country's North Coast has to offer. Fishermen flock to western Lake Erie, the Walleye Capital of the World, where the shallow waters are thick with oversize walleye and many other sport fish. The scene is intimate and informal, like one giant state park. In fact, each of the main islands has at least one state park or some other accessible, publicly administered land. And you don't have to fish to appreciate boating on the lake in the peak of an Ohio summer, with warm breezes, clear water, a rugged coastline, and a matrix of islands that call out for exploration. Nowhere else on the lake are there so many islands in one place.

The islands' most famous seafarer came early in American history. Commodore Oliver Hazard Perry dispensed with British naval captain Robert Barclay and his fleet of six, including the mighty brig *Detroit,* northwest of South Bass Island in 1813. **Perry's Victory and International Peace Memorial,** a 352-foot-tall Greek Doric column on South Bass, commemorates the battle and Perry's legacy and provides sweeping Lake Erie views from the observation deck (419-285-2184).

Perry also discovered a limestone cave 52 feet below the surface of South Bass. Now known as **Perry's Cave,** it was used by Perry's men as a supply cache and a source of drinking water during the war. A large underground lake there also once supplied drinking water for South Bass's Victory Hotel before it burned in 1919. The cave is now privately owned. Tours, including nighttime "lantern tours," reveal the origins of the cave and its history and provide a new perspective on the culture above ground.

The islands' riches drew early attention for their economic potential rather than their resort possibilities. Good farmland nurtured a nascent wine-making industry. Limestone quarries sprang up and are still there today. Visitors to Marblehead will notice the huge conveyor belts used to transport quarry rock for shipment.

Both Port Clinton and Sandusky are jumping-off points for excursions to the Lake Erie islands, though they're certainly worthwhile in their own right. Ferry companies offer service to the main islands from both cities, as does the town of Marblehead, and the most choices for restaurants tend to lie in those three places. Because it's connected to the mainland, Catawba Island tends to get lumped together with Port Clinton and Marblehead Peninsula. But until the Army Corps of Engineers diverted the Portage River, which enters the lake west of Catawba, it really was an island and has much the same character and opportunities as the other Lake Erie isles.

Two main draws, as elsewhere on the lake, are the wineries and the fishing. The island's name comes from the Catawba grape, and as you'd expect, grape growing and wine making are a way of life here. Cincinnati's Nicholas Longworth introduced the American Catawba vines to Ohio, and farmers soon learned that the Lake Erie climate was perfect for the grape. It's so favorable that the ultraproductive land along the shore is today known as the Lake Erie Grape Belt. **Catawba Island State Park** (4049 East Moores Dock Road; 419-797-4530) is the headquarters of the Lake Erie state parks (including **South Bass Island State Park; Oak Point State Park,** also on South Bass; Kelleys Island State Park; and Middle Bass Island State Park) and offers prime lake access via a four-ramp boat launch and a pier for those opting to fish from shore. In addition, outfits around the area offer boat rentals. Catawba has three well-protected harbors on the east side of the island, home to myriad marinas, and the added advantage of being accessible by car. Swimmers can journey a mile or two north to Gem Beach, a pleasant, sandy beach studded with vacation cottages and rentals.

South Bass Island, known simply as **Put-in-Bay,** epitomizes the Lake Erie islands experience. (Put-in-Bay is the name of the island's only village, as well as the crescent-shaped bay on the north side of the island.) The well-established tourism industry and nightlife on South Bass—its Beer Barrel Saloon has the world's longest bar—have earned it a reputation for out-of-control partying and debauchery, but the truth is you'll find what you look for here. There's great fishing, boating, kayaking, and plenty of other family-friendly activities and sites, including the Perry memorial, mentioned above. **Kimberly's Carousel** (160 Delaware Avenue; 419-285-2212) is a perennial favorite with kids and one of the last working carousels to use wooden horses—as well as zebras and fish. North of downtown Put-in-Bay, the Ohio Division of Wildlife runs the **Aquatic Resource Center** (1 Peach Point; 419-285-3701), which features displays of live fish and provides a free rod and bait for children to fish from the dock. Vehicles are permitted on the island, but at just over 3 miles wide, it's better suited to walking or using smaller-scale transportation. Vendors on the island rent golf carts and bikes.

Middle Bass Island is about half the size of South Bass and has far fewer amenities, although it has seen more development in recent years. This is the place to get

The walkable streets of Put-in-Bay cater to visitors.

away from it all. In 2001 the Ohio Department of Natural Resources turned 124 acres of the old Lonz Winery into **Middle Bass Island State Park** (419-285-0311). Plans for facilities are progressing slowly, so for now the island's biggest asset is a fifty-slip marina with some electrical hookups. Birders should head to **Kuehnle Wildlife Area** (no phone), a wetland rich with fauna, where the island's northeastern finger meets the main body. Adventurers can now enjoy a similar experience on formerly privately owned North Bass Island (also called Isle St. George), just 2 miles from the Canadian border. With help from federal funds, the state initiated a plan in December 2003 to purchase 589 acres, nearly 90 percent of the island, for primitive recreation and study. This will not be a state park, but visitors will have the chance to hike, fish, hunt, and explore the island hideaway.

Kelleys Island is the sleeper hit in the group, and it radiates the charm of a New England island retreat. Very much residential, the entire island is on the National Register of Historic Places. Kelleys is something of a Golden Mean between South Bass and Middle Bass. There are places to eat, drink, and revel, but that aspect is smaller, less intense, and balanced by peaceful coastal neighborhoods and 676-acre **Kelleys Island State Park** (419-746-2546). The park lies at the north end of the island, where broad, swimmer-friendly Sandy Beach awaits. Nearby are the **Glacial Grooves**, a 400-foot-long strip of glacier-carved limestone that proves the Lake Erie islands didn't escape the same Ice Age scouring that created Lake Erie. As on South Bass, visitors can rent bikes or golf carts to negotiate the island.

Unless ferry patrons at Kelleys Island are heading to Put-in-Bay, they'll likely end up in Marblehead, on the Marblehead Peninsula. This charming resort town is home to the venerable **Marblehead Lighthouse,** the oldest continually operating lighthouse on the Great Lakes, since 1822. It's one of the most photographed subjects on Lake Erie, and once you see it, it's not hard to understand why. The squat limestone lighthouse seems to grow right out of the rock. The site, which comprises 13 acres and a refurbished keeper's house, became Ohio's seventy-third state park in 1998. It's a fine place for a picnic.

For someone staying in Port Clinton, Sandusky, or on Catawba Island, driving down Marblehead Peninsula makes a peaceful afternoon trip. Don't miss Lakeside, a deliberately non-commercial retreat, a Chautauqua full of tidy rustic cottages and solitude. The eminent Lakeside Symphony offers additional cultural enrichment every summer. Much of the peninsula is residential or agricultural and provides a good orientation to your surroundings. To the north lie the islands, with Kelleys the closest. To the south is Sandusky Bay. And to the southeast, appearing in the distance as Kong-sized coils of razor wire, is Cedar Point, a coaster rider's ultimate challenge.

■ CEDAR POINT AND SANDUSKY *map page 258, C-1*

If **Cedar Point** sat along a fault line in the middle of the desert, it would still be an irresistible destination. Instead it occupies a sandy peninsula midway between Cleveland and Toledo (and not far from Detroit) that Disney would envy. But don't come looking for magic castles or monorails. What brings people from all over the country here are the thrill rides. Cedar Point has the highest concentration found anywhere. (The trade magazine *Amusement Today* has named Cedar Point the best amusement park in the world five years running.) There is also an 18-acre water park right on the beach.

In 2003 Cedar Point unveiled Top Thrill Dragster, the tallest, fastest roller coaster in the world. The Dragster launches riders down a strip of track that rises 420 feet, twists 270 degrees on the descent, and flings the passenger trains up to 120 mph before returning riders to the station to retrieve their stomachs and underwear. Better double-check that safety harness. Cedar Point has a long history of record-breaking coasters, including the 310-foot, 93-mph Millennium Force and the 205-foot, 72-mph Magnum XL-200.

Clearly this is a park that has no patience for being No. 2. But the dazzling location can also be a drawback from a park administrator's perspective. There isn't the endless surrounding acreage to plan new rides and seal off pedestrians from the flailing riders above as in some amusement parks. Structural skeletons and steel track frequently cross walkways and are sometimes in your face, which can make the vicarious experience all the more immediate. *One Cedar Point Drive; 419-627-2350.*

Expect a similar atmosphere at **Soak City,** Cedar Point's beachfront water park. Believe it or not, you never have to set foot in Lake Erie to get wet. Soak City has the requisite waterslides, tube rides, giant wave pool, and toddler area, as well as a swim-up bar for adults. Or patrons can also hit the real beach, on the east side of the peninsula, to sink toes in sand, play volleyball, or parasail on the lake. Two marinas, Cedar Point Marina and Castaway Bay Marina, allow boaters to dock near the park.

Sandusky is more than just a tourist town. Once upon a time, fishing was the city's greatest industry, and it continues in Sandusky's role as a Great Lakes shipping port. Sheltered Sandusky Bay provides safe harbor for countless watercraft. The **Maritime Museum of Sandusky** celebrates that legacy. Across from Battery

(above) Swimming has always been a favorite pastime at Cedar Point. (following spread) Marblehead Lighthouse has guided boats on Lake Erie since 1822.

Park, not far from where ferries arrive and depart, the museum features exhibits on passenger boats and freighters, information on early Ohio boatbuilders, artifacts, and special exhibits on Lyman Boat Works, a Sandusky institution from the twenties into the seventies. It also hosts boatbuilding classes and a lecture series. *125 Meigs Street; 419-624-0274.*

The **Merry-Go-Round Museum** is entirely at home in Sandusky. The museum takes visitors back to a simpler time, when an elegant carousel was the height of entertainment at Cedar Point. Opened in 1990, it has a fully restored, ready-to-ride Allen Herschell carousel, but it also emphasizes the artistry and craftsmanship involved in building these masterpieces. Often volunteer carvers will demonstrate how the wooden figures are made and discuss carousel art. Museum volunteers also restore antique carousel figures and parts, and visitors can watch the process. *301 Jackson Street; 419-626-6111.*

Ten miles east of Sandusky, the **Huron Playhouse** (325 Ohio Street; 419-433-4744) offers great summer theater in Huron, a charming lakeshore community.

(right) Riders can hit 93 mph on the Millennium Force.
(inset) The Leap Frog Scenic Railway at Cedar Point in 1920.

Small-Town Ohio

Not far from the lakeshore, the tenor of a town can change dramatically. In *Winesburg, Ohio,* author Sherwood Anderson wrote about a dark side to small-town life that residents of Clyde at the time wished he had ignored. Anderson grew up in Clyde, near Fremont and the Lake Erie coast, and he drew on his experiences there for the grim characters and sketches that make up *Winesburg, Ohio* and for other works, such as *Windy McPherson's Son* and *Poor White.* Anderson is better known for the writers he influenced, like Hemingway and Faulkner, than for his own work, yet Clyde as a town has welcomed Anderson back into the fold with a commemorative plaque. This excerpt comes from the chapter of *Winesburg, Ohio* that's titled "The Untold Lie, concerning Ray Pearson."

[Ray] began to think of the time, long ago when he was a young fellow living with his father, then a baker in Winesburg, and how on such days he had wandered away into the woods to gather nuts, hunt rabbits, or just to loaf about and smoke his pipe. His marriage had come about through one of his days of wandering. He had induced a girl who waited on trade in his father's shop to go with him and something had happened. He was thinking of that afternoon and how it had affected his whole life when a spirit of protest awoke in him. He had forgotten about Hal and muttered words. "Tricked by Gad, that's what I was, tricked by life and made a fool of," he said in a low voice.

As though understanding his thoughts, Hal Winters spoke up. "Well, has it been worth while? What about it, eh? What about marriage and all that?" he asked and then laughed. Hal tried to keep on laughing but he too was in an earnest mood. He began to talk earnestly. "Has a fellow got to do it?" he asked. "Has he got to be harnessed up and driven through life like a horse?"

Hal didn't wait for an answer but sprang to his feet and began to walk back and forth between the corn shocks. He was getting more and more excited.

Bending down suddenly he picked up an ear of the yellow corn and threw it at the fence. "I've got Nell Gunther in trouble," he said. "I'm telling you, but you keep your mouth shut."

Ray Pearson arose and stood staring. He was almost a foot shorter than Hal, and when the younger man came and put his two hands on the elder man's shoulders they made a picture. There they stood in the big empty field with the quiet corn shocks standing in rows behind them and the red and yellow hills in the distance, and from being just two indifferent workmen they had become all alive to each other. Hal sensed it and because that was his way he laughed. "Well, old daddy," he said awkwardly, "come on, advise me. I've got Nell in trouble. Perhaps you've been in the same fix yourself. I know what everyone would say is the right thing to do, but what do you say? Shall I marry and settle down? Shall I put myself into the harness to be worn out like an old horse? You know me, Ray. There can't anyone break me but I can break myself. Shall I do it or shall I tell Nell to go to the devil? Come on, you tell me. Whatever you say, Ray, I'll do."

Ray couldn't answer. He shook Hal's hands loose and turning walked straight away toward the barn. He was a sensitive man and there were tears in his eyes. He knew there was only one thing to say to Hal Winters, son of old Windpeter Winters, only one thing that all his own training and all the beliefs of the people he knew would approve, but for his life he couldn't say what he knew he should say.

—Sherwood Anderson, *Winesburg, Ohio,* 1919

■ LAKE ERIE VINEYARDS *map page 258, C-1*

It's hardly possible to discuss the Lake Erie vacationland without bringing up wine. Though southwest Ohio was known for grape growing first, the Lake Erie plains have long since surpassed it. Vineyards have been a staple here since the middle of the 19th century, when the region became a resort destination because of its sandy beaches and unique geography. Farmers found the vines did well, thanks to Lake Erie's warming effect. Despite being only 25 to 30 feet deep, the same relatively warm waters that produce trophy walleye also contribute to the longest frost-free season in the state.

In wineries, northwest Ohio's agricultural economy meets its tourism economy. A trip along the shore or on any of the islands will prove the prevalence of vineyards and the wineries that often accompany them. Among the players: Mon Ami on Catawba Island, Firelands in Sandusky, Heineman's in Put-in-Bay, and Kelleys Island Wine Co. on Kelleys Island. Just a few miles to the north, Canada's Pelee Island Winery is that country's largest estate winery.

When you want to get off the lake and spend a little time relaxing, the wineries are a good option. Many offer tours, restaurants, and gift shops. It's easy to spend half a day in one. North Bass Island, most of which the state recently bought in the name of preservation, doesn't have a winery, but it does have about 85 acres of vineyards that the Ohio Department of Natural Resources will continue to cultivate under contract for Firelands Winery.

At one time Ohio viticulture revolved around native grapes, but wineries today often use a range of species, American and European, that produce very drinkable, respected wines. Riesling, cabernet sauvignon, and chardonnay are among the choices. Some also are now making ice wine, a sweet dessert wine made by leaving grapes on the vine to freeze, which concentrates the sugars. It has a smooth, sweet finish. If hummingbirds could uncork a bottle, this is what they would drink.

■ TOLEDO *map page 258, B-1*

Toledo was once a city on the edge. Two years after the villages of Port Lawrence and Vistula combined to form Toledo in 1833, Ohio set off a border war with Michigan that had been festering for thirty years. Toledo was in Michigan Territory then, although that border was disputed, and Ohio planned to send its Miami & Erie Canal to the city. Michigan's governor sent a militia to the border, Ohio's governor countered, and things got heated. President Andrew Jackson, who favored Ohio, gave the state Toledo and awarded statehood and the Upper Peninsula to Michigan. The two states have hated each other ever since.

Turns out it was all a misunderstanding. Inaccurate maps used for the Northwest Ordinance of 1787 put Michigan's border farther north than it should have been, and this incorrect boundary was made official when Ohio became a state in 1803. Michigan resurveyed a few years later when it was planning for statehood and discovered the border mistake, but by then it was too late. Toledo went on to become an important canal link, a hugely successful port, and a perpetual burr in Michigan's saddle.

Later on, as railroads connected the city's port with interior markets and the country's population moved westward, Toledo suddenly found itself in the middle of everything. Edward Libbey and Michael Owens brought their New England Glass Company to Toledo to take advantage of cheap natural gas. They renamed it the Libbey Glass Company and spawned a towering legacy for Toledo. As Akron did with its rubber industry, Toledo adjusted to take advantage of the new markets that arose when glass became important for automobiles. Inside the triangle created by Chicago, Cleveland, and Detroit, Toledo grew into an important manufacturing and trade center as well as a safe house for gangsters on the run in those cities. If you needed to lay low for a while and shake the heat, you went to Toledo.

In the forties, Toledo's Willys-Overland Motors built an all-terrain military vehicle for World War II. The Jeep proved to have enormous commercial appeal after the war as veterans sought out the reliable vehicles that had gotten them through combat. Daimler Chrysler owns the company now, but Jeeps are still made in Toledo, and this connotes a rugged, modest, all-American image of the city that meshes nicely with reality.

In the seventies and eighties the city floated back toward the edge, an uncertain economic fate, that it once knew. Location alone couldn't offset the job losses and crumbling downtown core, and it lacked the sheer size of a first-tier city to carry it through tough times. Fortunately, officials took a hard look at the problems and in plotting solutions have emphasized the downtown core and overall livability, by adapting existing structures to new uses, encouraging residential living, and instituting pedestrian-friendly streetscapes.

(above) Toledo's river trade bustles in 1876. (following spread) A fire department rescue boat cruises down the Maumee River in downtown Toledo.

■ DOWNTOWN

Perhaps the most impressive thing about downtown Toledo is that there *is* a downtown. Many Ohio downtowns have returned from the brink of unredeemable decay in the past twenty years, but Toledo's downtown arguably had the furthest to go. Downtown Toledo was a shell twenty-five years ago, and residents held out little hope that it could be improved. Auspiciously, vacant buildings were spared renewal programs and simply stood empty until the time was right for redevelopment. Those old structures, including the Oliver House, Pythian Castle, and the Valentine Building, are now among downtown's greatest assets.

Toledo's downtown is not on Lake Erie but along the Maumee just before the river hits Toledo Harbor. One of the biggest fish in town is fiberglass giant **Owens Corning,** which has a $100 million glassed-in headquarters on the riverfront.

Just a few blocks away is the Center of Science and Industry, or **COSI Toledo** (One Discovery Way; 419-244-2674), which continued the downtown revitalization when it opened in 1997 in the old Portside development, a failed eighties shopping center. COSI is designed for kids and secretly makes learning fun with sections like Whiz Bank Engineering Learning World, where you can practice, for example, building bridges, animating with digital technology, and designing soda bottles.

Just outside COSI, **Promenade Park** runs along the river between Jefferson Avenue and Cherry Street. Promenade is the epicenter of outdoor activity downtown and is the place to be for events such as the Fourth of July fireworks and the Toledo Blues Festival. It's also a good place to take a breather and get your bearings as you navigate downtown. Around the corner, to the south, baseball fans are flocking to the Mud Hens' new home, **Fifth Third Field** (406 Washington Street; 419-725-4367). The stadium, in the Warehouse District, turned out right. It's both classic and contemporary and has an urban, in-the-middle-of-it-all feel—which, believe it or not, many downtown stadiums can't manage. Moreover, it's helping people remember downtown again, a legacy that the Mud Hens, the oldest and one of the best-known teams in the minor leagues, can be proud of.

By contrast, the **Erie Street Market** (237 South Erie Street; 419-936-2096) has been bringing people downtown for ninety years, minus a rough patch here and there. The market's history is a microcosm of downtown's. Once an open-air market, it was turned into Civic Auditorium in the 1920s when the city's need for meeting space grew. In the sixties it got mothballed amid competition from newer facilities. The renovated market debuted in 1997 and is more of a neighborhood mall and supermarket combo, in the best sense of the words; it features fresh seafood, a deli, a bakery, gift shops, an antiques mall, and a Libbey Factory Outlet. The adjacent outdoor farmers' market comes to life twice a week April through November.

Toledo has a lot of German descendants, but as Jamie Farr's Corporal Klinger indirectly explained, it saw legion immigration from Eastern Europe. On *M*A*S*H* Klinger was always stumping for **Tony Packo's** (1902 Front Street; 419-691-6054) and its "Hungarian hot dogs," which have been a local favorite going back to the 1930s. The original Packo's dog is split down the middle and served on a bun with mustard, onions, and a zesty chili. The Front Street location, east of the Maumee,

Hungarian hot dogs made Tony Packo's famous.

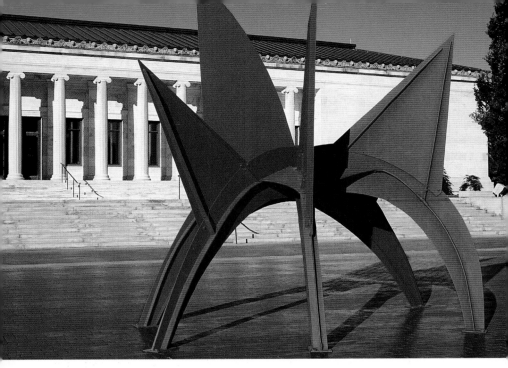

Alexander Calder's Stegosaurus *stands guard in front of the Toledo Museum of Art.*

is the same one used seventy years ago, with a little allowance for expansion. Here you'll find synthetic hot dog buns signed by an array of celebrities, a tradition Burt Reynolds started in 1972. A trip to Toledo without eating at Tony Packo's is not a trip to Toledo, you might say.

■ OLD WEST END

Perhaps better than anything else you could visit in Toledo, the homes and churches of the Old West End illustrate the city that was, with its grandeur, ostentation, and fabulously diverse Victorian architecture: Tudor, Queen Anne, Romanesque, Georgian, Dutch Colonial, and on and on. This was where people with money lived at the turn of the last century, before it became the *Old* West End to differentiate it from neighborhoods being built farther west. Neighborhood preservation caught on early, in the 1940s, before homes had a chance to deteriorate on a broad scale. Some call it one of the best-kept secrets in historical architecture.

The Old West End is bordered by Collingwood on the east, Monroe on the south, Detroit on the west, and Central on the north. The most elaborate and well-maintained showplaces tend to be in the southeastern section, although the entire neighborhood is on the National Register of Historic Places. To really do it justice, get out on foot and take in the homes at a slower pace. There are too many flourishes and details you'll miss from behind the wheel of a car. Dozens of homes warrant a closer look, and though they are mostly private residences, twice a year, in June and December, select homes are open for public tours. Don't miss **Mansion View** (2035 Collingwood Boulevard), a former bed-and-breakfast built with brick in the Queen Anne style; it is owned by the Old West End Association. Also worth strolling by are the **Edward Drummond Libbey House** (2008 Scottwood Avenue), a Shingle-classical hybrid belonging to the founder and president of the Libbey Glass Company, and the **Albin B. Tillinghast House** (2210 Robinwood Avenue), a Tudor-Gothic concoction with a mansard roof and three huge chimneys. Tillinghast never lived in the monstrosity, but automaker John North Willys of Willys-Overland (original makers of the Jeep) did.

Collingwood is the neighborhood's main drag. Although many of the homes that once lined the block have disappeared, the churches have not. There are seven on Collingwood alone, including the **Rosary Cathedral.** Credited with keeping Catholics in the neighborhood, the cathedral honors Toledo's namesake with its Spanish Plateresque style. As intricate and unusual as the exterior is, the interior matches its beauty and style. Generous use of stained glass and gold detailing creates a warm glow, while Felix Lieftuchter's sweeping ceiling frescoes illustrate the stories of Christ in blue and gold hues. It's a miracle the cathedral was ever finished. Construction began in 1925 but didn't end until 1940, and most of the building occurred during the Depression. *2535 Collingwood Boulevard; 419-244-9575.*

On the south side of Monroe, within sight of the Libbey house, is the **Toledo Museum of Art.** This is a fitting location, since Edward Libbey and his wife, Florence Scott Libbey, provided the impetus, spirit, and much of the funding for the original museum, subsequent expansions, and the collection. They also donated artwork. The museum showcases world-class works in all the usual genres—American, European, Asian, African, modern—but is also famous for its Art in Glass collection, a perfect reflection of Libbey and the Glass City. In mid-2006 the museum plans to open the Glass Pavilion, a cutting-edge, almost totally transparent building that will house the glass collection. (Note that much of this work won't be on display until the pavilion opens.) *2445 Monroe Street; 419-255-8000.*

■ MUSLIM TOLEDO

Toledo has been a landing spot for Arab immigrants since the beginning of the 20th century. For years the north side of Toledo, where Arab-Americans tended to congregate, was known as Little Syria, and in 1959 Toledo became the first major American city with an Arab-American mayor when Mike Damas, a Lebanese-American, was elected.

The early Arab immigrants were mostly Christians from Syria and Lebanon. The creation of Israel in 1948 and subsequent waves of conflict destabilized the Middle East and brought Muslim Egyptians, Palestinians, Jordanians, and others in great numbers. This would challenge notions of religious tolerance. In addition, a revised immigration policy in the mid-sixties opened the door to more Middle Easterners.

Toledo might seem a surprising choice for new immigrants, but it's only an hour's drive from both Detroit and Dearborn, which is the center of Arab America, a place where phone books, signage, and newspapers are often in Arabic as well as in English.

In the late sixties and early seventies, Toledo's Muslim population grew so fast that the original mosque at Bancroft and Cherry was becoming overcrowded, and leaders began making plans to build a larger one. That came to fruition in 1984 as the **Islamic Center of Greater Toledo** (25877 Scheider Road, Perrysburg; 419-874-3509), one of the most beautiful mosques in North America and a major platform for making connections to the larger community.

More surprising than Toledo's large Muslim population, which numbers around fifteen thousand, has been wider ignorance of its importance, or even its existence. Betsy Hiel referenced the Islamic Center in a *Toledo Blade* story in 2000 about the Arab-American experience. "When the 26,000-foot base and 60-foot-high dome of white brick was built, some local residents thought it was a palace for a farmer's wife. When the 135-foot twin minarets were being put in place, others thought they were missile silos. When the two-story, thirty-room structure with an octagonal carpeted prayer room was completed, still others thought it was a Mexican restaurant."

In the wake of September 11, Toledo Muslims have taken a leadership role in drawing distinctions between their religion and the political extremists who claim it. Toledoans figured prominently in the PBS documentary *Islam in America After*

The Islamic Center of Greater Toledo serves as an elegant ambassador.

September 11th, a film lauded for its nuanced portrayal of American Muslims' lives in the age of war on terror. Some Muslims have been in Toledo fifty years or more. But more recent immigrants also are well educated and often work in professional fields, as educators, engineers, and doctors. Many are business owners. The influence of Muslims on the city will only increase as the local Muslim population continues to grow.

■ TOLEDO OUTDOORS

Even if you count the Lake Erie islands as a separate destination, Toledo has an abundance of wildlife and outdoor recreational opportunities. (One of its nicknames is Frogtown, a nod to its ex-swamp status and the vociferous frogs that inhabited it.) Exhibit A is the **Toledo Zoo,** called one of the best in the country. The city's top tourist attraction, which lies about 4 miles south of downtown, exhibits four hundred species and is well known for its African Savanna, which includes the popular Hippoquarium. *2700 Broadway; 419-385-5721.*

On the west side of town, the **Toledo Botanical Garden** is a beautiful place to walk and marvel at 5 acres of perennials, ferns, herbs, and wildflowers. The Village Garden section has art studios and galleries to explore, and July and August bring a weekly Jazz in the Garden event. *5403 Elmer Drive; 419-936-2982.*

To study Toledo's coastal environment, you can head to **Maumee Bay State Park** (1400 State Park Road; 419-836-7758), which sits on the bay just east of Toledo, or **Crane Creek State Park** (13531 West Route 2; 419-836-7758), which is farther east, near Oak Harbor. Maumee Bay is a more developed state park, with a lodge and golf course. Crane Creek, a small state park, is a good base from which to observe and explore neighboring **Magee Marsh Wildlife Area** (13229 West Route 2; 419-898-0960), which was spared from development because of its value for duck hunting. In fact, both Maumee Bay and Magee Marsh present incredible birding opportunities. Egrets, herons, and several dozen other species might be spotted here in a single day. Directly north of Crane Creek is **West Sister Island,** the largest heron and egret rookery on the Great Lakes and the only federally designated wilderness area in Ohio. West Sister Island is part of the Ottawa National Wildlife Refuge and is not open to the public.

History runs deep in the northwest, and parks around Toledo preserve that too. **Side Cut Metropark,** in Maumee, for years held a plaque identifying the park as the site of the Battle of Fallen Timbers, the decisive American victory that paved the way for settlement and statehood. In 1995 a local anthropologist determined

Oliver Perry directs his men to the Niagara *during the Battle of Lake Erie.*

that the site actually lay a quarter mile away, so Toledo Metroparks has since purchased land on that site for incorporation into the park. *1025 River Road; 419-535-3057.*

Fort Meigs State Memorial also holds historic value. Built in 1813 to defend Ohio against the British, Fort Meigs is the country's largest log fort. The memorial hosts reenactments and interpretive events every summer. In 2003 it staged a grand reopening in time for the Ohio Bicentennial to show off recently completed renovations and a new visitors center. *29100 West River Road, Perrysburg; 419-874-4121.*

Sauder Village also lends an immediacy to history. Farmers and craftspeople here carry on their business just as they would have a hundred and fifty years ago. Many of the buildings are authentic structures that were relocated to create the village. This is an immersion experience. Watch the blacksmith, silversmith, potter, cooper, broom maker, and others make their wares, which are also available for sale. Little Pioneers Homestead provides hands-on activities for the younger kids. The village also has a restaurant, country inn, and performance center. *22611 Route 2, Archbold; 800-590-9755.*

■ NEIL ARMSTRONG MAKES HISTORY

On July 20, 1969, Neil Armstrong became the first person to walk on the moon. The *Apollo 11* mission that Armstrong, Edwin "Buzz" Aldrin, and Michael Collins flew, and specifically Armstrong and Aldrin's moon landing, reconstructed the human perspective about what is possible, our place in the order of things, and what lies beyond. Yet those who learned of these men's deeds from teachers and history books often lack an appreciation for that shift and for how daring and committed the astronauts and the entire NASA program truly were. Armstrong grew up in Wapakoneta, along I-75 about an hour north of Dayton, and walked on the moon just thirty months after NASA had suspended Apollo test missions in the wake of the death of three astronauts on the launch pad aboard *Apollo 1*. Collins himself gave the *Apollo 11* mission fifty-fifty odds.

The **Neil Armstrong Air and Space Museum** in Wapakoneta covers the astronaut's accomplishments but focuses more on the history of flight and space exploration. The *Gemini VIII* capsule that Armstrong and David Scott piloted is here.

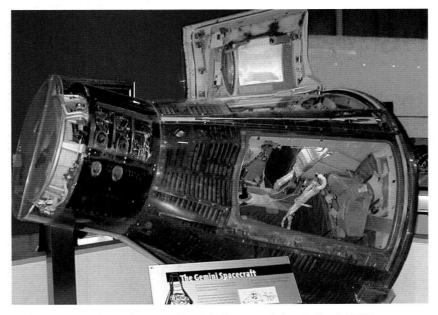

Neil Armstrong and David Scott completed the first space docking in Gemini VIII.

A New Space

We landed on the Sea of Tranquility, in the cool of the early lunar morning, when the long shadows would aid our perception.

The sun was only ten degrees above the horizon, while the earth turned through nearly a full day during our stay, the sun at Tranquility Base rose barely eleven degrees—a small fraction of the month-long lunar day. There was a peculiar sensation of the duality of time—the swift rush of events that characterizes all our lives—and the ponderous parade which makes the aging of the universe.

Both kinds of time were evident—the first by the routine events of the flight—whose planning and execution were detailed to fractions of a second—the latter by rocks round us, unchanged throughout the history of man—whose three-billion-year-old secrets made them the treasures we sought.

The plaque on the "Eagle" which summarized our hopes bears this message: "Here Men from the Planet Earth First Set Foot upon the Moon, July 1969 A.D."

We came in peace for all mankind whose nineteen hundred and sixty-nine years had constituted the majority of the age of Pisces—a twelfth of the great year that is measured by the thousand generations the precession of the earth's axis requires to scribe a giant circle in the heavens.

In the next twenty centuries, the age of Aquarius of the great year, the age for which our young people have such high hopes, humanity may begin to understand its most baffling mystery—where are we going? The earth is, in fact, traveling many thousands of miles per hour in the direction of the constellation Hercules—to some unknown destination in the cosmos. Man must understand his universe in order to understand his destiny.

Mystery, however, is a very necessary ingredient in our lives.

Mystery creates wonder and wonder is the basis for man's desire to understand. Who knows what mysteries will be solved in our lifetime, and what new riddles will become the challenge of the new generations? Science has not mastered prophesy. We predict too much for next year yet far too little for the next ten. Responding to challenge is one of democracy's great strengths. Our successes in space lead us to hope that this strength can be used in the next decade in the solution of many of our planet's problems.

—Neil A. Armstrong, September 16, 1969, before a joint session of Congress

So are Armstrong's space suit, a moon rock, and astronaut food samples. (Imagine freeze-dried baby food in foil and plastic.) There's an exhibit on Armstrong's career, a planetarium, and a Lunar Landing Simulator where you can test your skill at landing a lunar module. It's not hard to pick out the Armstrong museum from the interstate: it's the only building that looks like the moon rising on a stage. *I-75 and Apollo Drive; 800-860-0142.*

■ **BELLEFONTAINE** *map page 258, B-3*

You'd expect the highest point in Ohio to be in the Appalachian foothills, but instead it's an anomaly on the western plains around Bellefontaine. Campbell Hill, elevation 1,549 feet, and the limestone hills around it resisted the glacial forces that leveled the rest of the region. That's the beginning of a happy tale that's made Logan County one of the more scenic and popular travel destinations in the state.

In the winter, **Mad River Mountain** services skiers and snowboarders with twenty trails, five chairlifts, and the largest snowmaking system in Ohio. There's plenty of skiing in northeast Ohio, but this is the only place to hit the slopes in the west. Mad River Mountain tops out at 1,460 feet with a 300-foot vertical drop and offers some great views of the surrounding forested hills to boot. *1000 Snow Valley Road, Zanesfield; 800-231-7669.*

Just south of the Logan County line, **Ohio Caverns** has equally impressive but less-sweeping views. The same limestone responsible for the area's hills has succumbed to slightly acidic water underground to produce the state's largest and arguably most fascinating cave. Open year-round, Ohio Caverns has two types of formations, calcite and iron oxide (rust), which adds color and puts the cave in a select group. Only a few caves in the world are known to have both types of formations. *2210 East Route 245, West Liberty; 937-465-4017.*

Even a simple drive through the countryside east of Bellefontaine can be a pleasant and eye-opening experience. It's easy to picture this area as it was two hundred years ago. Its beauty impressed frontier legend Simon Kenton in 1778 even as the Shawnee were marching him to his death, which was to be a burning at the stake at Wapatomica, an Indian village on the Mad River east of present-day Bellefontaine. Kenton's friend and Shawnee ally Simon Girty arrived and talked the Indians out of it, and Kenton would later avoid being burned at the stake two more times. The Shawnee called the Mad River valley *mac ack ocheek,* meaning "smiling valley." Certainly someone was smiling on Simon Kenton.

Brothers Gen. Abram Sanders Piatt and Col. Donn Piatt matched Kenton's knack for survival with their penchant for eccentricity. After the Civil War the two returned to their property around West Liberty and built two of the most unusual houses the state has ever seen—castles, actually. They're known collectively as the Piatt Castles, which is convenient because it's easy to confuse the two. Abram had his finished first and named the Norman-inspired castle **Mac-A-Cheek** (10051 Township Road 47; 937-465-2821). Donn's castle, **Mac-O-Chee** (Route 245 at County Road 1; 937-465-2821), followed in a Flemish style. (The castles overlook Macacheek Valley and sit near Macochee Creek.) Both are open to the public and worth touring for their interiors. The homes have been passed down through the generations, and Mac-A-Cheek Castle holds heirlooms and artifacts that have been in the family for centuries. The cabin the two brothers grew up in, **Pioneer House** (10245 Township Road 47; 937-465-0757), remains standing near Mac-A-Cheek and has been restored as a homey gift and crafts shop.

■ TRAVEL BASICS

Getting Around: To really take in the landscape of northwest Ohio, you'll need to travel mostly by car. I-75 is the major north–south thoroughfare, though U.S. 23 is the best way to access the region from Columbus. The Ohio Turnpike is the major highway running east–west, just below the Lake Erie shoreline. If you have time, treat yourself to a scenic drive. From Bowling Green, 25 miles south of Toledo, head northeast to Catawba Island on Routes 105, 163, and 53. Another good bet: Travel southwest from Perrysburg, just 10 miles south of Toledo, on Route 65 to Route 424 to Defiance and Route 111 along the Auglaize River southwest of Defiance. Both trips are known for incredible fall foliage.

In Greater Toledo, you can drive or rely on the public bus system. One fun option is the Downtown Lunch Trolley, which has two loops to give you a lift to dozens of eateries. It operates mid-day during the week.

Climate: Like much of the state, northwest Ohio is warm and humid in the summer and cold in the winter. The thermometer rises above 80 degrees Fahrenheit frequently during June, July, and August, and it's not uncommon for winter temperatures to dip well below freezing. Winter winds on the plains, and those whipping off the lake, can numb the hardiest of souls. Seasonal transitions, however, are more moderate around Lake Erie. Toledo records more than its share of cloudy days. The entire region averages about 36 inches of precipitation a year.

PRACTICAL INFORMATION

■ AREA CODES AND TIME ZONE

All of Ohio is in the eastern time zone. The area code for Cincinnati is 513; for Dayton the area code is 937. In the southeast, including Zanesville, Dresden, and Marietta, the area code is 740. Columbus's area code is 614. The area codes for Cleveland are 216 and 440. Area codes 330 and 234 apply for Akron, Canton, Youngstown, and surrounding areas, and 440 applies for the rest of the northeast. For the northwest, including Toledo, area codes 419 and 567 apply.

■ METRIC CONVERSIONS

1 foot = .305 meters   1 mile = 1.6 kilometers   1 pound = .45 kilograms
Centigrade = Fahrenheit temperature minus 32, divided by 1.8

■ CLIMATE

Spring and fall are the best times to experience Ohio's varied landscape. You'll find mild temperatures that will allow you to truly enjoy the frequent festivals and fairs. There's no doubt that all four seasons come out in full force, with winter lows of -20 degrees Fahrenheit and summer highs reaching 100 degrees. Winters are often cold, gray, and windy, while summers are hot and humid. (Lake Erie keeps coastal communities cooler than the rest of Ohio in the summer.) Annual precipitation averages 38 inches, with a healthy dose of winter snowfall: extreme southern Ohio sees about 20 inches of snow a year, while areas east of Cleveland can get 80 inches or more of lake-effect snow. Most of the state receives 30 to 40 inches of snow a year. Better bring your umbrella and galoshes to be on the safe side.

■ GETTING THERE AND AROUND

BY AIR

Akron-Canton Airport (CAK), on I-77, 15 miles south of Akron and 8 miles north of Canton, receives flights from several domestic carriers. I-77, Exit 113; *888-433-2359;* www.akroncantonairport.com.

Cincinnati/Northern Kentucky International Airport (CVG) is in Kentucky, 13 miles southwest of downtown Cincinnati. *I-275, Exit 4; 859-767-3144;* www. cvgairport.com.

Cleveland Hopkins International Airport (CLE) is 13 miles southwest of downtown Cleveland. *I-71, Exit 170B;* www.clevelandairport.com.

Dayton International Airport (DAY) is 13 miles north of downtown Dayton and 60 miles north of Cincinnati. Airlines often offer substantially cheaper fares than at the larger Cincinnati airport. *I-70, Exit 32; 937-454-8200;* www. daytonairport.com.

Port Columbus International Airport (CMH) is 8 miles east of downtown, just inside the I-270 loop. It offers service from nearly every major airline. *I-270, Exit 35, or I-670, Exit 9; 614-239-4000;* www.port-columbus.com.

Toledo Express Airport (TOL) is 20 miles west of downtown Toledo off I-80. *11013 Airport Highway; 419-865-2351;* www.toledoexpress.com.

Youngstown-Warren Regional Airport (YNG) sits 11 miles north of Youngstown and 10 miles east of Warren. It connects to more than two hundred cities worldwide. *North of Route 82 on Route 193; 330-539-4233;* www.yngwrnair.com.

By Car

In the **northeast,** there's a tangle of highways running in and out of **Cleveland, Akron,** and **Youngstown.** From the south, I-71 and I-77 take you into the region, and the Ohio Turnpike cuts east–west across the area. Interstate 90 runs east–west along Lake Erie and merges with the turnpike.

In the rural **southeast,** your best bet is to get a detailed map and wander the myriad country highways. The major roads running through the area are I-70 east–west and I-77 north–south. Route 7 follows along the Ohio River for much of the region. U.S. 33 is a good choice for entering the region from Columbus; from Cincinnati use Route 32 for the near hill country, I-71/I-70/I-77 for the eastern hill country.

Interstate 71 and U.S. 23 are the main north–south routes through **central Ohio,** while I-70 takes you in and out of the state running east–west. Interstate 270 makes a loop around the **Columbus** metro area.

In **southwest** Ohio, I-71 and I-75 are the main north–south routes. You can circle the **Cincinnati** metro area on I-275 or take I-74 west to Indianapolis. Your best bet for connecting with rural southeast Ohio is Route 32.

Interstate 75 is the main north–south route through the **northwest** area of the state. The Ohio Turnpike takes you east–west not far south of the Michigan border and Lake Erie shoreline.

By Train

Amtrak serves numerous Ohio cities, including Columbus (with connecting buses only), Cleveland, Cincinnati, Sandusky, and Toledo. Stations in Akron and Elyria serve the Western Reserve, but no service is available for southeast Ohio. Taking the train makes the most sense for those coming from out of state through a major hub, such as Chicago or New York. *800-872-7245;* www.amtrak.com.

By Bus

Akron's **Metro Regional Transit Authority** provides bus service around Greater Akron. *330-762-0341;* www.akronmetro.org.

Central Ohio Transit Authority provides bus service in Columbus and Franklin County. *614-228-1776;* www.cota.com.

Greater Cleveland Regional Transit Authority is a countywide public transportation system with both buses and trains. *216-566-5100;* www.gcrta.org.

Greater Dayton Regional Transit Authority provides bus, trolley, and tram service around the Dayton metropolitan area. *937-425-8400;* www.mvrta.org.

Greyhound runs buses in and out of Ohio's largest cities, as well as Athens, Marietta, Portsmouth, Wooster, and Zanesville. *800-229-9424;* www.greyhound.com.

South East Area Transit provides service to Muskingum County, which includes Zanesville, Cambridge, and Dresden. *740-454-8573;* www.zbus.com.

Southwest Ohio Regional Transit Authority provides public bus service around Greater Cincinnati. *513-632-7575;* www.sorta.com.

Toledo Area Regional Transit Authority provides bus service around Greater Toledo. *419-243-7433;* www.tarta.com.

■ Food

Ohio's landscape consists mostly of farmland. With more than two hundred commercial crops, residents take their food seriously. It's practically a state pastime to visit local farmers' markets during the summer to stock up on fresh produce, and there's a growing movement called Discover Ohio Proud dedicated to cooking with Ohio goods. If you're looking for old-fashioned Midwestern comfort food, you won't be disappointed. Meat-and-potatoes-style home cooking is dished up at small cafés and restaurants around the state. This is, after all, the birthplace of Wendy's and White Castle. In Bidwell you can even enjoy your sausage and eggs at the original Bob Evans Farm—now famous for its restaurant chain and grocery store products.

In addition to the hearty fare, you'll find ethnic offerings of nearly every kind imaginable. Fabulous Indian and Thai food are easy to find, and other choices range from sushi and Ethiopian to first-rate Italian. Thanks to Polish and Czech immigrants, Cleveland offers a bounty of Eastern European eateries. You can't visit southwest Ohio without trying the famed Cincinnati chili, served over spaghetti and available at Skyline or any number of independent chili parlors. There's a wealth of independent restaurants in Ohio, as well as pockets of haute cuisine. In Cincinnati the restaurant Jean-Robert at Pigall's has been getting rave reviews in the national press for its French cuisine. Notable chefs and restaurants also dot the rest of the state, especially in the larger cities.

■ LODGING

Like those in much of the country, Ohio's lodging options are dominated by the large chain hotels. Visitors from outside the Midwest, however, will be pleasantly surprised by the reasonable prices found in most areas of the state. There are breathtaking historic options, too. Highlights include the Cincinnatian Hotel, Best Western Mariemont Inn, and Hilton Cincinnati Netherland Plaza in Cincinnati; the Lafayette in Marietta; and the Renaissance Cleveland Hotel Tower and Hyatt Regency Cleveland at the Arcade.

Bed-and-breakfasts dot the landscape in both rural and urban areas. These vary widely in both quality and price. Around Lake Erie resort towns, you'll find a plethora of vacation rentals readily available—from houseboats and small cabins to luxury condos and homes. The area surrounding Hocking Hills also boasts a number of rental cabins perfect for family trips. Another standout is Landoll's Mohican Castle south of Loudonville—it's a luxurious hideaway situated on an 1,100-acre estate.

■ RESERVATION SERVICES

Bed and Breakfast Inns Online. www.bbonline.com/oh.
Ohio Hotel and Lodging Association. *614-461-6462;* www.ohla.org.
Xanterra Parks and Resorts. (Includes lodge reservations for Ohio State Parks and Resorts.) *303-338-6000;* www.xanterra.com.

■ HOTEL AND MOTEL CHAINS

Best Western. *800-780-7234;* www.bestwestern.com.
Days Inn. *800-329-7466;* www.daysinn.com.
Doubletree. *800-222-8733;* www.doubletree.com.
Hilton Hotels. *800-774-1500;* www.hilton.com.
Holiday Inn. *800-465-4329;* www.6c.com.
Hyatt Hotels. *800-233-1234;* www.hyatt.com.
Marriott Hotels. *888-236-2427;* www.marriott.com.
Radisson. *800-333-3333;* www.radisson.com.
Ramada Inns. *800-828-6644;* www.ramada.com.
Ritz-Carlton. *800-241-3333;* www.ritzcarlton.com.
Sheraton. *800-325-3535;* www.sheraton.com.
Westin Hotels. *800-228-3000;* www.westin.com.

■ CAMPING

National Recreation Reservation Service. *877-444-6777;* www.reserveusa.com.
Ohio Campground Owners Assoc. *No phone;* www.ohiocamper.com.
Ohio State Forests. *614-265-6694;* www.dnr.state.oh.us/forestry/forests/forests.htm.
Ohio State Parks. *800-282-7275;* www.dnr.state.oh.us/parks.
Wayne National Forest. Athens Ranger District, *740-753-0101;* Marietta Unit, *740-373-9055;* Ironton Ranger District, *740-534-6500;* www.fs.fed.us/r9/wayne.

■ OFFICIAL TOURISM INFORMATION

Ohio Division of Travel and Tourism. *800-282-5393;* www.ohiotourism.com.
Akron/Summit County. *800-245-4254;* www.visitakron-summit.org.
Canton/Stark County. *800-533-4302;* www.visitcantonohio.com.
Dayton/Montgomery County. *800-221-8235, Ext. 281;* www.daytoncvb.com.
Experience Columbus. *800-354-2657;* www.experiencecolumbus.com.
Greater Cincinnati. *800-246-2987;* www.cincyusa.com.

Greater Cleveland. *800-321-1001;* www.travelcleveland.com.
Greater Toledo. *800-243-4667;* www.dotoledo.org.
Holmes County. *330-674-3975;* www.visitamishcountry.com.
Marietta/Washington County. *800-288-2577;* www.mariettaohio.org.
Sandusky/Erie County. *800-255-3743;* www.sanduskyohiocedarpoint.com.
Youngstown/Mahoning County. *800-447-8201;* www.youngstowncvb.com.
Zanesville-Muskingum County. *740-455-8282;* www.visitzanesville.com.

■ USEFUL WEB SITES

American Journalism Review. Search for Ohio's periodicals. www.ajr.org.
Arts in Ohio. A searchable event finder for the entire state. www.artsinohio.com.
Cincinnati.com. Explore Cincinnati through its largest media outlets. www.cincinnati.com.
Cleveland.com. News, sports, entertainment, and local media. www.cleveland.com.
Cleveland Magazine. Arts, entertainment, and restaurant listings. www.clevelandmagazine.com.
Columbus Dispatch. The city's largest newspaper online. www.dispatch.com.
Cuyahoga Valley National Park. www.nps.gov/cuva/index.htm.
Fodors.com. Ohio hotel, restaurant, and other listings. www.fodors.com.
Ohio Festivals and Events Association. Searchable event listings. www.ofea.org.
Ohio Historical Society. Historical sites, museums, and events. www.ohiohistory.org.
Ohio **Magazine.** Travel, living, dining, and events. www.ohiomagazine.com.
Ohio Public Library Information Network. A resource of Ohio research databases and information available through two hundred and fifty independent libraries statewide. www.oplin.lib.oh.us.
Ohio's Appalachian Country. Culture, events, and attractions. www.ohioappalachian.com.
Ohio University. Learn about frequent university-sponsored events. www.ohio.edu.
Ohio Wines and Wineries. Learn about state wines and search for wineries. www.ohiowines.org.
Toledo Blade. E-version of the city's newspaper. www.toledoblade.com.

■ FESTIVALS AND EVENTS

■ JANUARY
Lebanon Antique Show. Eighty dealers from around the country in Ohio's antiques capital. Also in October. *513-932-1817;* www.wchsmuseum.com.

McKinley Day, Canton. A celebration of McKinley's birthday on the Saturday closest to January 29. Civil War reenactors, living-history demonstrations, and a ceremonial wreath laying at the McKinley tomb. *330-455-7043;* www. mckinleymuseum.org.

■ FEBRUARY
Annual Arts Sampler Weekend, Cincinnati. An excellent introduction to the city's arts scene, with dozens of free events. *513-871-2787;* www.fineartsfund.org.

Clark Gable Birthday Celebration, Cadiz. Features a dinner dance and a memorabilia show and sale honoring his February 1 birthday. *740-942-4989;* www. clarkgablefoundation.org.

■ MARCH
Hueston Woods Maple Syrup Festival, Oxford. Warm up with good food and a tour of Hueston Woods State Park; then learn how sap is gathered from the trees. *513-523-6347;* huestonwoods_friends.tripod.com/friends.htm.

■ APRIL
Grant Days, Georgetown. Commemorating U. S. Grant's April 27 birthday, with a Civil War Grand Ball, carriage rides, and battle reenactments. *513-732-3600.*

Tri-C Jazz Fest, Cleveland. Some of the best musicians in the world come to play Tri-C, a fixture of Cleveland jazz for twenty-five years. Performers play a range of venues over two weeks. Sponsored by Cuyahoga Community College. *216-987-4400;* www.tricjazzfest.com.

■ MAY
Bead International preview and opening reception, Athens. International exhibition of award-winning, contemporary bead-centered artwork, held in even-numbered years. Late May–early September. *740-592-4981;* www.dairybarn.org.

Marching in the Findlay Market Opening Day Parade in Cincinnati.

Runners negotiate Cincinnati's hills in the Flying Pig Marathon.

Big Parade, Oberlin. A new town-and-gown tradition, featuring floats, dancing, and, of course, live music. *440-775-8102.*

Feast of the Flowering Moon, Chillicothe. A celebration of both native and small-town culture—traditional native dancing, mountain-man rendezvous, arts and crafts, a parade, and food. *800-413-4118;* www.feastofthefloweringmoon.com.

German Heritage Day, Sauder Village. Authentic German foods, German-language church services, and cultural programs. *800-590-9755;* www.saudervillage.org.

Pepsi Jammin' on Main, Cincinnati. One of Cincinnati's premier music festivals. Past years have featured Ben Folds, Peter Frampton, Joan Jett, and Morphine. *513-721-8883, Taft Theatre box office;* www.pepsijamminonmain.com.

Port Clinton Walleye Festival. Held every Memorial Day weekend in the Walleye Capital of the World. Once you've experienced it, they say, you'll be hooked. *419-732-2864;* www.walleyefestival.com.

Quilt National preview and opening reception, Athens. International exhibition of award-winning, contemporary quilts, held in odd-numbered years. Late May–early September. *740-592-4981;* www.dairybarn.org.

Strawberry Festival, Norwalk. Plenty of bands and food, plus a car show, parade, and strawberry-pie–eating contest during Memorial Day weekend. *419-663-4062;* www.norwalkjaycees.com.

Taste of Cincinnati. Ethnic foods and traditional Cincinnati concoctions from around the city, along with music, entertainment, and kids' rides. *513-621-6994;* www.tasteofcincinnati.com.

Tour of the Scioto River Valley (TOSRV). Classic annual cycling tour from Columbus to Portsmouth—and back. Two days. *614-442-7901;* www.tosrv.org.

■ JUNE

Art Tatum Jazz Heritage Festival, Toledo. A variety of jazz bands honoring Tatum, a Toledo native. Includes food vendors and a children's tent. *419-241-5299;* www.toledojazzsociety.org.

Columbus Arts Festival. Summer comes to Columbus with arts, crafts, entertainment, and fare from top Columbus restaurants. *614-224-2606;* www.gcac.org/artsfest.

Coshocton Hot Air Balloon Festival. Balloon competition draws twenty to thirty balloons annually. The festival also includes music, kids' bicycle races, and Little League tournaments. *740-622-5411;* www.coshoctonchamber.org.

Dean Martin Festival, Steubenfield. Includes an auction, film festival, and plenty of Dean Martin standards. *800-510-4442;* www.deanmartinsteubenville.com.

"Keeping the Tradition" Pow Wow, Xenia. Native dances, dress, and kinship at the Blue Jacket Outdoor Drama Amphitheater. *937-275-8599;* tmvcna.org/4powwow.htm.

Miss Ohio Pageant, Mansfield. Festival, Miss Ohio Grand Parade, preliminaries, and crowning. *419-522-6677;* www.missohio.org.

Muster on the Maumee, Fort Meigs State Memorial. A huge celebration of historical interpretation, from the Middle Ages to today, with craftspeople and performers illustrating cultures of yesteryear. *419-874-4121;* www.fortmeigs.org.

Northeast Ohio Polka Fest, Geneva-on-the-Lake. Ethnic food and music galore at the Old Firehouse Winery. *800-862-6751;* www.oldfirehousewinery.com.

Old West End Festival, Toledo. Huge arts fair, home tours, parade, and kids' games. www.oldwestendtoledo.com.

Parade the Circle, Cleveland. A Carnival-style parade and showcase of the diverse University Circle culture, with dancers, street performers, ethnic foods, and special activities run by community organizations. *216-791-3900;* www. universitycircle.org.

Roy Rogers Festival, Portsmouth. A tribute to the hometown hero, known to friends and locals as Leonard Slye. *740-353-0900;* www.sciotocountyohio.com/ royrogers.htm.

■ JULY

All-American Soap Box Derby, Akron. The final showdown for kids from around the world who come to race in the Rubber Capital of the World. *330-733-8723;* aasbd.org.

CITYFOLK Festival, Dayton. A multicultural celebration with a range of live music, performances, ethnic art, and fireworks. *937-223-3655;* www.cityfolk.org.

Cleveland Grand Prix. CART racing under the lights at Burke Lakefront Airport. *888-817-7223;* www.grandprixofcleveland.com.

Crooksville/Roseville Pottery Festival. Auctions, demonstrations, and exhibits. Coincides with Pottery Lovers Reunion. Crooksville and Roseville alternate hosting. *740-697-7021;* www.ceramiccenter.org.

Dayton Air Show. This two-day world-class air show is one of the highlights of the summer. *937-898-5901;* www.daytonairshow.com.

Islandfest, Kelleys Island. The island celebrates the apex of the vacation season with a street dance, crafts fair, music, food, and fireworks. *419-746-2360;* www. kelleysislandchamber.com.

KidsFest, Cleveland. The big summer event for kids. Hands-on exhibits, theatrical productions, street performers, and games at Tower City Amphitheater. *888-761-7469;* www.cleveland.com/kidsfest.

Lancaster Festival. Extended, eclectic music and arts celebration, featuring the Lancaster Festival Orchestra. *740-687-4808;* www.lanfest.org.

Pottery Lovers Reunion/Taste of Zanesville. Includes an auction, open houses, tours, demonstrations, and special sales. *800-743-2303;* www.visitzanesville.com.

■ AUGUST

Bucyrus Bratwurst Festival. It's big (a hundred thousand people), tasty, and very, very German. Features brats made only in Bucyrus. *419-562-2728;* www.bratwurstfestival.org.

Dublin Irish Festival. Traditional dances, music, food, storytelling, craftspeople, and Irish history. *614-410-4545;* www.dublinirishfestival.org.

Holmes County Fair, Millersburg. A five-day fair featuring truck and tractor pulls, motocross, bull riding, and a demolition derby in the heart of Amish Country. *Phone changes year to year;* www.holmescountyfair.com.

Northwest Ohio Rib-Off, Toledo. A nationally recognized rib event. *419-242-9587;* www.uhs-toledo.org/rib-off/ribinfo.htm.

Ohio Renaissance Festival, Harveysburg. Sixteenth-century England takes form with costumed performers, jousting, storytelling, and period food. Weekends August–October. *513-897-7000;* www.renfestival.com.

Ohio State Fair, Columbus. One of the largest and best state fairs in the country. *888-646-3976;* www.ohiostatefair.org.

Every taste is covered in the Ohio State Fair parade.

Ohio Tobacco Festival, Ripley. A celebration of Ripley culture with parades, a flea market, antique car show, and queen pageant. *937-373-3651.*

Portsmouth River Days. Huge traditional festival with music, midway rides, fish fry, sidewalk sales, and fireworks. Late August–early September. *740-353-1116;* www.riverdays.org.

Pro Football Hall of Fame Festival, Canton. Hall of Fame induction ceremony, Hall of Fame Game, and more than a dozen accompanying community events. *330-456-8207;* www.profootballhof.com.

Twins Days, Twinsburg. The world's largest annual gathering of twins. *330-425-3652;* www.twindays.org.

Vintage Ohio Wine Festival, Kirtland. Showcase of more than twenty Ohio winemakers along with catered food from the area's top restaurants. *800-227-6972;* www.ohiowines.org.

■ SEPTEMBER

Cleveland National Air Show. Among the premier air shows in the country, at Burke Lakefront Airport. The three-day event on Labor Day weekend brings more than forty military and civilian aircraft. *216-781-0747;* www. clevelandairshow.com.

Great Mohican Indian Pow-Wow, Loudonville. Authentic dancing, music, storytelling, and food. Also held in July. *800-766-2267;* mohicanreservation.com/powwow.

Johnny Appleseed Festival, Brunswick. Antiques show, children's activities, apple everything, and the first Bag Your Own Apples of the season. *330-225-5577;* www.mapleside.com.

Marion Popcorn Festival. Huge three-day festival with tons of food, entertainment, and music, including well-known national acts. *740-387-3378;* www. popcornfestival.com.

Oktoberfest-Zinzinnati. The largest Oktoberfest outside of Munich. Beer, food, and music galore. *513-579-3197;* www.oktoberfest-zinzinnati.com.

Piqua Heritage Festival. Crafts demonstrations, an Indian village, and more than one hundred artisans and crafters at Johnston Farm. Labor Day weekend. www. piquaheritagefestival.com.

The Ohio State Fair is among the largest in the country.

Riverfest, Cincinnati. End-of-summer celebration over Labor Day weekend. Also known locally as the WEBN fireworks. *513-352-4000;* www.webn.com/riverfest.

Sternwheel Festival, Marietta. This town's biggest event of the year, the weekend after Labor Day. Stern-wheeler races and a fireworks blowout. *800-288-2577;* www.mariettaohio.org.

Wellston Coal Festival. Everything coal, from the Coal Miner Olympics to coal mine tours. Its slogan? "Come watch us strip (mine)!" *No phone;* www. jacksoncountyohio.org/jw/visit/events.htm.

■ **OCTOBER**

Ashtabula County Covered Bridge Festival, Jefferson. A quilt show, draft horses, musical entertainment, and tours of those famous covered bridges. *440-576-3769;* www.coveredbridgefestival.org.

Autumn Lighthouse Festival, Marblehead. Arts, crafts, and tours of the oldest continuously operating lighthouse on the Great Lakes. *419-797-4530.*

Bob Evans Farm Festival, Rio Grande. Music, dancing, crafts, and food down on the farm. *800-994-3276;* www.bobevans.com.

Circleville Pumpkin Show. An Ohio classic, with the Largest Pumpkin Contest, pumpkin doughnuts, hamburgers, fudge, pie, and anything else you can think of. *740-474-7000;* www.pumpkinshow.com.

German Village Oktoberfest, Columbus. The central Ohio Oktoberfest celebration. 614-221-8888; www.germanvillage.com.

Ohio Swiss Festival, Sugarcreek. Swiss polka bands, Swiss Festival Queen contest, Steinstossen (stone throwing), and Schwingfest (Swiss wrestling) in Ohio's Swiss cheese capital in late September or early October. *330-852-4113.*

Tall Stacks, Cincinnati. This quadrennial signature event celebrating Cincinnati's riverboat heritage draws seven hundred thousand to eight hundred thousand people. *513-721-0104;* www.tallstacks.com.

■ **NOVEMBER**

Buckeye Book Fair, Wooster. Scores of authors, some nationally known, meet and sign for the public. Books are discounted, and proceeds benefit literacy programs. *330-262-3244;* www.buckeyebookfair.com.

Warren Harding Birthday Celebration, Marion. Includes a wreath-laying ceremony and reception at the Harding home on the Saturday closest to Harding's birthday, November 2. *800-600-6894;* www.ohiohistory.org/places/harding.

Two girls make history at Tall Stacks in Cincinnati.

■ DECEMBER

Candlelight Christmas at Malabar Farm State Park. Wagon rides, hot cider, caroling, and shopping. *419-892-2784;* www.malabarfarm.org.

Christmas at Stan Hywet, Akron. An elegant mansion becomes even more regal during this annual holiday exhibition. *330-836-5533;* www.stanhywet.org.

Clifton Mill's Light Display, Clifton. Three million lights at one of the world's largest water-powered gristmills still in operation. *937-767-5501;* www.cliftonmill.com.

Dillon House Victorian Christmas, Fremont. Celebrate a grand 19th-century Christmas at the Hayes Presidential Center. Extends into early January. *800-998-7737;* www.rbhayes.org.

First Night Columbus. Music and entertainment at dozens of venues. The largest celebration in the city. *614-481-0020;* www.firstnightcols.org.

INDEX

COMPASS AMERICAN GUIDES

Compass American Guides are available at special discounts for bulk purchases for sales promotions or premiums. Special editions, including personalized covers, excerpts of existing books, and corporate imprints, can be created in large quantities for special needs. For more information, write to Special Markets/Premium Sales, 1745 Broadway, MD 6-2, New York, NY 10019 or e-mail specialmarkets@randomhouse.com.

COMPASS AMERICAN GUIDES

Critics, booksellers, and travelers all agree: you're lost without a Compass.

"This splendid series provides exactly the sort of historical and cultural detail about North American destinations that curious-minded travelers need." —*Washington Post*

"This is a series that constantly stuns us...no guide with photos this good should have writing this good. But it does." —*New York Daily News*

"Of the many guidebooks on the market, few are as visually stimulating, as thoroughly researched, or as lively written as the Compass American Guide series." —*Chicago Tribune*

"Good to read ahead of time, then take along so you don't miss anything." —*San Diego Magazine*

"Magnificent photography. First rate."—*Money*

"Written by longtime residents of each destination...these handsome and literate guides are strong on history and culture, and illustrated with gorgeous photos." —*San Francisco Chronicle*

"The color photographs sparkle, the archival illustrations illuminate windows to the past, and the writing is usually of the utmost caliber." —*Michigan Tribune*

"Class acts, worth reading and shelving for keeps even if you're not a traveler. " —*New Orleans Times-Picayune*

"Beautiful photographs and literate writing are the hallmarks of the Compass guides." —*Nashville Tennessean*

"History, geography, and wanderlust converge in these well-conceived books." —*Raleigh News & Observer*

"Oh, my goodness! What a gorgeous series this is."—*Booklist*

ACKNOWLEDGMENTS

On trips around Ohio, I've received invaluable assistance from individuals at historical societies, museums, archives, and libraries; tour guides; convention and visitors bureaus; and helpful residents. In particular I owe thanks to Vicky Tabor Branson at the Ohio Historical Society for her generous help in obtaining archival images; Daryl Baldwin, director of the Myaamia Project at Miami University, for permission to excerpt from *myaamia mahsinaakani kaloosiona,* his Miami language dictionary; Tammy Brown at the Ohio Department of Tourism for her introductions and information; Susan Wenner Jackson for her insights and travel companionship; and Kevin Coleman of Intrepid Historical Services for his encyclopedic knowledge of Chillicothe. Special thanks to Michelle Taute for her research, assistance, and support and to Meg Leder, Judi Ketteler, and Jack Heffron for their editorial guidance.

Finally, I thank Bill Manning for evoking Ohio through his photographs; Paula Consolo for sharpening the text in ways broad and narrow; Danny Mangin for his keen vision and humor; Paul Eisenberg for managing the big picture; Melanie Marin for her nuanced eye and an outstanding collection of archival images; and Siobhan O'Hare for creating such a beautiful volume. I also thank Linda Schmidt for ushering it through production.

All photographs in this book are by William Manning unless noted below.

Page 8, Jeff Greenberg

Introduction:
Page 13, Jeff Greenberg
Page 14, Ohio Historical Society

History and Culture:
Page 21, Chicago Historical Society
Page 26, Ohio Historical Society
Pages 28-29, University of Chicago Library, Special Collections Research Center
Page 30, Library of Congress Prints and Photographs Division
Page 33, Library of Congress Prints and Photographs Division
Page 34-35, Library of Congress Prints and Photographs Division

Miami River Valleys:

Old Northwest:

About the Author

Brad Crawford is the former editor of an instructional photography book line at F&W Publications, publisher of *Photographer's Market*. He writes on a variety of topics, especially travel, science, and the outdoors, and has an Ohio travel column. He is also co-author of *My Sister Is Missing*, a true family drama written with Sherrie Gladden-Davis. Brad has worked as a magazine editor and acquisitions editor and as an advertising agency copywriter and copy editor. He graduated from the University of Missouri–Columbia School of Journalism and lives in Cincinnati.

About the Photographer

William Manning is an internationally known photographer whose work has been used by many national and international corporations and publishers, including American Airlines, BP Amoco, Rand McNally and Co., *National Geographic, ESPN* magazine, *Reader's Digest, Time* magazine, *Business Week,* the Sierra Club, John Hancock, Avon Cosmetics, Coldwater Creek, and many others. Travel and architectural photography, his areas of expertise, have taken him to many locations across North America, great cities across Europe, locations in New Zealand, and the east African countries of Kenya and Tanzania. Manning leads many photographic tours and workshops throughout the world, sharing his insight and experiences with other photographers. His work can be viewed on his Web site, www.williammanning.com.